I JUST CAN'T HELP BELIEVING

I JUST CAN'T HELP BELIEVING

Going Down:
The Relegation Experience

CHARLIE CONNELLY

MAINSTREAM
PUBLISHING

EDINBURGH AND LONDON

First published in Great Britain in 1998 by
MAINSTREAM PUBLISHING COMPANY (EDINBURGH) LTD
7 Albany Street
Edinburgh EH1 3UG

ISBN 1 84018 076 5

A catalogue record for this book is available from the British Library

Typeset in Van Dijck MT
Printed and bound in Great Britain by Butler & Tanner Ltd, Frome

Contents

Acknowledgements

I went into this project a wide-eyed innocent in the ways of authorship. Now that I have emerged at the other end a squinting cynic with bags under my eyes that would make Parker from *Thunderbirds* look like an advertisement for Optrex, I must hand out the plaudits to those who've helped and encouraged me whilst doing their level best to stifle yawns in the face of rabid assertions regarding the fates of Hereford United and Lincoln City over the past few months.

Special thanks are due to Mark Perryman of *Philosophy Football* who sat through my early ideas, suggested refinements and has been a constant source of advice and encouragement despite the fact that this book deprived him of an occasional employee.

Thanks to those individuals and fanzines who responded to my cautious enquiries for help and information: Chris Jones, *Talking Bull*, David and Tracey Norton, Jackie Mooney, *Seaside Saga*, Marko Poutilainen of ToffeeWeb, Peter Howls, Robert Nichols, *Fly Me to the Moon*, Geoff Vickers, Middlesbrough Supporters South, Lee Warren, Gary Parle, *The Deranged Ferret*, Tony Smith, Mick Hupalowsky, Simon Edwards, Paul Rumbles, Anna Merriman, *The 69er*, Huw Evans. I'd also like to mention Rick Everitt, Colin Cameron and Richard Redden, whose books about Charlton Athletic I have ravenously plundered to add flesh to the bare bones of my memories.

For their advice, encouragement, inspiration or even just feigned interest I would like to thank the following: Anne Coddington, Sally Davison, Avis Greenaway, Sarah Williams, Bertie Vitry, Vanna Derosas, Heather Walker, Ian Walden Rashbrook, Richard Martin, Chris Bassett, Pat McGarvey, Dan Hart, Tim O'Brien, Ma and Pa Sands, Mum and Dad (Connelly Office Supplies), Konrad Caulkett, Paul s'Jacob, Emma Harvey, Sharon Lennox, Amanda Collins, The Relegated Followers of Fashion, Kelly Sands, Nan (who always thought I 'did lovely with the writing'), David 'Harry' Crystal, Bill

Campbell, Cathy Mineards, Fiona Brownlee, and the music of the Coal Porters, the Byrds and the Beach Boys for keeping me going during those long red-eyed, stubbly chinned nights.

Thanks to Charlton Athletic Football Club for all the pain, heartbreak and redemption. And to Sasa Ilic: thanks for Wembley 98.

Special thanks to Tim Bennett for his role in inspiring a love for books about football in the days long before *Fever Pitch*. Keep swinging on the metaphorical crossbar.

Finally, all my love and thanks to Katie, who has lived through every word of this book with a superhuman lack of moaning. Thanks for smiling all the way, even when spending Valentine's Day watching Brighton play Doncaster Rovers, for not strangling me when we drove four hours to Doncaster to find that the game was all-ticket, and for preventing me from aiming a Cantona-esque flying kick at my ancient coal-fired computer when it finally gave up the ghost five days before deadline day.

Going Down

THE RELEGATION EXPERIENCE

In the opening titles of *Hong Kong Phooey*, Penry the mild-mannered janitor changes into his super-hero garb of mask and dressing-gown, does a few nifty moves, leaps on to an ironing board and is catapulted face first into the wall. From there he slides down into the basement to embark on his next ill-fated adventure.

Rarely can Middlesbrough Football Club have been compared to a floppy-eared talking dog with a penchant for the martial arts, but the goings-on at the Teesside club during the 1996–97 season were a classic example of how a club can look the part and throw all the right shapes, yet still astonish their legions of fans by spectacularly cocking up at crunch time. The only difference being that Bryan Robson wears more than a little red cap and purple T-shirt to his day job. Or so we assume.

Those of us who support teams that don't have a spiffing new ground and squillions to spend on top foreign imports (and Mikkel Beck) can be forgiven for allowing ourselves a wry chuckle at the demise of Middlesbrough. The abiding belief that money can buy instant and lasting success was held at bay for another season as relegation, the great leveller, triumphed and Middlesbrough sheepishly rejoined the ranks at whom they had thumbed their noses on the way up two years earlier.

Relegation helps to keep football sane. As many, if not more, clubs are involved in what the media uncharitably labels relegation dogfights every year as are involved in what are perceived to be the more noble battles at the top end of the table. No matter how much is spent on squad strengthening and snazzy all-seater stadia for the post-Italia 90 fan, a collection of highly talented and expensive individuals cannot guarantee success. Derby County struggled to get out of a distinctly mediocre First Division despite heavy investment on the playing side, Wolverhampton Wanderers, under the 'Golden Tit' Jack Hayward, have found the same, and the revamped Newcastle United squad did not exactly set the division alight on their way up under Kevin Keegan.

The progress of Fulham will be closely monitored. Thanks to their sudden cash injection, Fulham have turned from a club of fine tradition for whom many had a bit of a soft spot to one that most people dearly hope will lose every week and come a spectacular cropper. Their downfall in the play-off semi-final to glamorous Grimsby Town was the epicentre for ripples of mirth which spread throughout the land. A bit of a new experience for friendly old Fulham.

Now that football is hip and trendy (but fashion being what it is, it might not be by the time you read this – in which case, you're a square), club owners and marketing professionals have had the pound signs springing up in their eyes ever since Gazza blubbed and Waddle missed in 1990. Thanks to money, the First Division isn't the First Division any more. There is a First Division, but it's really the Second Division. The Second Division is really the Third Division. There isn't a Fourth Division. Well there is, but it's now the Third Division. The First Division is now the FA Carling Premiership, and everyone in it has oodles of cash.

The good old days of *Match of the Day* on a Saturday night and *The Big Match* on Sunday afternoon are long gone, as the traditional Saturday afternoon pursuit becomes a Friday night/Saturday afternoon/Sunday lunchtime and/or afternoon/Monday evening pursuit. Thanks to satellite television, which has pumped millions of pounds into a small proportion of the game, the needs of the armchair fan (although I suppose that with the recent intellectualisation of the game they are probably more likely to be futon fans) are considered greater than those of the fan at the turnstile. The perhaps inevitable move towards pay-per-view television (don't Sky subscribers already pay to view matches?) means that Saturday football, a tradition steeped in working-class culture, could disappear altogether.

Much has been made of the impact of television money on the game. However, most of the money goes to the clubs who need it least: those whose success generates extra income through gate money and who have slick merchandising operations which ensure that their club's shirt is on display in the shop windows of small market towns hundreds of miles away from the ground. Clubs in the lower reaches of the Premiership (about sixth place downwards) rely on the extra income from satellite TV and miss it immensely when they are relegated, despite the 'golden parachute' handed out to relegated clubs designed to ease their way back to the real world. They find their coverage suddenly reduced from half a dozen full-length matches complete with in-depth discussion from leading football thinkers (and Richard Keys) every season, to ten minutes of highlights the following day with commentary from a local madman in a threadbare overcoat who started out on the local *Evening Telegraph* in the '50s, yet still struggles to string a couple of sentences together without splitting infinitives and mixing metaphors. Or the goals on ITV at 1 a.m. on a Tuesday morning.

Despite the big clubs' efforts to create a closed shop and secure a financial fortune for life, relegation still lurks mischievously at the bottom of every division, a rare bastion of the democracy that made football great. If you weren't good enough, you couldn't play with the big boys any more; you had to go away and practise and practise and practise until you were good enough to play with them once again. It is still theoretically possible for clubs to 'do a Wimbledon', but is it equally likely that clubs could 'do a Bristol City' and tumble from top flight to bottom flight in successive seasons?

This is highly unlikely, because so great are the financial risks involved in dropping from the Premiership to the First Division alone that a club would go bust before turning up to its first game in Division Three unless they had a phenomenal core support that would continue to turn out in force even as their club dropped into the bottom division.

The top ends of each division have been tinkered with to bring in more cash, so now to enter the European Cup you just have to have a big bank balance. It is possible to be the champions of Europe without actually ever having been champions of your own country. Outside the Premiership, the play-offs ensure that a club finishing sixth can reach a Wembley final and be promoted behind teams who have earned that right by finishing in the top two, having waved to their fans and gone home to watch two clubs that finished below them enjoy a sun-drenched day out at Wembley.

Relegation, however, remains sacred. No play-offs for the teams who missed out on automatic relegation to keep the interest going to the end of the season, no day out at Wembley to decide who else is going down. Finish below the dotted line and that's your lot, sonny. Andy Gray will now walk past you in the street and pretend not to know you. Which is probably no bad thing, come to think of it.

The fact that Middlesbrough went down shines like a beacon for the future of football. No one is safe. As yet, no one has come up with a way of ensuring definite survival: the prospect of a Manchester City v. Macclesfield Town fixture in the Football League was unthinkable not five years ago. So when the Moss Rose former part-timers show up at Maine Road, every football fan should pause momentarily and give quiet thanks to the unrepentant ogre of relegation.

The marketing people can mess with some of our sacred cows: the FA Cup is sponsored, albeit apologetically, and the FA Cup draw has turned from an occasion of solemn importance, velvet bags and old men with cobwebs trailing from their heads to a showbiz bonanza with a cheap bingo machine, banter between Rodney Marsh and Barry Fry, and Graham Kelly smiling (for God's sake!). Clubs can change their shirts several times a season (here's a tip for parents moaning about shelling out 40 smackers for the latest abomination for their little Johnnies or Janets: don't buy the bloody things), convert their supporters' club drinking dens into American-style sports bars or get rid of their traditional club record in place of 'Simply the Best', but if you finish low enough you're going to go down. End of story. For all the glitz and razzmatazz that has latched on to football's coat tails, clambered up its back and sat squarely on top of its head, relegation has loftily ignored everything around it.

And I think it's brilliant. I'm not alone, either. Compare the number of column inches given over to Arsenal's championship victory in 1997–98 with the number of trees felled in order to allow hacks to pontificate upon the relative fates of Manchester City, Everton, Spurs, Newcastle United and Reading (okay, forget the last one). On the last day of any season, the *Match of the Day* devoted to the relegation situation makes far more compelling viewing than watching a bunch of overpaid prima donnas waving the Premiership trophy at their slavering supporters (most of whom will have been going for, ooh, three years at least). In the modern football climate, relegation is the last interesting thing left in the game. Save for those season-ticket holders at Old Trafford, Highbury, Anfield and Ewood Park, no one particularly cares who wins the Premiership. By the end of the 1997–98 season we were too busy willing Spurs and Newcastle to go down to worry about who was doing what at the top end. Arsenal's winning of the championship and subsequent securing of the double was not the talk of the season. It was the laments of 'oh, I wish Spurs and/or Newcastle had gone down' that could be heard in the pubs and bus queues of England. The latter would have been worth it just to see the look on Alan Shearer's face. Mind you, the Toon Army would probably just have seen the back of his (oddly square-shaped) head as he jogged down the tunnel after the last game and sped out of St

James' Park to pastures new quicker than you could say Jack Robinson (or should that be 'Wor Jackie' Robinson?).

Relegation is one of the last bastions of the true spirit of football. Like most brilliant ideas, it flourishes through its simplicity, and its consequences are far-reaching. In tennis, for example, Tim Henman can tumble down the world rankings yet still end up playing Pete Sampras a week later. If he drops to two hundredth place he's not stuck playing on cratered tarmac courts in his local park, dodging dog turds and fending off stones thrown by local schoolchildren. He's still in with a shout of gracing the Centre Court at Wimbledon a few weeks later. A relegated football club, however, knows that it has at least a year before rejoining the level from which it has fallen, a year spent with a number of bedfellows of lesser status. A bit like Ulrika Jonsson's love life, in fact.

Even when a team is labelled 'too good to go down', the network of figures that makes up the league tables is ultimately what counts. Looking back at tables for 1997–98, no one will be able to tell from the stark rows of numbers how Barnsley almost escaped, how Newcastle struggled to hold on to their dignity, how Everton came within a whisker of being relegated or how despite sticking five past Stoke away from home in the last game of the season Manchester City still dropped into the Second Division. The muddied battles, the remorselessly ground-out backs-to-the-wall draws, the ill luck of a last-minute scrambled shot shaving the outside of the post, the desperate last-ditch clearance off the line, none of these count for anything when the pack stops shuffling at the end of another league campaign.

Relegation is a cold, emotionally neutral phenomenon. If you don't win enough points, tough. You might have played the best football in the world, but you're still going to Stockport next year. Or Bury. Or Millwall. Or Scarborough. You pay for a bad season with at least one whole season at the lower level. A couple of good results early in the campaign don't put you back up with the big boys; you've got to show your worth over nine long months.

When a big club is struggling at the wrong end of the table, the media, and television in particular, labours under the bizarre misapprehension that the nation at large is solemnly bowing its head and hoping that the poor little rich club will extricate itself from the mire and reinstate itself to its rightful place near the top of the table. The situation at Spurs in 1997–98 was for some reason deemed to be 'tragic'. No it wasn't. It was absolutely hilarious. Watching a bunch of overpaid, pampered pretty boys having their hides whipped week in week out on *Match of the Day* was one of the consistent highlights of the season. The collective whingeing from the Spurs camp and the rumours of dressing-room strife and players having clauses written into their contracts forbidding the coach to drop them led to barely controlled mirth everywhere outside Tottenham High Road and certain corners of Wapping. Everyone wanted them to go down, in the same way that everyone bar their own fans wants to see Manchester United get hammered in Europe every season.

Why would it have been more tragic for Spurs to go down than, say, Barnsley? Relegation proves that no team, however rich, successful or otherwise, has a right to be in the top flight *per se*. Surely the demise of Barnsley was more of a 'tragedy' for the game: at last a club regarded as unfashionable had broken through into the top flight and scared the wits out of a few of the bigger clubs. They were a side assembled on a relatively small budget (how many Barnsley players can you name?) who battled against the established order showing a passion and spirit rarely seen amongst the élite clubs. Their fans, players and manager Danny Wilson were much more of a credit to the Premiership than Spurs, with their gutless performances and interminable whingeing behind the scenes.

If Barnsley had survived at the expense of Spurs or Everton it would have been fantastic for the game. It would have illustrated how you can pump all the money you like into the game and the clubs, but at the end of the season it's the figure in the last column of the league table not the balance sheet that's important. The loss of Spurs from the Premiership would have caused television executives to throw their hands in the air in horror. Millions would have been wiped off Spurs' share price. The fancy dans would have been scouring their contracts for loopholes and get-out clauses, and it would all have been hugely funny to watch.

On the last day of the 1997–98 season, as Everton entertained Coventry City whilst sitting a point behind Bolton Wanderers, who travelled to Chelsea, in the last relegation spot, the images of the respective fans arriving at the grounds spoke volumes for the different attitudes of traditionally big clubs and their lesser counterparts. Everton fans walked up to Goodison that day like a bomb-disposal squad approaching an unidentified holdall making loud ticking noises. There was much wringing of hands, gnawing of finger-nails and gnashing of teeth, and the silence in the streets surrounding the ground was deafening. At Stamford Bridge, however, Bolton fans arrived determined to party, faces painted, wigs agogo. No matter that if you paint your face in club colours, don a curly wig and then lose you look faintly ridiculous on the way home, the Bolton fans, used to something of a yo-yo existence, were determined to party. They knew at the start of the season that survival would be a bonus. So if they stayed up, brilliant. If they went down, well, life in the First Division isn't so bad. They know they'll do well again.

For Everton relegation represented a trip into the unknown. They were terrified. Okay, if they'd gone down then maybe there would have been the odd pang of remorse amongst statisticians that such a proud long service record in the top flight had come to an end, but beyond that what were they so worried about? The chances of Everton staying in the First Division for more than one season, let alone emulating Manchester City and dropping into the Second, were pretty slim.

What did they expect? Ramshackle wastegrounds full of flesh-eating vampires? Teams of 17-stone bruisers with low foreheads looking at each other and grinning ruthless, gap-toothed smiles whilst preparing to kick the finely tuned athletes from the top flight into oblivion?

At the end of the game, as Everton secured the point they needed to stay up at Bolton's expense, the Goodison turf was swamped by jubilant Evertonians cavorting about the place as if they'd won the European Cup. Bolton fans shrugged their shoulders, pondered awhile and looked forward to the swift return that they normally engineer every time they fall into the Nationwide League.

Relegation might have been good for Everton. A season of tonking the likes of Bury and Crewe to surf back into the Premiership at the first attempt on a tide of delirium might have stimulated the club into a position to challenge for major honours once again. You never know, the supporters might actually have enjoyed themselves. Never again, said everyone on the blue side of the Mersey. Just as they had four years earlier when Goodison witnessed its first ever last-day escape from the jaws of doom, as described later in this book. Of course it will happen again. That is Everton's fate, bartered in exchange for the success of the '80s.

There are myriad reasons for relegation, and this book will hopefully demonstrate some of them, but in the modern climate it all comes down to that old devil called cash. Whether it be overspending beyond a club's means, not having enough money to start with, or having a regime in charge more interested in making the stuff for themselves than in seeing success on the field, money is the root of all relegation. Well, okay, money is the root of everything involved with football these days, but in no other aspect of the game can misinvestment or mismanagement have such grave financial consequences, particularly with so many clubs now floating on the stock market.

The fact that Manchester City and Stoke City, traditionally big clubs with magnificent stadia, lined up at the start of the 1998–99 campaign in the same division as Macclesfield Town speaks volumes for the standard of football in the First Division as well as being a damning indictment of whatever went wrong at both clubs. Yes, the gap is widening between the Premiership and the First, but those coming down from the top flight find that it's a hard division to leave by the front door. Sunderland, for example, fully expected to return to the Premiership at the first attempt. Yet despite clocking up 90 points, enough to win the title in most other seasons, they found themselves in the play-offs where, despite scoring four goals at Wembley and not losing in open play, they were still ousted by Charlton Athletic on penalties.

At the other end, Manchester City and Stoke City would never in a million years have expected to be playing out the last few minutes of the season knowing that both were already relegated. Despite their flashy grounds and relatively big crowds, their executive air-conditioned team coaches will still be crawling around the back lanes of Essex in 1998–99 looking for the rickety wooden fascia of Colchester United. Thanks to relegation, you're only as good as your last season. And their last season just wasn't good enough. You can have the best ground in the world, the most supporters and brilliant individual players, but that doesn't save you from going down if you haven't won enough games.

For all the moans about the state of football in England, it's nothing compared to what goes on in Brazil. In the alleged home of the beautiful game, relegation is not the unshakeable monolith it is in Britain. The Brazilian football authorities bend over backwards to help out big clubs who have fallen on hard times. At the end of the 1991 season, Gremio, one of Brazil's leading clubs, were surprisingly relegated. In order to aid their return to the top flight, the Confederacao Brasilerei de Futebol decreed that no fewer than 12 clubs would be promoted the following season. Gremio were one of them, but as a result joined a top flight consisting of a rather unwieldy 32 clubs.

Four years later, the CBF were up to their tricks again. They decreed that the bottom two clubs in the top flight would be relegated. If, however, one or both of those clubs had ever won the Brazilian championship, they would play off against the lowest-placed team or teams that had never won the league. In other words, past glories that could conceivably have been attained before any of the team's current squad were born are deemed a good enough reason to overlook contemporary shortcomings on the field. A team finishing fifth from bottom could have found themselves demoted because a team that finished four places below them had waggled the championship trophy at their supporters 50 years before. Fortunately, neither of the clubs occupying the two bottom spots had ever won the title, ensuring that such lunatic play-offs were not necessary.

In 1996, Bragantino and the famous Fluminense occupied the bottom two places in the table, but this time, rather than mess around with unwieldy and time-consuming trivialities like play-offs or suchlike, the CBF, in another burst of philanthropy to their more historically successful charges, just let both clubs off, extending the top flight by two teams.

These oddball events have left the Brazilian Championship in chaos, with no one prepared to play at the lower level after such precedents have been set. It's no wonder that Pele resigned as Brazilian Sports Minister: football, which he had christened 'the beautiful game', has lost its sport. Money talks, and those who can shout the loudest get the breaks.

At least *Sky* would never try and tamper with the English relegation system; the farcical events in Brazil could never be repeated here. Would they? Could they?

Today, promotions and relegations are measured in terms of pounds, shillings and pence rather than kudos. At the conclusion of the 1998 First Division play-off final, for example, when Charlton's Sasa Ilic saved Michael Gray's spot-kick to earn a place in the top flight for the south London club, the *Daily Mail* dubbed it 'the £10 million save'. Similarly, in February 1997 Coventry City chairman Bryan Richardson told *FourFourTwo* magazine that 'if you go down you are probably looking at losing between £3 and £4 million a year'. No talk, then, of consolidation, of rebuilding, of taking stock and launching a new assault on the top flight. Nope, it's a question of how many noughts will be wiped off the club's share price.

Despite the huge financial stakes, the battle against relegation remains one of the pure sporting issues in a world gone money-mad. It's one of the few things left in the game still unsullied by the marketing people determined to squeeze as much money from the game as they possibly can. Pictures of grieving fans have been used in advertising campaigns (and, indeed, on the cover of this book, but hey, that's different), but generally relegation is the last bastion of what made football great that remains untainted. The FA Cup final has been turned into a cheap American-style orgy of razzmatazz and thus becomes no more special than an episode of *Gladiators*. At the bottom of the table, away from the glitz, fireworks and power-pop anthems, it's 11 against 11 for survival, not honours.

So many great moments in football have come from relegation dogfights. Denis Law's goal against Manchester United remains an enduring image, as does David Pleat's jigging, skipping run across the Maine Road turf after Raddy Antic's goal four minutes from time had kept Luton up at the expense of Manchester City. Some of the most poignant images ever photographed at a football match came at the Hereford United v. Brighton and Hove Albion game in May 1997.

Since the abandonment of the test matches in the 1890s (see chapter two), the principle of relegation has never changed. It even has its own rituals. In the town of Bamber Bridge, Lancashire, support is divided between the two local clubs, Blackburn Rovers and Preston North End. Since the 1950s a curious ritual based around the Withy Trees pub has taken place whenever one of the teams has been relegated. A small coffin, bedecked in the colours of the demoted club, is carried through the streets of the town and funeral cards are given out to the 'mourners'. It's even been known for players to turn out for the wake.

Appropriately, for a concept held in such spiritual and reverential regard, there are myriad reasons why a club ends up being relegated, some of which are documented in the ensuing chapters. But can we identify a series of circumstances that point to inevitable relegation?

In the current Premiership climate, promotion from the Nationwide League seems to be a good indication that relegation isn't too far behind. At the end of 1997–98, those who argue that the gap between the Premiership and the Nationwide League is ever widening were vindicated by the fact that the three relegated clubs, Bolton Wanderers, Crystal Palace and Barnsley, were the same three clubs that had come up the previous year. They were replaced by Nottingham Forest, Middlesbrough and very nearly by Sunderland, who came within a poorly taken penalty in the play-off final of making it a quick return for all three clubs relegated from the Premiership in 1997. Although Charlton Athletic, promoted instead of Sunderland, start the 1998–99 season favourites for the drop, the progress of Boro and Forest will be followed closely. With both clubs having experienced the drop relatively recently, relegation for either will not be greeted so tolerantly this time by supporters.

But besides the chasm developing between the Premiership and the Nationwide League, there are a number of pointers that would seem to suggest that relegation is on the cards. Clubs with high-profile, not to say unpopular, chairmen definitely seem to struggle. Crystal Palace's remarkable yo-yo journeys between the top flight and the First Division came under the tutelage of Ron Noades. Remember the team of the '80s? Jim Cannon? Jerry Murphy? The side that was supposed to dominate the '80s in the same way that Liverpool had dominated the '70s? Well, that team, under Ron Noades, were comprehensively relegated in 1981. Since then Palace have been relegated three times. It will be interesting to see how Mark Goldberg's reign at Selhurst Park develops. With Noades taking over at Griffin Park, Brentford fans will wait with baited breath: another relegation for them will be disastrous.

Steve Gibson's high media profile at the Cellnet Riverside culminated with Middlesbrough's demise, whilst Peter Swales and Francis Lee at Manchester City both saw their periods in the hot seat end with relegation. Robert Chase at Norwich City and David Kohler at Queen's Park Rangers both saw their sides relegated whilst they were under pressure to vacate their boardrooms, whilst the on-field tribulations of Newcastle United coincided with the saucy shenanigans of Douglas Hall and his hapless colleague Freddie Shepherd.

Similarly, the departure of a long-serving, successful manager tends to indicate that relegation is not far behind. Manchester United were relegated six years after Sir Matt Busby retired having guided the Red Devils to the European Cup. When Bill Nicholson retired in 1974, Spurs were relegated within three years. Even that man Graham Taylor, having guided Watford to runners-up spot in the old First Division, saw the Hornets relegated one year after he had departed Vicarage Road in 1987.

Newcastle United, whilst not actually relegated, have struggled since the departure of Kevin Keegan, and it certainly might be worth having a couple of quid on them to go down. While Brian Clough was still in charge when Nottingham Forest went down in 1993, no sooner had they regained their place in the top flight after the retirement of their idiosyncratic boss than they were down again in 1997.

Off-the-field problems are an obvious contributory factor to relegation. Boardroom takeovers, groundsharing, chairmen unpopular with supporters . . . there are a whole number of possible causes. Not having enough money to invest in players, investing too much money and spending beyond a club's means . . . so many different factors can contribute to the demise of a football club come the end of the season.

It is impossible to pinpoint fail-safe criteria for relegation. As this book will hopefully show, there are a number of factors which can be identified with hindsight but rarely with foresight. If it were possible to identify a formula that guaranteed relegation, someone would have sussed it by now. Obviously the appointment of Alan Ball as manager should set alarm bells ringing at any club (how has he managed to carve out such a long career in football management when he obviously can't even manage a stall at a jumble sale?), but short of sending out a team of one-legged players, no one can say for certain at the start of any season that a club will be relegated. Doncaster Rovers are probably the closest we can get to any such assertion.

It can soon become clear, however, that it is not going to be your season. You can lose a few games in August and September but still think that the team just needs time to gel, to get their act together. Sometimes it happens, but sometimes the defeats carry on through October until, by Christmas, you realise that the team your manager had assembled during the close season, that interesting blend of youth and experience that was raring to go and fully expected to be in contention for honours come May, was actually in contention for nothing more than the worst defensive record in the entire Football League. There is usually one game, one turning point when the realisation dawns that it's not going to be your season. The cold, creeping sensation that the bunch of cart-horses on the pitch have neither the fight nor the ability to lift you above the mire moves slowly up your body. It might be a spineless capitulation to a team that hasn't won for two months, or it might be a game against one of the high-flyers that you have dominated throughout, only to lose to a last-minute deflected goal. The moment where you finally turn to the person next to you and say, that's it, I think we're going to go down here. The moment you realise that it's unavoidable, that it's written in the book of fate in big red letters. You're going down.

There are many instances of this detailed in these pages. For Lincoln City in 1987 the realisation dawned after all the other teams had finished their season, whilst for Manchester City it was a game at Birmingham City at Christmas, where they took the lead with two minutes remaining but contrived to lose to two goals conceded in a lengthy period of injury time. For Nottingham Forest in 1993 it was a 3–0 defeat at Everton in March, when they realised that, contrary to what everyone had been telling them, they weren't too good to go down.

But there is one team which has never had that feeling, that realisation at one particular point of a particular game that you're sunk. That no matter how hard the players try, it's all pointless. You're doomed. It's a feeling that Coventry City supporters have never known.

The Sky Blues have made the avoidance of relegation an art form, one that only they have mastered. Southampton have come close a few times, but only Coventry have survived by the skin of their teeth so many times. Ten last-day escapes in nineteen seasons certainly suggests that there is some magic formula peculiar to Highfield Road.

The sequence began in 1967–68. Two days before the start of that campaign, Coventry manager Jimmy Hill left to take up a post at London Weekend Television to be replaced in the hot seat by Noel Cantwell. Following a long spell of success under Hill, City struggled that season and went into the final game away to Southampton knowing they had to do better than Sheffield United, who were at home to Chelsea. The Sky Blues fought out a tense 0–0 draw, Sheffield United obligingly lost to Chelsea, and the Sky Blues were safe.

The following season, Leicester City needed to win their last game at Manchester United to stay up and send Coventry, who had completed their league campaign early, down to the Second Division. The final score was Manchester United 3 Leicester City 2, the Foxes went down, and Coventry stayed up.

It wasn't until 1977 that the Sky Blues next flirted with demotion. As detailed later, Coventry, Sunderland and Bristol City were all level on points going into the final day of the season, and Coventry entertained the Ashton Gate side knowing that if Sunderland lost, a draw would be enough for both sides to stay up. A five-minute delay to the kick-off to allow spectators into the ground meant that Sunderland's game kicked off first. Coventry took a 2–0 lead over Bristol City, but the West Country club fought back to 2–2. Then it was flashed up on the electronic scoreboard that Sunderland had lost to Everton and the 2–2 scoreline would be enough to keep both clubs up. The remaining minutes saw both sides politely passing the ball to each other until the referee put an end to the charade, and Coventry had survived again.

In 1980–81, City needed to avoid defeat at Nottingham Forest on the last day to stay up. They drew 1–1. Three years later, a late run of conceding nineteen goals in four games left Coventry needing to beat Norwich City on the last day of the season to preserve their place in the top flight. They fell behind early in the game but came back to lead 2–1. With two minutes remaining, Norwich striker Robert Rosario hit a shot past Les Sealey that cannoned off the inside of the post, flashed across the goalmouth and was eventually cleared. The Sky Blues had lived to fight another day.

The following season Norwich lived to rue Rosario's miss. In a campaign ravaged by a fierce winter, the Sky Blues still had three games to play when the Canaries had finished their programme. Coventry occupied the highest relegation spot, whilst Norwich were eight points ahead of them. The Highfield Road side needed to win their last three games to stay up and condemn the East Anglians to the Second Division. A Stuart Pearce penalty at the Victoria Ground was enough to beat Stoke City, even though the home side missed a spot-kick in the dying minutes, and that game was followed by a scrappy 1–0 win over Luton Town at Highfield Road. The winning goal came just six minutes from the end when Brian Kilcline drilled a free-kick through the Luton wall and into the back of the net.

This meant that City had to beat the champions Everton in their last game to stay up. Everton had only lost once since Christmas. Four minutes into the game, Coventry went a goal up through Cyrille Regis. A quarter of an hour later Micky Adams made it two, only for Paul Wilkinson to pull a goal back for the champions before half-time. In the second half, barely 90 seconds had passed when Regis pounced on a loose ball in the area to make it 3–1, and 12 minutes from time Terry Gibson rounded Southall for the fourth. The Sky Blues had done it again. The following season, City sealed their third last-day escape in three seasons with a 2–1 win over Queen's Park Rangers.

Six years were to pass before Coventry's next great escape in 1992. They went into the last match of the season knowing that a draw at Aston Villa would keep them up. Luton, level on points with Coventry but with an inferior goal difference, travelled to Notts County. Ex-City player Cyrille Regis put Villa ahead after just 20 seconds, and Villa added to that lead early in the second half. It became clear that a draw was beyond the Sky Blues, and their luck seemed to have run out when news came through that Luton were a goal up against County. Amazingly, the Hatters threw away their lead, County won 2–1 and the Sky Blues had cheated the drop again.

In 1995–96, Coventry were involved in one of the most infamous relegation scraps of all time. The Sky Blues, Manchester City and Southampton were all in line for the last relegation spot. Coventry were level on points with Manchester City but had a superior goal average. Coventry drew 0–0 with Leeds but word somehow got through to Maine Road that the Sky Blues had lost. Alan Ball instructed his side, drawing 2–2, to hang on to the ball, the final whistle went, and Manchester City were relegated. Coventry's luck seemed to be never-ending. The following season, 1996–97, City went into their last game at Spurs knowing they had to win and Sunderland and Middlesbrough had to draw or lose. On this occasion, despite the form book, Coventry were given odds of 9–1 on to go down. Naturally, they won and survived again.

Luck does, undoubtedly, play a significant part in any season, and Coventry City have certainly ridden theirs over the years. Most clubs have not been so fortunate. If only that last-gasp shot had gone in instead of hitting the post; if only the floodlights hadn't failed when you were 2–0 up, only for you to lose the rearranged game 4–0. If only you'd turned up at Blackburn Rovers instead of staying at home with a doctor's note. The list of close-season laments can be endless.

Take Aston Villa, for example. They went into the last match of the 1958–59 season needing a point to stay in the First Division. They travelled to The Hawthorns to face Midlands rivals West Bromwich Albion and looked to have ground out the 0–0 draw they needed when, in the last minute, they gave away a corner. Despite packing the goalmouth, the cross came over and, you've guessed it, the Baggies scored. The ref blew the final whistle and Villa were down.

So can we see it coming? At the start of the season, how many of us can say that our club is going down?

Before the 1997–98 season commenced, *FourFourTwo* magazine published a comprehensive preview, asking a correspondent from each club how he or she rated the club's chances for the forthcoming season. Of the clubs relegated from the Premiership, the Bolton fan thought they'd finish tenth, the Palace fan, warning readers not to underestimate their guts and raw talent, predicted a sixteenth-place finish for the Eagles, whilst the Barnsley fan pleaded with tongue in cheek for a mid-table finish.

In the First Division, the Reading correspondent was sanguine about his club's chances, not actually saying that they'd go down but hinting that it was probably quite likely, the Stoke fan could see no reason why the Potters wouldn't do well and predicted a play-off finish, whilst the Manchester City supporter somewhat rashly predicted that the Blues would finish top, or in the play-offs at the very least. Whoops.

In Division Two Southend United, who experienced their second successive relegation, were expected to finish mid-table, the Carlisle United supporter predicted a play-off spot at the very least, the Plymouth fan correctly foresaw that Argyle would be relegated, whilst the Brentford fan surmised that the Bees, defeated in the 1997 play-off final by Crewe Alexandra, would be in for a long, hard season. In the Third Division, the Doncaster correspondent called for stability but, reading between the lines, wasn't holding out much hope for Rovers' survival.

Only three correspondents predicted that their sides would go down. The Plymouth fan was correct, whist the Oxford United and Swindon Town supporters were overly pessimistic about their sides' chances. So if that evidence is anything to go by, then, no, on the whole we can't see it coming.

But what motivates us to keep watching a team that is obviously not good enough for the standard of football in which they compete? Take Stoke City, for example. In 1985 they were relegated from the First Division having accumulated the lowest points total in the history of the top flight, a measly 17. They also scored the fewest number of goals, 24, and chalked up the lowest number of wins, a princely three. Yet still over 10,000 people turned up every week to watch the Potters get thumped out of sight and be relegated by a country mile. Why? If the Stoke City side of 1984–85 had been a West End play it would have closed within a fortnight. So why did people keep going? Season-ticket holders had some sort of excuse, I suppose; they'd forked out the cash in advance and so were almost obliged to show up. But what possessed the more casual fans to keep turning out in their thousands?

Football fans are often portrayed as eternal optimists – you know, the 'this week we'll turn it around' brigade. However, I think most of us are actually committed pessimists. A certain proportion of Stoke fans probably went down to the Victoria Ground to have a laugh. Another proportion probably went to chant 'sack the board', but most probably went out of that inexplicable, oft-debated blind devotion to their football club that defies logic and makes football supporters ripe for fleecing by the game's money-makers.

I can remember standing in a chip shop near Selhurst Park on New Year's Day 1991. Charlton had just drawn 0–0 with Blackburn Rovers in a game that did not produce a single chance at either end. It was freezing cold, we all had raging hangovers, Charlton were looking set fair to drop into the Third Division the season after being relegated from the First and we were all utterly miserable. I don't know why, but at the same moment my cousin and I looked at each other over a battered sausage and asked each other the same question. Why do we do this? We've just watched a rubbish team participate in one of the worst games of football we've ever seen, we're cold, hungry and hungover. That's it, we said, we're not coming any more. But we both knew full well that we'd be back there the following week.

Ten thousand Stoke fans must have felt the same thing. Relegation. It stares you out, it taunts you, it teases you for a whole season. But still you keep going, and keep hoping that the corner will be turned and the drop avoided. We just can't help believing, that's our trouble.

Finally, no book about relegation would be complete without mentioning Simeon Hodson. Simeon, having begun his career at Notts County, signed for his home-town club Lincoln City in January 1986. The following season, of course, Lincoln became the first team ever to be automatically relegated from the Football League. Rather than drop into non-League football, Simeon spent the close season casting around for a new club, before signing for Newport County. Newport then became the second club to be relegated automatically from the Football League. Then they went out of business. Aghast, but desperate to stay in the Football League, Simeon then moved on to The Hawthorns. Fortunately for him the Baggies managed to retain their Football League place.

As a postscript, Simeon finally made the drop into non-League football with Telford United in 1997. In 1998 Telford finished third from bottom of the Conference and were relegated. However, fortunately for Simeon Slough Town withdrew from the Conference and Telford were reprieved.

God bless you, Simeon Hodson, wherever you are . . .

From Test Matches to Four-Pointers

THE HISTORICAL PERSPECTIVE

Relegation started out as a northern thing.

Not because teams from the north were particularly bad, but because in the early days, wherein lie the roots of the bizarre Football League/Football Association duality, League football was a distinctly northern preserve.

Football's north-south divide had developed right from the inception of the FA Cup competition, launched in 1872. The trophy was competed for by teams from the south (Queen's Park excepted), which were largely composed of former public schoolboys. It was these men, drawn from the upper classes, who had formed the Football Association in 1863 in order to codify the games they played on their school fields and turn them into a recognisable competitive sport.

The concept of 'muscular Christianity' which prevailed amongst the upper classes in the late nineteenth century had it that running around a field chasing an inflated pig's bladder was, in the eyes of God, a good thing. It was noble, sporting, courageous and amateur. However, each public school had developed its own variant of the traditional folk game that became football, meaning that inter-school matches and, indeed, games at the universities, when ex-pupils came together from different schools, did not have a single set of rules by which they could be governed.

The noble characteristics of these pastimes were undermined, however, when Blackheath refused to join the Football Association in protest at the outlawing of hacking, a process by which your opponent was dispossessed through the sportsmanlike practice of a good crack on the shins and a stamp on the foot. Blackheath stomped off in a huff and went on to become one of the leading lights in a sport that adapted such thuggery into ear-chewing and head-stamping, rugby union.

The public-school nature of the Football Association is no better illustrated than in the make-up of the Wanderers team which beat the Royal Engineers in the first FA Cup final of 1872: four Harrovians, three Etonians and one player each from Westminster, Charterhouse, Oxford and Cambridge. In 1883, though, a team of grimy northern industrial types called Blackburn Olympic came down to the capital, having had the temerity to reach the final. Then, to make matters worse, Blackburn Rovers carried off the cup for the next two years. It would take the toffs ages to wipe the soot off the trophy.

With the introduction of Saturday afternoon leisure time and the progress of the Industrial Revolution, football had grown to become an immensely popular pastime amongst working men. It was cheap and easy to play, and also cheap and exciting to watch. Huge crowds gathered to watch teams, particularly those based around the workplace. The traditional 3 p.m. Saturday kick-off derived from the fact that the factories would turn out on a Saturday lunchtime, so the afternoons were the only time the working man could feasibly watch or play football. Nowadays, of course, television dictates that games can be played at any time.

It was in 1888 that a Birmingham shopkeeper and Aston Villa fan called William McGregor called a meeting of interested parties in order to put forward a plan for a regulated series of fixtures between the major clubs. And so it was that in August that year the Football League came into existence, made up entirely of clubs from the north and Midlands: Everton, Preston North End, Blackburn Rovers, Bolton Wanderers, Aston Villa, Notts County, Burnley, West Bromwich Albion, Wolverhampton Wanderers, Accrington Stanley, Stoke City and Derby County.

Such was the popularity of the new Football League that four years later, in 1892, a Second Division was introduced, comprising Ardwick, Bootle, Burton Swifts, Crewe Alexandra, Grimsby Town, Lincoln City, Small Heath Alliance, Walsall Town, Burslem Port Vale, Northwich Victoria and Sheffield United. Once again, the Football League showed its impeccable northern credentials.

Even before the inception of the Second Division, the Football League was not a closed shop, in theory at least, with the bottom club being required to apply for re-election. This idiosyncratic system was to remain in place at the bottom of the League for almost a century, and was not abolished until 1986 when the Football League introduced direct promotion and relegation between the Fourth Division and the Conference.

The re-election system, which was to hinder the progress of ambitious non-League clubs for years to come, was, however, open to abuse. In the third season of the League, for example, Aston Villa and Bolton Wanderers occupied the bottom two places with 19 points. Bolton were placed last, having an inferior goal average, but, amazingly, there was a dispute over the result of their match with Notts County the previous October. The referee had reported the result as 4–0 to Notts County, but Bolton suddenly claimed that it had been only 3–0, a result which could have sent Villa out of the League in their stead. County agreed that they only recalled scoring three goals, but the referee was adamant there had been four. In a display of official wishy-washiness that was to characterise the League in future years, McGregor and his committee decided that the best way to defuse the situation was to exempt both clubs from the necessity of applying for re-election. In the words of *Shoot!* magazine's 'You are the ref' column, the League chose option c) take no action.

The random nature of re-election was underlined the following season when West Bromwich Albion finished second from bottom. With the League's expansion to 16 clubs that season, the bottom four clubs were all required to apply to keep their place the following season, and the Baggies were joined in their predicament by Darwen, Stoke City and Accrington Stanley. Remarkably, West Brom were given exemption from applying for re-election because they had won the FA Cup that season, a competition totally separate from the League.

At the end of the 1891–92 season it was clear to the League that the re-election system wasn't working. The introduction of the Second Division also necessitated a rethink on how to ensure that the best teams were allowed access to the top division. A system of 'test' matches were introduced, the forerunner of the play-offs of the modern age. But, instead of a knockout competition, a random system was introduced whereby the top three teams from the Second Division would meet the bottom three from the First. Thus Darwen beat Notts County and Sheffield United beat Accrington Stanley to go up and send their opponents down, but Small Heath, later to become Birmingham City, the first champions of the Second Division, lost to Newton Heath, aka Manchester United, in a replay. This resulted in the champions of the Second Division staying there and watching two teams that they had proved themselves to be superior to over the course of the season take their places in the top flight, whilst the team who'd finished bottom contrived to stay up. Piqued by this, relegated Accrington refused to play in the Second Division and joined the Lancashire League instead, whilst County thought long and hard before agreeing to take up their place in the lower division.

The test-match system clearly wasn't satisfactory in its present format, but it took another two seasons to introduce the mini-league system whereby the six clubs all played each other rather than playing one game against one opponent. Two years later, in 1897, the test-match system was streamlined to encompass the top and bottom two rather than three clubs from each division. At the end of the 1897–98 campaign the First Division's bottom club Stoke City met Second Division champions Burnley in the final round of matches. Both teams had accrued four points from their previous matches, whilst the other two teams involved, Newcastle United and Blackburn Rovers, had two points each. It didn't take Stoke and Burnley long to work out that a point apiece would ensure their places in the First Division the following season.

So it was that on 30 April 1898 Stoke City and Burnley took part in what must be a contender for the worst football match ever played – and, let's face it, there's been some tough competition.

With the pitch in a dreadful condition due to constant heavy rain in the days preceding the match, the two teams contrived to put on the most tedious match ever played. By half-time there had not been a single shot on goal. During the second half the crowd twigged what was going on and enthusiastically booed both teams. The charade continued unabated with both teams strolling around the field, politely passing the ball around. Eventually the crowd resorted to hanging on to the ball if it went out of play because, let's face it, the players certainly didn't need it. The game ended to a cacophony of abuse from the touchlines, still without a single effort on goal from either side. The players hadn't even pretended to try and win the game. Despite the obvious collusion and disgraceful shilly-shallying by both sides, the result was allowed to stand and Newcastle and Blackburn, who'd been engaged in a rather more exciting 4–3 victory for the Lancashire side that afternoon, missed out.

However, the expansion of the League to 18 clubs in each division the following season meant that the Stoke and Burnley collusion had in fact been meaningless, as they were both included in the top division anyway. The remaining two places the League decided to put to the vote. Manchester City, Newton Heath, Woolwich Arsenal and Small Heath put themselves forward, but Newcastle and Blackburn Rovers came top of the poll to earn a First Division place. One can only wonder what sort of a reception Stoke and Burnley received when they turned up in Newcastle and Blackburn the following season.

Soon afterwards, the first automatic promotion and relegation was introduced between the two divisions and in 1899 Bolton Wanderers and Sheffield

Wednesday became the first teams ever to be relegated automatically in English football. In a precedent of what was to come in the Premier League a century later, both teams went straight back up the following season, a campaign which produced the first major football scandal of the age which was a direct result of determination to avoid relegation at all costs.

As the twentieth century dawned, the season that straddled its turn was drawing to an uneventful close. Aston Villa had won the Football League; Bury had won the FA Cup. Glossop North End had finished bottom of the First Division, nine points adrift. The other relegation place would go to either Preston North End or Burnley, one of the villains of the test-match fiasco two seasons earlier. Needing to beat Nottingham Forest in their final game of the season, the Clarets crashed 4–0 and were relegated, to the delight of Newcastle and Blackburn fans everywhere. That appeared to be that, but the Nottingham Forest captain later alleged that as the two teams had lined up for the kick-off, the Burnley captain and goalkeeper Jackie Hillman had offered him two pounds a man to throw the game, claiming that at half-time, with Forest 2–0 up, he'd increased the offer to five pounds. Hillman admitted making the offer but claimed that he'd done it as a joke. The FA stopped laughing just long enough to ban him for one season.

Meanwhile, the re-election system in Division Two was still proving to be a farcical way of conducting business. In 1908, Tottenham Hotspur applied for election to the Football League from the Southern League, which had been set up as an amateur response to the professionalism of the new Second Division. The southern clubs, still largely public-school and amateur, resented the growth of the professional League, and the Southern League was seen as a more noble competition than that involving the money-grabbing northern professionals.

Unhappy that Spurs should want to leave and jump into bed with the Football League, the Southern League insisted that the club, who in 1901 had become the only Southern League team to win the FA Cup, resign their membership whatever the outcome of their application, leaving Tottenham with the possibility of not having a league to play in for the coming season. These fears appeared to be confirmed when Grimsby Town and Chesterfield were both re-elected and Lincoln City were replaced by Watford, all at Tottenham's expense.

Things looked ominous for Spurs, but then Stoke City, struggling on meagre crowds in the Potteries, suddenly announced their resignation from the League. In June a meeting was called at League headquarters, where Spurs and Lincoln City would put their cases for election and the vacant place would be put to the vote. Just before the meeting Stoke announced that they'd changed their minds and would appreciate very much having their place back please. Instead of turning them down, the League took the strange decision of including them in the ballot too. The votes were cast. Stoke finished last but Lincoln and Spurs ended up with the same total. To break the deadlock, the clubs who'd voted for Stoke were asked to vote again for either Tottenham or Lincoln City, and, wouldn't you know it, both teams ended up with 20 votes. It was turning into a long meeting. Various ways were considered to separate the two sides, but the League eventually brought an end to the farce by announcing that they'd give the place to Spurs. If the finger of fate had pointed at Lincoln City instead then, who knows, maybe the Imps would have done the double in 1961, gone on to win numerous FA Cups and be taken over by the stubbly chinned boss of an international computer company. Instead Lincoln had had the misfortune to be relegated twice in the same season.

The following campaign saw Nottingham Forest involved in yet another relegation scandal. On the last day of the season they faced Leicester Fosse knowing that they had to win by two clear goals to stay up and send Manchester City down instead. Fosse were already down, whilst Forest occupied 19th place with 34 points, the same as City but with an inferior goal difference. The game finished, rather suspiciously, 12–0 in Forest's favour, with three players (Hooper, Spouncer and Enoch 'Knocker' West, whose name was to crop up again in another relegation scandal) claiming hat-tricks. Manchester City, relegated by this result, not surprisingly went ballistic and complained to the Football League, who immediately launched an enquiry.

What they discovered was not some sort of fix; no brown envelopes had changed hands in shady corners of smoke-filled public houses. The Leicester Fosse players, already resigned to relegation, had on the evening before the game attended the wedding reception of one of their former team-mates, R.F. Turner, who had since joined Everton. It turned out that the Fosse players, far from having been bought off to lose the game, were just suffering from the most horrendous hangovers and could barely put one foot in front of the other, let alone play 90 minutes of competitive football. Maybe the League enquiry should have concentrated on how Forest only managed to score 12 against a team of stumbling, stubbly, sweaty players reeking of stale booze, vomiting on the sidelines and wandering around holding their heads and moaning 'never again'. As Fosse nursed their Alka Seltzer, the result was allowed to stand and City were condemned, sulking, to the Second Division.

When war broke out in 1914, football was widely criticised for not ceasing its programme and releasing players and spectators to go over to France and be killed knee-deep in mud. In the early stages of the war, recruitment was still essentially voluntary, and the football authorities' apparent refusal to suspend the game was seen as an obstruction to the recruiting drive. For some reason the prospect of staying at home to watch Derby County play Burnley was more appealing than being blown to pieces on the Somme.

The last offical game before football was suspended was the 1915 FA Cup final between Sheffield United and Chelsea, known as the 'khaki' final because of the number of military uniforms in the crowd, but three weeks previously relegation had been the shadowy figure behind the latest match-fixing scandal. On Good Friday 1915, Manchester United met Liverpool in a crucial league match for United, who lay third from bottom and were in serious danger of going down.

The match kicked off in the pouring rain and, roared on by a crowd of 15,000, United took an early lead through Anderson, who made it 2–0 early in the second half. However, with Liverpool looking strangely uninterested in salvaging the game or even having a serious attempt on goal, it was when McPherson hoofed a United penalty out of the ground that it became clear United and Liverpool had already agreed upon a 2–0 scoreline. The crowd soon realised what was going on and voiced its derision. The penny dropped for the referee after McPherson's penalty, which made Chris Waddle's in Turin look like a narrow squeak, but he was powerless to do anything whilst the game was in progress. When Fred Pagnam, who turned out to be the only United player not party to the affair, hit the crossbar late in the game, he was berated by a number of his team-mates.

The man behind the arrangement turned out to be Enoch 'Knocker' West, a striker with a tremendous goalscoring record for Sheffield United, Nottingham Forest and Manchester United, whom he had joined in 1910. West's performance in the match had been extraordinary: every time he received the ball he would more often than not thump it as far out of play as he could. On one occasion, when he found himself near the Liverpool goal with the ball at his feet, he turned away from goal and lofted the ball on to the roof of the grandstand.

The result was enough to keep United in the First Division. The FA concluded that the match had been fixed, and that several players would have won a lot of money through bets placed on the result if the bookies hadn't realised what was going on and refused to pay out. However, as football had officially ceased for the duration of the war and many players had joined up and gone to the front, the League had little alternative but to allow the result to stand. Chelsea were relegated in the position that United would have occupied had they lost to Liverpool that day. Spurs were also down. Many players received bans, but were pardoned at the end of the war having served their country during the hostilities. West, despite his relentless protestations of innocence, saw his ban remain in place until 1945.

Chelsea found themselves reprieved when football recommenced after the war during which the Football League had decided to increase the complement of clubs to 22 in both divisions. Chelsea were allowed to stay up, whilst the remaining place was contested between Spurs, who'd finished bottom, Barnsley, Birmingham City, Arsenal, Hull City, Nottingham Forest and Wolverhampton Wanderers. Arsenal came top of the poll despite having finished behind Barnsley, Wolves and Birmingham in the last season before the war. That first season after hostilities was marred by yet another scandal involving a club in danger of relegation, a scandal that didn't emerge until a Sunday newspaper exposed the story three years later.

The 1919–20 season had proved to be a disastrous one for Coventry City. In their first campaign as a Football League club they had not been out of the bottom two all season and went into their final two games, both against Bury, needing at least two points to stay up at the expense of Lincoln City, who had returned to League action since the Spurs fiasco. The bottom two clubs would have to apply for re-election and there was a widespread feeling in the game that any application from Coventry would be unsuccessful.

Coventry were a point behind Lincoln with a game in hand, but Lincoln had a superior goal difference. The match at Gigg Lane finished 2–2, and on 1 May 1920 the two teams met at Highfield Road. A crowd of more than 23,000 gathered to see Coventry come back from 1–0 down to win the match 2–1 and rise out of the relegation places for the first and only time all season. Lincoln failed to win re-election and were not even elected to the Third Division which was introduced the following season.

Although the match was the subject of rumours, it wasn't until 1923 that the League decided to act. They announced that the game had been fixed, both sides were fined £100 and ten players and officials received life bans. The full facts of the matter were not made public for many years (indeed, it turned out that when making their decision, the League were actually talking about the wrong match) until the former Coventry captain George Chaplin finally revealed all to a local newspaper in 1938. It turned out that prior to the two games with Bury, Chaplin and Coventry chairman David Cooke went to visit the Gigg Lane club and £200 changed hands. The result was assured and Coventry were off the hook. Lincoln lost out yet again.

In a few short years, then, relegation had become a prospect so daunting that clubs were prepared to buy their way out of trouble. Even in the years long before the top-heavy financial situation of League football, the stigma and lower wages engendered by relegation were enough for clubs to try to avoid it by fair means or foul.

More and more clubs experienced the ignominy of going down until, by the mid-'30s only Aston Villa and Blackburn Rovers of the original members of the Football League had never been relegated. Ironically they went down together in 1936, having played each other on the last day of the season. Blackburn won 4–2, but other results didn't go their way and they joined their opponents in the Second Division the following season.

The climax to the 1927–28 season, meanwhile, produced one of the most exciting relegation dogfights in football history. Going into the last game of the season, no fewer than ten First Division teams were looking nervously over their shoulders at the drop. In the end Middlesbrough and Tottenham Hotspur went down, with Boro finishing bottom on 37 points, but so close was the division that Derby County in fourth place had only seven points more. Spurs finished with 38, having been in sixth place at the end of March. Their 2–0 defeat at Liverpool on the last day of the season sealed their fate. Above the drop zone no fewer than seven clubs finished on 39 points, one ahead of Spurs.

As the years went by, the Football League settled into a four-division format. By the end of the 1950s, the regionalised third divisions were replaced with national third and fourth divisions, and a two-up, two-down, system was introduced. The bottom four clubs of the Fourth Division were still expected to apply for re-election every season, but it was viewed as little more than a formality. Despite the postwar boom in attendances, admission prices stayed affordable for even the poorest of working men – and it was mostly men packing the terraces in those days – whilst the maximum wage imposed on the players meant that the four divisions were kept within reasonable reach of each other. Players could not be lured away by the promise of vast sums of money, and tended to stay with one club for most of their career. But with the abolition of the maximum wage, as well as the increase in TV coverage and the boost to the domestic game of England's 1966 World Cup win, the clubs at the top began to grow richer, and relegation became something to be avoided at all costs.

Before the big clubs came to dominate the game entirely, the League still kept competition as open as possible, introducing the three-up, three-down system for the top two divisions, with four clubs moving between the Third and Fourth Divisions. Thus it became easier for clubs to move up and down the divisions, and the interests of more clubs were kept going for longer each season as there was an extra promotion and relegation place to fill. So it was that in 1974, Southampton, Crystal Palace and Cambridge United found themselves relegated in a position which would have made them safe the previous season. Bury, York City and Carlisle United, the last winning promotion to the First Division for the only time in their history, were the first beneficiaries of the extra promotion places.

Since then, the two major changes affecting relegated clubs have been automatic promotion and relegation between the Fourth Division and the Conference, introduced in 1986 to do away with the annual charade of re-election, and the inception of the Premier League. Much as the bigger clubs would like it to be a closed shop, so far the three-up, three-down system has survived numerous attempts at tinkering by the fat cats of the Premiership, and the door is open, albeit only a crack, for the smaller clubs, as teams like Bolton, Palace and Forest yo-yo between the top two divisions and dominate the promotion and relegation places.

So thank you, Stoke City and Burnley. If you hadn't strolled around for an hour and a half on the last day of April 1898, giggling behind your hands, killing time in the most outrageous display of collusion, a game which made West Germany v. Austria in the 1982 World Cup look like a fiercely fought cup tie, then maybe we wouldn't have the annual scrap for survival, the inten-sity of emotion that fills the ensuing pages here. The glee at seeing the big boys come a cropper, the fear of the last-minute corner in the last game of the season when you think you've got the point you need, the joyful taunts of 'going down, going down', the essential trappings of watching football. Thank you, Stoke and Burnley, for demonstrating to us that the intensity of emotion is just as strong in the slough of despond as the Elysian fields of joy. We are forever in your debt.

Knocker West and George Chaplin, we salute you. We salute you for recognising what a dreadful and terrible thing relegation is by trying to cheat your way out of it. And succeeding.

You can keep your Champions' League. Relegation, the basement, that's what football is really all about. Relegation is keeping the game alive. And it's bloody great.

Anyone Who Says They Remember the '60s Is Probably a Northampton Town Supporter

'Any team moving from the Second Division to the First needs half a million pounds spare to buy players. The club must also have an average home gate of at least 30,000, because the First Division is in effect two divisions in one: the élite top ten and the rest who make up the numbers.'

These words were spoken by far-sighted Northampton Town manager Dave Bowen after his side were relegated at the end of their only season in the top flight in 1966. More than 30 years later, they ring as true now as they did then; only the names and the price have changed. The circumstances in which they were spoken, however, will, in the present climate, never be repeated. The élite clubs and makers of fast bucks have seen to that.

Northampton Town had a remarkable decade in the '60s. The club that played its home matches on the car park of Northamptonshire County Cricket Club, a quirky, ramshackle, three-sided ground never popular with away supporters and not particularly popular with home supporters either, began and ended the decade in the Fourth Division. In the intervening years, the Cobblers rose through the divisions to earn a place in the top flight. One season later they were back in Division Two, and within two seasons they had returned from whence they had come, and where they were to remain for most of the ensuing years. In the early 1990s, the club came within a whisker of losing their Football League place and going out of existence altogether, but, unusually for a lower-division club, this tale has a happy ending.

When the Southern League was absorbed into the Football League as Division Three (South) in 1920, Northampton Town, bewildered at finding themselves suddenly elevated to League status, chugged along in respectable mid-table fashion throughout the '30s, '40s and most of the '50s troubling no one, local trophy-engravers in particular. They had the odd good season, as well as the odd stinker, but for the most part solid mid-table obscurity was held down with relentless monotony. In 1958, however, the Football League abandoned the regional set-up of its lowest divisions and introduced two national tiered divisions. The teams finishing in the top halves of the Third Divisions North and South at the end of the 1957–58 season would constitute a new national Third Division, whilst those finishing below halfway would make up the Fourth Division. Although the Cobblers' season was enlivened by an FA Cup run that included a famous 3–1 victory over Arsenal (whose side included ex-Cobbler and future boss Dave Bowen) and a visit to Anfield, Northampton found themselves struggling to cling on to their Third Division status. A late-season run that saw just one defeat in nine games (including a 7–2 hammering of Millwall and a 9–0 tonking of Exeter City) was undone by defeat in the last two games of the season which resulted in the County Ground side finishing in 13th place, one place below that required to attain Third Division status.

During the close season manager Dave Smith sought to strengthen his backroom staff to build upon the team's impressive end-of-season form, and suggested to the Northampton board that Dave Bowen be brought back from Arsenal to the County Ground as player-coach. Great idea, said the board, but we've got a better one. We'll bring him in as player-manager. Thanks for all you've done, Smudger, but can you clear your desk by the end of the week?

It was a move of astonishing boldness and foresight by the board, as Bowen was to become easily the most successful manager in the club's history. Which wasn't, in fact, saying much at the time, but his achievements were to be considerable by the standards of any club. In his first season, the novice manager steered the Cobblers to sixth position, missing out on a promotion place by just four points. The side he had assembled was a mixture of players brought up through the club's ranks and the results of shrewd dealings in the transfer market. For his first managerial appointment, Bowen was coming on like an old hand.

The 1960–61 season saw local rivals Peterborough United elected to the Football League, joining the Cobblers in the Fourth Division at the expense of Gateshead. Both sides set the pace in the division, with 23,000 people watching their first league encounter at London Road, where the Cobblers threw away a 3–0 lead to draw 3–3. By Easter, the four teams who were to be the first to leave the Fourth Division were well clear of the rest, with Peterborough eventually being crowned champions, followed by Crystal Palace,

Northampton Town and Bradford Park Avenue. The Cobblers had gained the first promotion in their long history. It was something they were to develop a taste for in the next few seasons.

The 1961-62 season started badly for Northampton Town, as they failed to score in their first six hours of Third Division football. Bowen then pulled off a public-relations masterstroke by signing the former Arsenal striker Cliff Holton from Watford. On a whim, Bowen telephoned Holton on the day of an away match at Crystal Palace in September 1961 and tentatively asked if the ex-Gunner fancied turning out for Northampton that evening. Holton, out of favour at Watford because of his business interests outside the game, agreed, met Bowen in London, signed the necessary papers, travelled on to Selhurst Park, pulled on a claret jersey and banged in a hat-trick as part of a 4–1 win. That evening Holton, who'd woken that day a Watford player, scored three times as many goals as the entire team had managed in their previous five games. He went on to score 36 times that season as the Cobblers finished in a respectable eighth place.

The following season saw the club race out of the blocks: an undefeated first ten games included an 8–0 thrashing of Wrexham and a 7–1 spanking of Halifax Town. Holton left halfway through the season to join Crystal Palace, claiming that his business commitments in the capital made it necessary for him to join a London club. He had, he said, driven two cars into the ground wearing a track up and down the motorway. Two cars that belonged to Northampton Town, but that's hardly the point. No wonder he was a successful businessman.

Holton's replacement Bert Llewellyn was carried off in his first game for the club at Queen's Park Rangers, during which a Rangers fan ran on to the pitch, attacked two Northampton players in a rare display of passion at Loftus Road and was eventually pinned to the goalpost by Cobblers keeper Chic Brodie. Brodie was later to have his career ended by another pitch invader, a dog which careered into him as he gathered the ball whilst playing for Brentford, smashing his kneecap.

Llewellyn's replacement, meanwhile, was watching the Northampton striker's exit on a stretcher from the White City stands. Frank Large was a QPR player that day, but Bowen signed the unsettled striker in what was to be another managerial masterstroke. Large went on to chalk up 18 goals during the second half of the season, as Northampton finished the campaign as Third Division champions. Promotion was confirmed with a 3–0 win over Brighton in mid-April in front of 17,000 people at the County Ground, and the title was assured in the best possible way for Cobblers fans, a 4–0 win away at Peterborough United.

The summer of 1963 saw the title euphoria tempered a little by the resignation of Dave Bowen as manager. In a bizarre crisis of confidence, Bowen asserted that he had taken the club as far as he could, and it was the job of a more experienced boss to take the club into the Second Division. Assistant Jack Jennings took over on a caretaker basis, and the Cobblers went straight to the top of the table, starting the season with three wins out of three, including a 2–0 win at Roker Park in front of 40,000 screaming mackems. For the next game, at home to Derby County, Dave Bowen had exorcised his demons and resumed control to steer the team to a 1–0 reverse. Despite the odd highlight, such as turning Sunderland over 5–1 on a snow-covered pitch at the County Ground, Northampton finished the season in consolidatory 12th place, with little hint as to what was to come. The only clues were to be found in the club's formidable reserve team packed with young players who were to develop the following season into First Division contenders.

An early-season run of 17 games unbeaten placed the Cobblers second in the division at Christmas 1964. The team that Bowen had assembled for £16,000 was reputed in some circles to be worth around a quarter of a million pounds. Bowen's investment in youth was paying off: not only were the club in a strong position on the field, they also had a 22-legged bank account running around on the pitch each Saturday.

With four games remaining, the team travelled to Gigg Lane knowing a win over Bury would be enough to win promotion to the First Division. The Shakers included a young Colin Bell in their side. Joe Kiernan opened the scoring with a 20-yard shot and the Cobblers were two up in a quarter of an hour through Bobby Brown. Bury pulled a goal back, but Don Martin ensured promotion with two second-half goals. The Cobblers went up in second place behind Newcastle United following a 'tame' 1–1 draw with Portsmouth at the County Ground on the final day of the season. The point ensured Portsmouth's Second Division safety in Jimmy Dickinson's 764th and final game for Pompey.

Northampton Town, who just four years earlier had never even been promoted, were now, incredibly, a First Division football club. If Dave Bowen's words at the head of this chapter could have been taken out of any modern newspaper, so could the treatment meted out to the Cobblers following their triumph. They were roundly castigated by the press for their robust long-ball style, their lack of support and their bizarre home ground. Sound familiar? Up sticks and move to Dublin, anyone? Northampton were widely expected to be totally out of their depth amongst the big boys, and no one expected them to stay longer than one season in the top flight.

Bowen, who caused incredulity in the press by turning down a big-money move to Sunderland, refused to be cowed by criticism and invited the thrill-seeking Northampton public down to the County Ground to see First Division football with the words 'Don't think that we are going to put entertainment in front of running the risk of losing', and promptly rewarded the squad by taking them on a glamorous close-season tour of . . . Eastern Europe.

The 1965–66 season opened at Goodison Park in front of 48,000 people. Holding their own at 2–1 down with 15 minutes to go, the Cobblers eventually went down 5–2. 'We shall respect everyone in this league,' commented Bowen afterwards. 'The lads found the pace even faster than they expected. Everton's ability to turn defence into attack within seconds came as a bit of a surprise.'

Appropriately, Northampton's first home game was against Arsenal, the team the Cobblers had dumped out of the FA Cup a few years earlier, and where Dave Bowen had spent ten successful years as a player. Herbert Chapman had cut his managerial teeth at the County Ground before turning Arsenal into the enormous institution they had become as a result of his management. The game finished 1–1, with the Cobblers gaining the same result a week later against Manchester United.

The first win of the season was achieved against a West Ham side containing the Moore, Hurst and Peters trio which within months would be the backbone of England's triumphant World Cup team. The victory came at the end of a week during which Bowen had failed to tempt Celtic winger Jimmy Johnstone to the County Ground.

The Cobblers were then at the wrong end of a number of hammerings: 6–1 at Leeds, 6–1 at Blackburn (who were to finish bottom of the table), 5–0 at Liverpool, when Bill Shankly commented 'I don't agree that Northampton are the worst team in the First Division', and two 6–2 defeats, at Manchester United and Stoke City, on successive Saturdays. But despite these reverses, they also picked up useful points, winning 4–1 at Fulham and 2–1 at Villa Park, as well as beating Leeds 2–1 in the return and holding eventual champions Liverpool to a goalless draw at the County Ground.

The crucial game came on 23 April against fellow strugglers Fulham. With three games to go, and Blackburn already down, 11 clubs were in theory still in danger of occupying the remaining relegation place. A record crowd of 24,423 packed into the County Ground to see the Cobblers take a 2–1 half-time lead. Early in the second half, George Hudson's lob bamboozled Jim McLelland in the Fulham goal and the ball appeared to cross the line before Fulham scrambled it away to safety. However, the linesman, in a sublimely ill-timed moment of slapstick, had slipped, fallen flat on his face and completely missed the incident. The Cobblers had another goal disallowed when Mackin's free-kick was ruled out for an alleged foul on the beleaguered Fulham goalkeeper. Two other chances had been cleared off the line and Moore had hit the bar. With 25 minutes to go, however, Northampton were still 2–1 up when Steve Earle equalised for the Londoners. Two goals in the last two minutes gave Fulham the points and all but confirmed Northampton's swift return to the Second Division. Despite beating Sunderland the following week, defeat at Blackpool on the final day brought the Cobblers' odyssey to a close. Against all likelihood, Northampton Town had competed at the highest level and all but survived. A five-year journey from the bottom division had been ended by two late Fulham goals and a linesman who came over all Norman Wisdom at the wrong moment.

What the club had achieved was extraordinary. Joe Mercer concurred, commenting, 'The miracle of 1966 was not England winning the World Cup but Northampton Town reaching the First Division.' He also told Dave Bowen that until you have been relegated, you have not been initiated. For the Cobblers, however, it was not so much an initiation as the start of a slide that was to lead to the calamitous events of the 1990s. The glory days were well and truly over.

The 1966–67 season literally brought the club to its knees. By February 1967, as the summer of love approached, it was a spring of surgery for North-ampton. No fewer than 11 players underwent cartilage operations during the season (was the County Ground pitch made of concrete?), and Dennis Brown lost a kneecap in a car accident. The low point came in October when the Cobblers leaked 26 goals in six games, including 6–1 shaftings at Hull and Ipswich. Remarkably, between the Ipswich result and a 4–0 home defeat by Wolves, Northampton chalked up a record 8–0 win over Brighton in the League Cup.

After this dismal period, skipper Theo Foley returned from his personal cartilage battle and Frank Large rejoined the club from Oldham. Large helped to bring about an upswing in fortunes and a 2–0 win over Cardiff in March lifted the Cobblers from the bottom of the table for the first time all season. A 3–1 lead over Carlisle turned into a 3–3 draw to keep the club up to their neck in trouble, followed as it was by a 3–0 reverse at Blackburn Rovers. A trip to the Valley in a relegation four-pointer saw Charlton triumph 3–0, and Northampton were condemned to the Third Division. 'We just hadn't got it,' said Bowen, having seen the players he'd brought up through the ranks depar-ting the club in such numbers that a revolving door was almost commissioned for the club's main entrance.

Early in the Third Division campaign of 1967–68, Dave Bowen relinquished his managerial duties for good. Former Spurs winger Tony Marchi joined as manager and cleared the decks of the remaining players from the First Division season. Don Martin joined Blackburn for £36,000, and Frank Large departed again, reluctantly joining First Division Leicester City for £20,000. Despite bringing in several new players, the Cobblers finished the season in 18th position. Marchi received his marching orders, and complained that he'd been brought to the club to halt the slide, and he'd halted it. Surprisingly, 18th place in the Third Division two seasons after being in the First was not considered much of an achievement by the board and Marchi stomped off in a huff.

The following season, former Wolves and England player Ron Flowers stepped up to the manager's job from his previous position as coach. With little option but to blood young players, Flowers's experience on the field could only benefit youngsters like full-back Phil Neal, who was to go on to great things with Liverpool and England, eventually landing a plum job repeating everything Graham Taylor said on the England bench.

By mid-March the Cobblers were conceivably in with a shout of promotion, but a terrible run saw eight defeats in ten games and a 1–1 draw with Oldham on the last day of the season was not enough to save them from a return to the Fourth Division they had left nine years earlier. The final home game, against Crewe Alexandra, attracted a crowd of 4,406. Three years earlier, when the Cobblers had concluded their home First Division programme with a 2–1 win over Sunderland, they had pulled in just under 18,000 people.

In the increasingly liberal-minded '60s, Northampton Town's footballing odyssey must have seemed like some weird, drug-fuelled fantasy. Logically, it just shouldn't have happened: one of the League's most committed underachievers, who only found themselves in the Football League by accident when the Southern League was deemed dangerously successful and enticed into the fold in the 1920s, had catapulted themselves into the highest echelon of English football. Having careered into the top flight, the Fourth Division bunjee rope twanged them back into the basement as fast as they had left it. In February 1970, Manchester United arrived at the County Ground for an FA Cup tie. Four years earlier, the Cobblers had been United's First Division bedfellows and eked out a 1–1 draw. On this occasion, however, any lingering pretensions that Northampton may have had to belonging outside the lower divisions were pounded into the mud as an inspirational George Best helped himself to six of United's eight goals.

The increased gates of the glory years, as well as the profits the club made in the transfer market, should have left Northampton in a position to finally up sticks and leave the County Ground. Their history was littered with suggestions and plans for new locations that were never pursued. As early as 1930, plans were mooted for a move to an old military site and a complex which would have included a sports centre and accommodation for over 20,000 people, nearly half of whom would be seated. It came to nothing, as most of these schemes do. How many times have plans for fantastic stadia been unveiled, depicting sleek stands, little trees and strange stick people walking around in pairs, casting long shadows? How many times do these plans come to nought, and the new ground turns out to be a soulless affair more suited to a Subbuteo stadium?

Whatever profit the Cobblers made on the way up, it didn't go into a new stadium. The club's rapid fall from the pedestal of the First Division negated any grandiose plans for relocation and the County Ground was to remain the home of both Northampton cricket and Northampton football for the foreseeable future.

If Dave Bowen's comments about the 'two divisions in one' were true in the pre-World Cup mid-'60s, the situation is even worse in the 1990s. Northampton's rise and fall would probably be fatal in the modern climate. A club rising through the divisions with such rapidity would have to invest heavily in playing staff and facilities and hope for at least a few seasons in the top flight to recoup that investment through television income and to build an increased fanbase. Wimbledon, although their crowds are higher than most people give them credit for, have suffered for their meteoric rise from the Southern League because they didn't have a wide historical fanbase; they rose too quickly to establish themselves in the local community above their traditional status. Northampton didn't have time to do that in the '60s. In 1959–60 they averaged around 8,500 for home matches; ten seasons later, back in the bottom division, the club was pulling in just over 5,000. In between, they averaged over 18,000 during their First Division season. So, during the Cobblers' slide, 13,000 people found better things to do in Northampton on a Saturday afternoon and never returned. Maybe another two or three seasons in the top flight would have established a wider fanbase through the club's higher position and higher media profile. The coffers would have been swelled, a new ground could have been built, and the history of Northampton Town could have been quite different. And it's all down to a linesman who, on a fateful afternoon in April 1966, decided that short studs would do.

Bristol City, Swansea City and Wolves suffered similar falls from grace to Northampton Town in the '70s and '80s and almost paid for it with their existence. Wolves and Bristol City had traditional support which helped save their clubs from extinction, but Swansea City, who like the Cobblers yo-yoed through all four divisions, did not. Somehow they survived, the legacy being a bizarre-looking Vetch Field, with half a futuristic stand overlooking a more traditional, decaying ground.

In the 1990s, with the financial stakes raised higher than ever before, any club with aspirations to follow Wimbledon takes a phenomenal gamble with its entire existence. So if, in four years' time, Rochdale reach the Premiership, their freefall will be arrested by the Official Receiver before they can complete a season in the Second Division.

After their adventurous decade, Northampton Town spent the following seasons in the Fourth Division, save for a couple of seasons in the Third. The 1987–88 campaign saw the club miss out on promotion to the Second Division on the final day, but by the end of the decade they were back in the Fourth. The '90s, however, were to prove as eventful as the '60s.

In April 1991, the club introduced a businessman named Michael McRitchie to the media, a chirpy Brummie who had, it turned out, bought the club. McRitchie's business activities were shrouded in mystery; all that was known about him was that he had begun his career as a market trader in Birmingham. When a local reporter asked him if he should be described as a 'property entrepreneur', McRitchie stroked his chin, looked out of the window and replied that yes, he liked the sound of that. When he took over the Cobblers, the club was purportedly £50,000 in debt, with the local constabulary threatening legal action for the recovery of a reported £30,000 in unpaid bills. And when the police take you to court, your chances of winning are probably pretty slight.

As the 1991–92 season progressed, rumours circulated through the town that the club was in considerable financial difficulty. On the pitch, Northampton were struggling; off it they appeared to be floundering. Managed by one of the mainstays of the successful '60s side, Theo Foley, they were following a mid-table finish the previous season by threatening a much lower position in 1992. The first round of the FA Cup saw them turned over 4–2 by Crawley Town of the Beazer Homes League, whilst Leyton Orient racked up five goals to end the club's interest in the Rumbelows Cup (remember that?) at the first attempt.

McRitchie was becoming increasingly paranoid, and relations with the local press were deteriorating by the week. A group of supporters concerned for the future well-being of the club suggested a public meeting to air their grievances and give McRitchie and the club the opportunity to clarify the Cobblers' financial position. A venue was booked in the town, and the meeting was announced for 2 January 1992. Northampton Town then announced that the club wouldn't be there. McRitchie, who had successfully unloaded the rest of the board to leave himself and his wife in sole charge of the club, was not interested in what the supporters had to say, nor was he inclined to fill them in on the situation behind the scenes at the County Ground. Meanwhile, things were getting worse. The printers of the club's programme were threatening court action — supporters arriving at the County Ground for the match against Burnley in November 1991 were offered a pathetic sheet of A4 folded in half as a match programme — and the players refused to train when they weren't paid. They were then humiliated when McRitchie made them queue at the club's burger outlet while he paid them in pound coins. The PFA eventually stepped in to pay the players' wages for November and December, a figure in the region of £60,000. They made it clear to the club that this was a loan, not a gift, and they would be expecting the money back before too long. Despite protestations from the McRitchie family occupying the boardroom that things weren't as bad as they looked, honest, the club was obviously up to its neck in it. McRitchie didn't help his own personal profile at the height of the rumours by leading the team on to the field against stricken Aldershot alongside the Shots' chairman as the PA played 'Always Look on the Bright Side of Life'. He may have thought this was funny. Cobblers fans, wondering what the hell was going on at their club, certainly didn't.

On the day of the meeting, the club suddenly announced that it would be there after all. Chairman McRitchie didn't show, crying off apparently through illness. However, as the meeting took place, McRitchie was seemingly well enough to attend a dinner-dance in Luton. Representing the club would be beleaguered manager Foley and commercial director Paul Clark.

Six hundred fans packed the Exeter Rooms to hear former director Martin Pell announce from the floor that as a shareholder he had access to the club's accounts, which made alarming reading. Pell revealed that Northampton Town Football Club was fractionally under £1 million in debt, and was losing something in the region of £7,000 every week. The supporters were stunned: they knew things were bad, but had no idea that they were this bad. Michael McRitchie, as he waltzed his wife around a Luton dance floor, had some explaining to do. Foley announced that top scorer Tony Adcock had been sold that day to rivals Peterborough, along with another Cobblers hero, Bobby

Barnes, for £65,000. A nine-match unbeaten run had put the team on the fringe of the promotion race, but with Adcock and Barnes gone the next eight games produced only five points and just two goals.

On the night of the meeting, plans were hatched for the Northampton Town Supporters' Trust, organised by a group of lifelong fans determined that their club should not go the same way as Aldershot. They announced an independent fundraising organisation which would plough any money raised back into the club. A business plan was put together based on the issue of shares at five pounds each, but McRitchie wasn't interested, opining that money from the Trust had been taken from the supporters, and wasn't the Trust's to give away. The fact that Northampton Town FC had been banking supporters' money at the turnstiles, in the bar, at the refreshment stalls and in the club shop and had still ended up with a six-figure debt was an irony that appeared to be lost on the increasingly paranoid chairman. McRitchie even went as far as barring the Trust from collecting money at the County Ground, money given to the Trust by supporters concerned for the future of their club. Volunteers with collecting buckets were thrown out of the ground at the first home game after the public meeting, a 2–2 draw with York City.

In its first two months, the Northampton Town Supporters' Trust raised over £12,000. The feeling amongst supporters was that the Football League had some hidden agenda whereby unsuccessful and financially unstable clubs should give way to ambitious clubs with good facilities and sound finances from the GM Vauxhall Conference. A cricket ground car park and a bank account almost £1 million in the red would not endear Northampton Town to the authorities, with Woking and Kettering Town knocking on the door waving bank statements, tugging on Graham Kelly's sleeve and pointing to neat, well-appointed stadia.

In the light of this grim prognosis, serious consideration was given by the Trust to forming a new club to enter the United Counties League (a feeder league below the Beazer Homes League) the following season, even going so far as to ensure the use of the County Ground for 1992–93 should Northampton Town go to the wall. Such moves were forestalled when McRitchie conceded to the inevitable and brought in the Birmingham firm Pannell Kerr Foster to take over the administration of the club. Nine players and the entire management team were immediately sacked on 3 April, the day before an away match at Barnet. Defender Phil Chard was put in charge of team affairs and had to put a side together from the remaining first-team squad, plugging the gaps with members of the youth team. In the event a 3–0 defeat was almost respectable, with the team receiving an impressive ovation from the travelling supporters who detected the first moves towards the removal of the McRitchie regime.

Despite the redundancies, some of whom were long-serving players such as Peter Gleasure, the last remnant of the 1986–87 Fourth Division Championship side, as well as the popular Foley, the supporters were becoming more optimistic about the club's future prospects, particularly when McRitchie resigned within days of the arrival of the administrators. Following the resignation of McRitchie, Pannell Kerr Foster had suggested a new board of directors comprising members of the Trust and ex-directors, people who, it was felt, had the interests of the club at heart, with the opportunity for genuine supporters' representation at board level. The news was even better at the end of April, when Northamptonshire County Council announced that the construction of a new community stadium was going ahead, and that Northampton Town FC would be offered the opportunity to play there. The stadium would be ready for the start of the 1994–95 season.

In the space of four months, the fortunes of Northampton Town had swung from a club with such crippling debts that the future appeared to lie in the lower reaches of the non-League pyramid, to one that had become a model for supporter involvement with a brand new stadium being prepared by a supportive local authority. If things were suddenly promising off the field, however, the Cobblers still had innumerable problems on it. Chard, a managerial novice, was having trouble assembling a squad, and his side scored just nine times in the last 17 games of the season to finish in 16th place. Not a bad achievement for a motley bunch of old pros and youth-team upstarts, particularly considering the turmoil in which the club was immersed off the field, but clearly the situation on the pitch could not be allowed to continue.

During the summer of 1992 the administrators announced the new board, comprising Barry Ward of Parnell Foster Kerr as chairman, Trust representatives Brian Lomax and Phil Frost, and former board members Barry Stonhill, Barry Hancock, Martin Church and Mark Deane, who reclaimed their seats in the boardroom. Unfortunately, the new board could not find money for new players, and the team was destined for a season of struggle. Even youth coach Paul Curtis, only just the right side of 40, was to be pressed into action at right back during the season. In September 1992 the Cobblers entertained Hereford United, who had four players sent off but still managed a 1–1 draw with seven men, Northampton's goal coming from the penalty spot. By Easter, Northampton Town were favourites for the drop, and trips to Welling United and Northwich Victoria in the GM Conference loomed.

Chard was under pressure: former Wolves boss John Barnwell was called in in an advisory capacity.

Early April saw the Cobblers grind out 1–0 wins against Bury and Rochdale and pick up valuable draws with Walsall and Doncaster Rovers. A 2–0 defeat at home to Wrexham, a result which clinched promotion for the Racecourse Ground side, meant that on the last day of the season it was between Northampton and Halifax for the drop. The Cobblers were two points ahead of Halifax, and visited Gay Meadow to take on a Shrewsbury Town side looking to confirm a place in the play-offs. Gay Meadow had always been something of a bogey ground for the club, and so the supporters' hopes seemed to rest on Hereford avoiding defeat at the Shay.

Two thousand Northampton supporters descended on Shrewsbury on 8 May to see Northampton, on the brink of security off the field, fight for their Football League life. Despite a ticker-tape welcome, Town found themselves 2–0 down within half an hour, with playmaker Martin Aldridge stretchered off shortly afterwards. The score remained unchanged until half-time, and with Halifax and Hereford drawing 0–0, Cobblers fans despaired. There seemed no way back from 2–0, and years of watching football suggested that Halifax were bound to beat Hereford at the Shay, probably through a dodgy last-minute penalty or comical own goal. The evening news would doubtless finish with scenes of joyous Halifax fans cavorting around the pitch and hugging players, whilst Cobblers fans wept on the terraces at the wholly inappropriately named Gay Meadow.

Six minutes into the second half Phil Chard, who had given away the free-kick which had produced the Shrews' first goal, pulled a goal back for Northampton, latching on to a through ball from Pat Gavin. Then word filtered through that Hereford had taken the lead at Halifax. The away end erupted. With 20 minutes remaining, Gavin capitalised on an error in the Shrewsbury defence and buried the ball in the back of the net. Cobblers fans were stunned. Suddenly their collection of barely mobile veterans and enthusiastic but inexperienced youths were matching high-flying Shrewsbury and playing the game of their lives. But there was still more to come.

If the Cobblers' 1960s slide was triggered by a moment of high comedy, their League survival was assured by another in the 1990s. With six minutes remaining, Pat Gavin set off in pursuit of a backpass to Shrewsbury keeper Paul Edwards. Edwards hared out of his goal to reach the ball first. As he drew back his right foot to launch the ball in the direction of Shrewsbury High Street, no doubt pursued by the famous Bloke in a Coracle, Gavin jumped and turned balletically in the air. Edwards thumped the ball square against Gavin's ample backside and the ball bounced into the empty net to seal the unlikeliest of victories. Saved from the bottom by a bottom. In years to come Northampton may have its own Turin Shroud, when an old pair of football shorts will turn up with a faint 'Mitre' imprint on the rear. Controversy will rage over the authenticity of the 'Shrewsbury Arse'.

At the Shay, Halifax fans watered the pitch with their tears, while Northampton fans danced on the terraces of Shrewsbury. In the space of three-quarters of an hour, Cobblers fans had gone through the entire range of football emotions. The foreseeable future would be spent in the Football League, and when the euphoria had died down, the phrase 'this must never, ever happen again' echoed around the streets of the town. And they weren't talking about their well-earned hangovers, either.

In the build-up to the 1993–94 season, the last at the County Ground, player-manager Phil Chard released several players, the heroic Pat Gavin amongst them, as he sought to put together a new squad to lift Northampton away from the danger zone. However, his plans were undone when the League slapped a transfer embargo on the club until the PFA loan had been paid off.

The season started predictably badly. A mere two points were picked up from the first seven games, the low point being reached with a dreadful, gutless performance that culminated in a 2–0 home defeat by Wigan Athletic. Ironically, one of the Wigan goals came from Pat Gavin, set up by a young Keith Gillespie. Chard was furious with his side, who appeared to show no desire, no fight, no inclination to exert themselves in the name of Northampton Town. The supporters despaired. Surely the club had learned its lesson from last season? Chard was relieved of his managerial duties but remained with the club as a player, whilst John Barnwell took on the manager's job.

Barnwell's first game in charge saw a battling performance against Lincoln City which ended in a narrow defeat at 4–3. A win over Darlington and a draw with Wycombe was followed by a 5–1 thumping of Mansfield Town. Suddenly things seemed to be looking up. Supporters travelled to Scunthorpe talking of a play-off place and, in hushed tones, even promotion. That evening they returned to Northampton with all illusions shattered, as Scunthorpe rattled in seven goals without reply, the first of a 15-match run without a win. The Cobblers tumbled down the table from fifth place to bottom. The PFA was eventually paid off, enabling Barnwell to sign players including Diodinne Efon Elad, a Cameroonian Under-21 international signed from Fortuna Cologne. Results didn't improve until February, however, although the League made it clear that if Kidderminster Harriers won the Conference they would not be promoted, having failed to make their ground grading in time. They confirmed that this would mean a reprieve from the drop for whoever finished the season propping up the Football League. The smart money was on Northampton Town.

The penultimate game of the season was billed as the final match at the County Ground. The new stadium, christened Sixfields, was due for completion in time for the 1994–95 season, and League football at the new ground was guaranteed, ironically not by performances on the field but through the deficiencies of another ground, the Aggborough Stadium, Kidderminster.

Chester were the visitors, and the final match resulted in three important points for the Cobblers as Wilkin scored the only goal of the game straight from the kick-off. What was intended to be the last football match at the County Ground was a subdued affair. Not many tears were shed; Cobblers fans instead looked forward to the new residence as a new beginning. Visiting fans were not likely to rue the move from the County Ground either. A three-sided ground always lacks atmosphere, and the away end was undoubtedly one of the worst in the Football League. The club's introduction of hanging baskets in the 1980s couldn't disguise the fact that the ground could no longer support League football. With a number of new stadia springing up around the lower divisions such as the Bescot Stadium, Walsall, and Glanford Park, Scunthorpe, the County Ground was becoming more and more of an anachronism in the new, glamorous world of English football. Whilst Northampton fans bade a quiet farewell to the place that had seen thousands of hopes shattered over the years, any feelings of nostalgia were swamped by excitement and the birth of a new era at Sixfields. If the County Ground was associated with failure, Sixfields gave the club the chance of a fresh start.

The Chester result left the Cobblers one place off the bottom with a game to play, a point ahead of Darlington. The fact that Kidderminster had been confirmed as Conference champions meant that nothing was at stake but pride, but the Cobblers were unable to salvage even that as they capitulated 4–0 at Chesterfield. Darlington's 1–0 win over Bury ensured that Northampton Town finished bottom of the Football League for the first time in their history.

As it turned out, Northampton hadn't seen the last of the County Ground, as it was announced during the summer of 1994 that Sixfields would not be ready for the start of the season. The Cobblers would play their first four home games on the old ground, leading cynical fans to suggest that the club fancied another bumper payday from a second 'last' game.

The real last game culminated in a disappointing defeat to Mansfield at a less-than-full County Ground. Four days later 7,500 people crammed into the new Sixfields stadium for the visit of Barnet. At last Northampton Town had a ground to call their own, a compact, neat stadium that perfectly suited their needs, a stadium to be proud of. The opening game finished 1–1, with the Cobblers hitting the woodwork three times. However, the new surroundings were not the Emperor's new clothes for the ailing team, and a succession of poor results culminating in a dreadful performance against Scunthorpe, who scored the only goal of the game with their only chance, spelled the end of John Barnwell's tenure at Sixfields. Ian Atkins, who'd laid the foundations for Colchester's return to the Football League, was appointed and immediately set about the long-overdue rebuilding of the side. A number of shrewd signings, including veteran striker Garry Thompson, propelled the Cobblers into the safety of 17th place. The last game of the season, against Exeter City, served as a reminder to Northampton fans how far they had come from the gloom of the McRitchie era. Exeter were two weeks away from the distinct possibility of going out of business, needing to raise £350,000 in that time to survive. A huge banner reading 'Don't Let Our Club Die!' was unfurled at the Exeter end and was warmly applauded by Cobblers fans. At the end of the game, a 2–1 win for Northampton, both sets of fans met in the centre of the pitch in a fantastic spirit of solidarity. Exeter fans, having just witnessed what could have been the club's last ever match, embraced their Northampton counterparts, looked around the Sixfields stadium and dreamed of a rosier future. With a new manager, a new ground and a new future, Cobblers fans paused to reflect upon how far they had come on the 30th anniversary of promotion to the First Division.

Exeter survived, of course, and the Northampton story ended happily in May 1997. Atkins's rebuilt side made it into the play-offs and met Swansea City at Wembley, having overcome Cardiff in the semi-finals. A crowd of 48,000 saw a closely fought game heading for injury time when John Frain hit a free-kick from 25 yards into the far corner of the Swansea net. Dave Bowen, the man who had given Northampton Town supporters a glimpse of the big time in the '60s was not there to see it, having passed away during the 1980s. But the club he guided into the top flight are currently in a better position than at any time in their history. It's highly unlikely that they will ever reach the Premiership, but they appear to have found their niche at a compact stadium that suits the needs of a small-town club perfectly.

Sixfields, like similar stadia to be found in the lower divisions and the higher reaches of the non-leagues, may lack character, but Cobblers fans don't mind that. Away fans can now look forward to a trip to Northampton knowing that they'll be able to see the whole pitch, for a start.

It appears that nearly 30 years after cascading through the Football League, Northampton have finally taken stock and learnt from their experiences, although it took them going through the traumas of near-extinction and facing relegation from the League to do so. It's ironic that the County Ground will be remembered more for the achievements of a Beatle-cropped genius at the height of his powers tearing apart a demoralised crop of lower-division journeymen than anything achieved by Northampton Town. The same will never be said of Sixfields.

From Europe to the Orient

MANCHESTER UNITED 1973–74

Wandering around the Manchester United Megastore is a unique football experience. From Ryan Giggs duvet covers to Manchester United wine, via a startling selection of replica kits, United fans arrive by the coachload to scoop up armfuls of goodies to take back to those hotbeds of Mancunian support like Suffolk and Herefordshire, to wear or display to neighbours and friends as they park their Manchester United jogging pants-encased backsides on their armchairs, Manchester United mug of tea in one hand, Manchester United mobile phone in the other, and watch the latest instalment in United's doomed European odyssey. If you've got all the gear, it's the next best thing to being there. All you need to complete the authentic Old Trafford experience is a brawny individual in a fluorescent overcoat shouting at you to sit down every time you get up to adjust the aerial.

United fans travel to their Theatre of Dreams from all over the country – often it's the only time they'll ever visit Old Trafford – and never actually visit the ground. Straight off the coach, into the Megastore, a cartload of souvenirs and back to the shires. An experience as artificial as the material used to make the shirts.

But amongst all the shrines to Sheringham and altars to Butt, there is unquestionably something missing from the Megastore. The dump bins of hats, pennants and keyfobs, the bath towels and flags hanging from the walls, they are all telling you that everything you need is here – but this is all about Manchester United plc, not Manchester United Football Club. Each club logo is appended with a tiny TM; the assistants at the checkout have little nametags; you're offered a shopping trolley, for God's sake. It's all so sanitised; there's nothing of the soul of football. The Megastore is nothing to do with supporting Manchester United, it's a conveyor belt designed to relieve you of your cash as quickly and efficiently as possible. No thought or imagination has been put into design or layout; it's a philosophy of pile 'em high, ship 'em through the doors. The club have reduced the Old Trafford experience to the level of buying a pot of paint and a bag of nails. Nothing in the Manchester United Megastore has anything to do with football any more. 'I'm not inspired,' says Konrad Caulkett, not a Manchester United fan but someone who'd taken time out to visit the store on a trip to the city. 'I wouldn't be proud to be a Manchester United supporter looking at all this. It's just all so hyped up.' Pointing out a family of four Japanese tourists, he says, 'They were on my train up from London this morning. They had no luggage with them. They must have come up here on a day trip to load up with gear.' The family, laden with souvenirs, bustles towards the checkouts as another coach pulls up outside and disgorges its occupants on to the tarmac. 'I've even seen United aftershave in here,' says Caulkett. 'What next? Probably United old rope, because that's what they're getting money for.'

The token hats and scarves are still there, but everything else is aimed at the home. A range of leisurewear, bedding, even wallpaper and bath accessories illustrate how Manchester United have become an armchair obsession for so many of their followers. If you can't get to Old Trafford, then the more regalia with which you can deck out your home, the better.

The missing element from the millennial Manchester United is its glorious past. On the fast-track to relieve you of your cash, Manchester United have wiped out their history. The very thing that made United great, the legacy provided by Matt Busby in his 50-year involvement with the club, isn't there. You can find dozens of items in the Megastore with Paul Scholes's face gazing back at you, but whither Martin Buchan? Bobby Charlton? David Sadler? Duncan Edwards? Charlie Roberts? Billy Meredith? The marketing of Manchester United has exploited the tradition of the club, the world-wide fanbase it created, and smothered it with a pile of Peter Schmeichel pillowcases.

But United do have a history, a glorious one, one that revolves around Matt Busby's European dream finally achieved in 1968 in an emotionally charged evening at Wembley Stadium, when a mercurial George Best and an astonishingly mature 19-year-old called Brian Kidd were inspired by the ghosts of Munich to become the first English club to lift the European Cup. Within six years of that triumph, however, Manchester United were lining up at Brisbane Road, Leyton, to take on Orient in the Second Division on the opening day of the 1974–75 season. Busby's team had aged or departed, and United's followers set about dismantling a set of stadia ill-equipped to handle the huge numbers of travelling fans which blindly followed United throughout the dark days of relegation from the First Division.

Manchester United have not always been the monolith of capitalism that they are today. In fact, their roots are the complete antithesis of the corporate ogre they have become. Formed as Newton Heath in 1880, the club was founded by workmen of the Lancashire and Yorkshire Railway Company, who became Manchester United in 1902. A few years ago, in an attempt to acknowledge their roots and to hang on to the coat tails of the old-fashioned football-shirt industry spawned by widespread disillusionment with the overpriced, shoddily made abominations passing as team strips in the 1990s, Manchester United introduced a shirt purportedly representing the Newton Heath green and yellow of the 1890s. They got the colours the wrong way around.

In the first decade of the twentieth century, just as in the last, United were arguably the strongest team in the country. The FA had made Manchester City's highly successful team of the turn of the century scapegoats for the widespread illegal payment of players prevalent in the game and decimated the team, banning them from ever playing for Manchester City again. Much of the side immediately joined Manchester United, including Billy Meredith, probably the best player of his day. Born of strong working-class stock, the Manchester United team were the driving force behind the growth and development of the players' union, spreading the message of the new unionism to all the clubs they visited, seeking the abolition of the maximum wage and the removal of the constricting retain and transfer system. Hard to imagine such left-wing radicalism involving the modern Manchester United plc. Completely impossible to imagine, in fact.

By the 1930s, however, Manchester City had regrouped and were on the ascendant. United were in decline, winning a relegation head-to-head battle with Millwall on the last day of the 1933–34 season to send the Lions down and retain their Second Division place by a whisker.

After the war, one of the key players of the successful City side of the late '30s was appointed manager of United, a Scot named Matt Busby with kind, sparkling eyes. Bombed out of Old Trafford and camping out at Maine Road, Busby led a shoestring United team to victory in the 1948 FA Cup and set about constructing a youth policy that was to change the fortunes of Manchester United in the most spectacular fashion. With a network of scouts across Britain, United assembled a formidable youth team which was to ensure that Busby needed to buy only one player between 1951 and 1958.

Unbelievably, given what he was later to achieve, Busby's job was on the line for a while in 1952, when United sat fourth from bottom after losing six of their opening 11 games of the 1952–53 season. He pleaded to be given more time, pointing to the success of United's youth team who, with Edwards, Whelan, Pegg and Scanlon in their ranks, went on to beat Wolverhampton Wanderers 9–3 on aggregate in that season's FA Youth Cup, a trophy that was to be a familiar piece of silverware in United's trophy cabinet over the next few years. United's first team, meanwhile, finished eighth, their lowest position since the war. Fortunately the United board, recognising the wealth of talent emerging from the youth team, decided to stick with Busby.

In October 1953, Busby took a young side to Rugby Park for a friendly which saw United, including a 17-year-old Duncan Edwards, beat Kilmarnock 3–0. This game entered United folklore as the day which saw the birth of the Busby Babes. No doubt Manchester United plc's marketing department would dearly like to rewrite history to turn a midweek friendly at Kilmarnock into a clash-of-the-titans encounter with Real Madrid at a packed Old Trafford, but, sorry guys, that's not the way it happened.

The team took a couple of seasons to mature, finishing fourth in 1954 and fifth the following year, although they won the Youth Cup on both occasions. In 1956 United had walked away with the League title by mid-April with a squad whose average age was just 23. United's patience with Busby had been vindicated: they were unquestionably the best team in the land, and looked set to remain that way for some years to come.

The European Cup competition, brainchild of French football writer Gabriel Hanot, was held for the first time during the 1955–56 season. The FA loftily ignored it, and the only British entrant was Hibernian, who went out in the semi-finals to Stade de Reims. The competition was won by Real Madrid, undoubtedly the dominant team in Europe at the time, who beat the French side 4–3 in the final despite conceding two goals in the first ten minutes.

Ironically, given the modern climate, the first European Champions' Cup was not restricted to the champions of each European nation. This criterion was introduced immediately after the first tournament and turned the European Champions' Cup into the glorious competition that it became, a tournament of champions. Then television became involved, and bank accounts spoke louder than performances on the field. You can now once again become champions of Europe without even being champions of your own country.

Busby liked what he saw, however, and was delighted when United were invited to compete in the 1956–57 tournament. A football visionary, Busby knew that his side could and should compete with the best teams in Europe, that Manchester United needed fresh, tougher challenges. They had proved themselves on the domestic front; now Busby wanted to conquer Europe. He accepted the invitation, much to the chagrin of the Football League, and United were drawn away to Anderlecht of Brussels in the first leg of the preliminary round. A 2–0 win saw Anderlecht travel to Maine Road (Old Trafford's floodlights were not yet ready) and leave again after a remarkable 10–0 hammering at the hands of the Busby Babes. United went on to reach the semi-finals, going out to Real Madrid over two legs.

The following season's European adventure ended in the snow at Munich airport on 6 February 1958. The team Busby had worked so hard and so successfully to build lay dead, torn and injured in the slush, mud and oil of a Munich runway on a freezing winter night. Busby himself took months to recover, but the mental scars were to drive him on with a relentless obsession to make Manchester United the champions of Europe. It was an obsession which was eventually to lead to United's relegation in 1974.

The day after the tragedy, as Britain awoke to the full scale of the disaster and Busby fought for his life in an oxygen tent, another event took place that was to have a huge impact on the future of Manchester United. Louis Edwards, boss of a Salford meat-packing company, was elected on to the Manchester United board. George Whittaker, United's long-serving secretary, had vetoed Edwards's election to the board just a few days earlier, but Whittaker's death at Munich had removed any opposition as a shell-shocked board struggled to carry on some semblance of business as usual

Edwards had grown up in the streets of Salford, close to Old Trafford. He had worked for the firm his father had named for him and his brother Douglas, Louis C. Edwards and Sons, and the two boys took over the company on the death of Louis senior in 1943. An extravagant personality known to his friends as 'Champagne Louis', Edwards was well-known on the social circuit in Manchester and had become friendly with Busby through mutual friends in the entertainment business. Busby had invited Edwards and his wife to Old Trafford and they watched matches from the directors' box on numerous occasions. Edwards was a football fanatic and a fervent United supporter, but the perks provided by Busby led him to desire a place in the United hierarchy. United's hospitality wasn't enough: Edwards wanted a piece of the action.

Manchester United had become a limited company on joining the Football League in 1892. Shares were issued only in times of need: before the First World War, and again in the 1930s, when James Gibson stepped in to bail the club out of a financial crisis and fund the development of Old Trafford. A total of 4,000 shares were issued, Gibson holding a controlling interest with much of the rest divided amongst individuals holding a handful each. As time passed, many of these shareholders died and their shares were carried over to their heirs and descendants.

On joining the board, Louis Edwards was offered ten shares in Manchester United. He immediately became deeply involved with the day-to-day running of the club, attending many funerals of the victims of Munich and often accompanying Busby on trips to sign new young players. In 1962, after four years on the board, Edwards's involvement in United was driven more by a passion for football and the club than any business motives, although his shareholding had grown slightly to 17.

During that year, however, Louis C. Edwards and Sons was floated on the stock market, instantly making the Edwards brothers very rich men. Louis now had the time and money to become even more involved in Manchester United. Edwards had plans for the club, plans that could only be carried out if he had more control, and over the next two years he employed one of his underlings, Frank Farrington, to search out and buy as many United shares as he possibly could.

Farrington wore out several pairs of shoes as he pounded the pavements of Manchester, knocking on doors and offering impressive sums for shares that many households had forgotten they even owned. Manchester United shares had been looked upon by those original small investors as being of sentimental value only; it made them feel part of the club in its early, formative years. Now, with many of them having passed away, widows and mothers found the svelte and charming Farrington's offer on behalf of Louis Edwards hard to resist. Ironically, given the late United secretary's reported opposition to Edwards's involvement in the club, George Whittaker's wife sold her husband's 443 shares to Edwards, his offer of £12 per share impossible to turn down for a widow struggling to make ends meet. This sale in particular made Louis Edwards the third biggest shareholder in Manchester United, and within a few weeks he had the controlling interest.

The United board, nervous of one person attaining such a vast stake in the club, passed a resolution in the early part of 1963 designed to prevent Edwards accruing an even higher stake. Although there was no suggestion that Edwards had malevolent intentions underpinning his amassing of shares, the board saw themselves as custodians of the club, not owners, and were reluctant to allow one individual to attain too much power in the boardroom. Edwards successfully circumnavigated this by introducing his brother Douglas, now a leading Conservative politician, and his close friend Denzil

Haroun into the fray. Amazingly, the board approved all of this, apparently missing the obvious implications of these two new shareholders, neither of whom had previously shown the slightest interest in Manchester United.

Finally, and most significantly, in 1963 James Gibson's son Alan sold Edwards 500 of his shares for £12,500 to give Edwards just under half of the entire share issue in the club. With Douglas Edwards's and Denzil Haroun's shares taken into account, this trinity effectively controlled the club. When United chairman Harold Hardman died in 1965, it was inevitable that Edwards would succeed him. Edwards now had complete control of arguably the biggest football club in Britain and possibly Europe, and it had cost him approximately £30,000. Or roughly the price of one of Denis Law's arms, if you compare it to his £115,000 transfer to United from Torino.

Busby, on the verge of quitting the game as he lay in hospital in 1958 but persuaded to stay on, unquestionably became obsessed with winning the European Cup. Although the rebuilt side failed to emulate their lamented predecessors in the League, a number of high-profile European friendlies were arranged, with opposition such as Benfica, Real Madrid and Bayern Munich visiting Old Trafford. Domestically, the arrival of players such as Law and Pat Crerand steered United away from the relegation zone in 1962–63, the FA Cup providing some consolation for the poor league showing. The following season, the FA Youth Cup was won for the first time since the Babes in 1957 by a side that featured a shy, homesick, fragile youngster from Belfast named George Best.

United finished second in the League again in 1964, clinching the title the following season. In the 1965–66 European Cup they reached the semi-finals, having become the only team ever to beat Benfica in a European Cup tie in Lisbon with a 5–1 win in the previous round. However, a return to Belgrade, from whence the ill-fated BEA Elizabethan had come in 1958 after United's 3–3 draw at Red Star, saw United go out 2–1 on aggregate to Partizan. Busby was distraught, and once again considered giving up the game. Persuaded otherwise by his team, the European flames were fanned again when United won the League in 1967, clinching the championship with a 6–1 win at West Ham, a ground where in later years United were to throw away more than one League title.

Hibernians of Malta, FK Sarajevo and Gornik Zabrze were all overcome on the way to the semi-finals where United met Real Madrid, the team whose early dominance of the European Cup Busby had so envied. After winning the first leg by the only goal of the game, United found themselves 3–1 down in the second and looked to be going out of the competition again. Two late goals, however, saw the Old Trafford club through to the final to meet Benfica at Wembley.

Once again United left it late. At 1–1 with a few minutes remaining, Alex Stepney pulled off a remarkable save from Eusebio to save Busby's dream and force the game into extra time. Three goals in the extra half-hour meant that, ten years on, the demons haunting Busby could be laid to rest: United were the champions of Europe. Busby's mission had been accomplished. The players and officials who had lost their lives pursuing their manager's dream of European glory had not died in vain.

Although no one predicted it at the time, the European Cup was won at a considerable price. United were destined not to win the League again for nearly three decades, and within six years of their Wembley triumph they would be relegated to the Second Division. Busby's blinkered drive towards the European Cup had left the framework of the club in a fragile state: even Busby, who had built United's success on the firm foundations of a solid youth policy, had not invested in the future. The decline set in almost immediately. Busby's subsequent retirement left successor Wilf McGuinness, promoted from reserve-team coach, with an ageing team, United's legendary youth policy in tatters and the momentous achievements of the Busby tenure hanging heavily over his head. George Best commented that, 'For Matt and for Bobby Charlton, for Bill Foulkes and Denis Law . . . they'd done it. And then they sat back and you could almost hear the energy and ambition sighing out of the club. It was like being in at the winding-up of a company.' For Busby, there were no more challenges. Anything after Wembley '68 would have been an anti-climax, and within eight months of United's European Cup triumph the manager announced that he was stepping aside.

McGuinness, who had no experience of managing a Football League side, let alone the champions of Europe, inherited a team containing players – Foulkes, Brennan and Charlton – who were actually older than he was. United's players had had the greatest respect for Busby, who had been a father figure as well as a manager, respect drawn from his achievements, experience and age. McGuinness had none of these attributes and yet hoped to follow in the footsteps of one of the greatest club managers in football history. It was, to put it mildly, a formidable task.

McGuinness sought to assert his authority, particularly over the caucus of older professionals. Unfortunately he came to the conclusion that humiliation was the best way to engender respect, and promptly dropped Foulkes, Law, Brennan and Charlton. Foulkes, the last survivor of the Munich side still on the playing staff, never pulled on a United shirt again. McGuinness once even made Bobby Charlton, one of the most respected professionals in the British game, do 20 press-ups on a muddy pitch whilst dressed in his club blazer and tie for the heinous crime of putting his hands in his pockets during a team talk.

McGuinness was in a no-win situation. Few could have envied him the task of following Matt Busby at Old Trafford, particularly with the playing staff rapidly ageing and becoming increasingly restless and surly. Some undoubtedly had managerial ambitions of their own, and perhaps sought to undermine McGuinness whilst he kept the seat warm for them. He wouldn't be the last manager to have problems with George Best, who was cracking under the pressure of carrying the team with his fragile skills, whilst United's fans were becoming noisily perturbed about the resurgence of Manchester City. Their championship win in 1968 had been overshadowed by United's European success, but the Maine Road side went on to win the FA Cup in 1969, and the Cup-Winners' and Football League Cups in 1970. It can't have helped much that Busby was still very much a day-to-day figure at Old Trafford, having taken on the job of general manager. Not only was the spectre of Busby's achievements a constant burden to McGuinness, but his physical presence still permeated the club.

McGuinness's ill-fated reign came to an end just after Christmas 1970 with United fifth from bottom of the First Division. A sensitive, well-intentioned man, the trauma of his tenure at Old Trafford later caused him to lose all his hair. Busby took over for the rest of the season, and ensured United's First Division survival.

In April 1971, Busby had secretly met Jock Stein at a service station on the M6 with a view to bringing the Celtic manager to Old Trafford the following season. Although agreeing the deal in principle, Stein used the United offer to win an improved contract at Celtic instead, having doubted that he would be allowed the independence he would need at Old Trafford. In his stead United appointed former Torquay and Leicester boss Frank O'Farrell. Busby returned to his desk as general manager and accepted a long-standing invitation to join the United board.

United began well under O'Farrell and by Christmas 1971 the team sat five points clear at the top of the First Division. The turn of the year saw results turn for the worse, culminating in a 5–1 defeat at Elland Road to an ascendant, arrogant Leeds United. O'Farrell, quick to spot the decline but too slow to arrest it, sought salvation in the transfer market. Alan Ball was leaving Everton and hinted strongly that any interest from United would be enough to take him to Old Trafford. Inexplicably, O'Farrell failed to act until

Ball was actually on his way to London to sign for Arsenal for £220,000. Frantic messages were left across the country, but it was too late.

Of the existing squad, Best was struggling. Unhappy that some of the older players were still around when they were clearly past their best by a number of years, he fought valiantly to carry the team and the hopes of the Old Trafford supporters on his own. As well as his troubles at United, his sister had just been shot in the leg in Belfast and Best missed a game against Newcastle United following death threats issued against him and his family. Even business interests outside football were not going to plan, with Best's chain of boutiques feeling the pinch of the less-than-buoyant economic climate. The pressure was getting on top of him, and Best turned increasingly to a frantic, alcohol-fuelled social whirl to escape the traumas which haunted his professional life.

One day in January 1972, Best failed to turn up for training. The older players insisted that the wayward star be dropped from the team, pointing out that that is what Busby would have done. Instead, perhaps determined not to do things the Busby way, O'Farrell fined Best, ordered him to undergo extra training and made him move out of his purpose-built luxury dwelling in the Cheshire countryside and back with the landlady who had taken him in when he first came over from Belfast as a teenager. The older pros raised their eyebrows and tutted.

As well as having to cope with a sulking Best, O'Farrell was trying to build a new United side. He brought in defender Martin Buchan from Aberdeen and striker Ian Storey-Moore from Nottingham Forest. The atmosphere at the club was deteriorating rapidly, with the Busby-era players a disruptive, malevolent influence. They appeared content to live off the Wembley '68 reputation and seemed ill-disposed to secure the future of the club that had turned them into European Cup winners. Law, Charlton and Best were not getting on at all, and the atmosphere in the dressing-room was dreadful. Charlton, whose early career had been spent in more austere times than the early '70s, was appalled by Best's behaviour and considered leaving the club altogether. Best, meanwhile, had lost all respect for Charlton, even to the extent of refusing to play in the striker's testimonial at Old Trafford and enjoying a night on the town instead.

Unsurprisingly, dressing-room friction was affecting results. Third Division Bristol Rovers came to Old Trafford in the FA Cup and won, whilst Tottenham Hotspur stuck four past Alex Stepney at home in the League. Pressure was mounting on the beleaguered O'Farrell, who, like McGuinness, could not shake off the Busby legacy, especially as he had to pass the man himself in the corridors of Old Trafford every day and try and gain the respect of his stroppy former protégés. Surely Busby must have recognised what was going on? The club he had built almost single-handedly was rapidly disintegrating under his nose within a few years of their greatest triumph, yet he appeared disinclined to act. Maybe he felt that stepping in would undermine O'Farrell's authority, but all the while he was at the club, O'Farrell – indeed, any manager – would not gain the respect of the senior professionals. O'Farrell had no authority to undermine.

The situation worsened as the 1972–73 season progressed. Ted MacDougall, signed from Bournemouth, where he had a prolific striking record, in order to boost United's impotent firepower, complained that he was treated as an outsider by the established players. They looked down upon him as a lower-division player who was not good enough to wear the United shirt, even though he was showing a lot more passion and commitment to the United cause than some of the squad. Most of the United players had grown up together, coming up through the ranks under the paternal eye of Busby. It was rare for United to sign players, so anyone coming in was automatically an outsider and would struggle for acceptance, particularly when faced with a disruptive, sanctimonious clique. Especially a player brought in by a manager for whom the senior pros had not an ounce of respect.

Indeed, O'Farrell's authority was undermined further when Best went walkabout again. Busby and Louis Edwards eventually resolved the situation, but not once did they consult the manager. Manchester United had become nothing more than a cliquey old-boys' club, feeding off a fading reputation. Pumped full of their own importance, the class of '68 were unable – or just unwilling – to see the damage they were inflicting upon the club.

In late December 1972, United travelled to Selhurst Park to play a Crystal Palace side widely regarded as the worst team in the First Division. Palace cruised to an emphatic 5–0 victory. United couldn't sink any lower. O'Farrell was dismissed a few days later, the scapegoat for a deeper malaise within the club. Watching the game at Selhurst was Scotland manager Tommy Docherty. Docherty claimed to be there watching Palace's defender Tommy Taylor, but given that United's Scottish internationals Denis Law and the popular Willie Morgan had recommended to Busby that Docherty would be the ideal man for the United job, it appears a convenient coincidence that Docherty happened to be there. Before the game Busby asked if the Scotland boss would be interested in the United job, should it ever become vacant. Replying in the affirmative, a few days later Docherty discovered that, surprise surprise, there was a vacancy, and he was offered the job.

He jumped at the chance, and immediately set about reorganising the Old Trafford playing staff. For a club not used to buying players, Docherty must have seemed like a chequebook-wielding dervish when he arrived at Old Trafford. He immediately signed Scottish international Alex Forsyth from Partick Thistle and the promising Jim Holton from Shrewsbury Town to shore up United's leaky defence, as well as Lou Macari and George Graham to add some grit to the midfield. Within four months Docherty had signed as many players as United had in the six years since the European Cup triumph. Keen to be a new broom, he clearly had his eye on those players who'd been at Old Trafford too long. Charlton took the hint and announced his retirement with dignity intact.

United had fought their way clear of the relegation zone, ensuring their safety by winning at Leeds and drawing 0–0 with Manchester City. The last game of the season, at Chelsea, was Bobby Charlton's last in a United shirt after 606 games and 199 goals.

If Charlton's dignity was preserved, Denis Law's was to be blown to pieces. Docherty and Law both knew that the striker's advancing years meant that his days as a player at Old Trafford were numbered. Docherty, however, had promised Law a job for life at United, a standard progression for long-serving United pros being a place on the coaching staff or similar. Professional footballers had not yet discovered ways of making enough money during their career to set themselves up for life, and for someone who had made such a contribution to United's success, it would have been a fitting reward for Law to have been given the security of a coaching post at Old Trafford. It was with not inconsiderable incredulity, then, that Law learned via a television set in the corner of a bar in Aberdeen where he was visiting friends that he had been signed by Manchester City on a free transfer. It was the first of many curious acts by Docherty, and one which would return to haunt United later in the season.

During the summer of 1973, Docherty brought yet more players to Old Trafford. Gerry Daly joined from Bohemians, Brian Greenhoff and Arthur Albiston arrived and another young Irishman, Sammy McIlroy, graduated to the first-team squad. With the dead wood now removed and the basis of a good young squad playing for a new, proven manager, United looked forward to the season with more optimism than at any time since 1968.

They made a solid start to the 1973–74 campaign, losing the opening game at Arsenal but beating Stoke City and Queen's Park Rangers. A poor run of results followed, with United struggling to score goals. Bizarrely, goalkeeper Alex Stepney found himself at the top of the first-team goalscoring charts with three successful penalty conversions, a ridiculous situation for a Sunday morning pub team, let alone a supposedly ambitious First Division side.

Defensively United were sound, but they lacked anything remotely resembling firepower up front. Best made a brief comeback in United colours, with over 7,000 people turning out to see his first game for United's reserves at Old Trafford, but the mercurial genius's talismanic skills had deserted him, and as the season progressed he drifted out of football at the frighteningly early age of 27.

By October, when United failed to register a win throughout the whole month, gates were falling to below 30,000, unheard of in postwar United history. George Graham, who was in truth past his best when he joined the club but had done the job he was brought in to do, lost his place. Brian Kidd's form slumped and he departed for Everton, never to fulfil his early promise. Best's last game for United was a defeat at Queen's Park Rangers on New Year's Day 1974. United struggled to overcome Plymouth Argyle in the FA Cup and finally hit the bottom of the table in February after a spineless 2–0 defeat at home to Leeds United. A crunch relegation four-pointer was lost in the dying seconds at Birmingham in March and United, unthinkably, were favourites for the drop. Suddenly, when all seemed lost, United clicked. At Chelsea at the end of March an injury to Steve James forced Brian Greenhoff back into defence, giving United's formation a different shape. Moving upfield using short passes, the visitors ran out surprise 3–1 winners. Norwich and Newcastle were also defeated, whilst high-flying Everton were turned over 3–0 at Old Trafford. Manchester United were actually enjoying their football for the first time in a number of years and a chink of hope had appeared. But at this late stage United were dependent on other results as well as their own. With three games remaining, they travelled to Goodison for the return match with Everton, whilst relegation rivals Birmingham City entertained Queen's Park Rangers. United lost by the only goal of the game, and Birmingham beat QPR 2–0 at St Andrews.

On 27 April 1974, United had to win at Old Trafford and hope that Birmingham didn't beat already-relegated Norwich City. United's opponents were Manchester City, whom they hadn't beaten at Old Trafford for eight years and who included in their line-up Docherty's reject Denis Law. Manchester derbies are always highly charged, but never had so much been at stake for United than this, the 97th occasion the teams had met in a league fixture. After two pitch invasions before the game had even started, the atmosphere was crackling at kick-off, particularly when news filtered through that Norwich had taken the lead against Birmingham after two minutes. United were in control against City but struggled to create clear chances. The game was a scrappy affair played at a frantic pace, and so bad-tempered that referee Clive Thomas took the players off for seven minutes and instructed both teams to cool down. Macari and City's Mike Doyle had already been sent off, and there were constant battles on the terraces. Dennis Tueart went close for City, but at half-time Old Trafford heard that Bob Hatton and Ken Burns had put Birmingham City 2–1 ahead at St Andrews. United's heads visibly dropped, Mike Summerbee hit the bar for City, Stepney pulled off a great save from Tueart and, with ten minutes to go, City sensed that the game was theirs for the taking. In the 83rd minute, Summerbee fed Lee on the left-hand side of the penalty area, who played a quick pass to Law, six yards out with his back to goal. With an instinctive flick of the heel, Law propelled the ball into the United net.

Without looking round, Law knew from the reaction of the City fans that he had scored. A shocked Old Trafford watched Law meander away from the goal, stunned, unable to turn and look at the ball nestling in the United net. Whooping, delighted City team-mates surrounded him, slapping his face and throwing their arms around him, but Law was oblivious as he walked away from the goal with awkward short strides, his face expressionless, betraying neither a hint of happiness at having scored the only goal of the Manchester derby nor the anguish of effectively sealing United's relegation, the club whom he had served for the best years of his career. Wiping his eyes with the hem of his shirt, Law trudged to the edge of the pitch and was immediately substituted. It was to be his last touch in club football.

Within seconds, United fans swarmed across the pitch and the match was abandoned, the result standing. Birmingham had beaten Norwich, so United's defeat was academic: they were a Second Division club. Law's goal was, in a statistical sense, meaningless. In other ways, though, it was the dénouement of the neglect that had set in at Old Trafford immediately after the European Cup win. One reflex backheel illustrated the demise of United more than a thousand articles and books ever could. Manchester United was a sick club, and surely now Busby knew it. He was sanguine about relegation, telling Docherty towards the end of the season that if United were to go down, they should do so in style and come back up the same way. He recognised that Docherty was a wise choice as manager, a strong personality with his own ideas about tactics and players. Tommy Docherty was probably the only manager in the game at the time with the confidence and character to succeed Matt Busby. In fact the ghost of Busby would not be exorcised until well into the reign of Alex Ferguson, another dour Scot treated patiently by the United administration with spectacular results.

Relegation in a sense took a great deal of pressure from Docherty. Once it was all but certain, United were able to play football rather than fight for their lives every Saturday. In players such as Daly, McIlroy and Stuart Pearson, the nucleus of a fine team was developing. Not a team that would threaten the achievements of the '58 and '68 sides in the short term, but nonetheless the foundations of a rebuilding operation made necessary by the all-out campaign to win the European Cup for Matt Busby and his Babes. Such an all-or-nothing onslaught had reaped the glittering prize, but the pedestal on which it stood was visibly rotting away. McGuinness and O'Farrell were never given the chance to rebuild, in terms of either time or resources. It's doubtful whether either of them would have succeeded whatever the circumstances, but the legacy they followed, in which they had their noses rubbed every day, made them impotent from the start. Docherty was different, a more resilient, assertive character who could stamp his authority on the players and the club and win respect. He undermined that authority, however, with a self-destructive streak that was to become apparent in his remaining time at Old Trafford and beyond.

There was never much doubt that United would bounce straight back. Their end-of-season form was that of a First Division team, and the growing confidence of the young players was clearly visible. Docherty kept faith with the same squad that had shown such character and mettle in the relegation run-in, and United ran out at Orient on the first day of the season to be welcomed by a phenomenal 10,000 of their fans. United were used to being big fish in the First Division; in the Second they were enormous. The reputation of their supporters was legendary, and the Second Division 'firms' and clubs had little answer when the marauding United fans came to town. The Red Army swarmed across the pitch before the game, ignoring even Matt Busby's tannoy pleas for calm. It was to be a familiar ritual wherever United went. That day, a late Stewart Houston goal clinched a 1–0 victory and United were soon well clear at the top of the table.

Few clubs could approach United, with Buchan and Holton impassable at the back and the midfield of Daly, Greenhoff and Macari buzzing around the opposition defences. United powered their way around the country, leaving bewildered opponents in their wake and a number of casualties on the terraces. In December 1974 at Hillsborough, 106 people were arrested at the game where Jim Holton broke his leg and effectively ended a career that had seemed destined for long-term international success.

At the turn of the year United's promotion challenge wobbled slightly with defeats at the hands of Bristol City, Oxford United and Aston Villa, but thanks to an unbeaten run which stretched through the months of March and

April, they clinched their return to the First Division with a victory at Southampton just after Easter, and the Second Division Championship was assured with a 2–2 draw at Notts County. Before their final game of the season, a 4–0 win over Blackpool at Old Trafford, United displayed the Second Division Championship trophy. In the photographs, the grim looks on the players' faces betray the fact that not a great deal of pleasure was taken from the club's success that season. The Second Divison was a place where United should never have been. Leaving it at the first attempt was a stepping stone to greater things, the success to which United felt they had established a right, not something to celebrate.

During the close season, Docherty took his United players to the Far East to recuperate from the rigours of a hard, highly pressurised season. He had already demonstrated his unpredictable side with his bizarre handling of Denis Law, and also when he leaked details of a supposedly personal arrangement with George Best to the newspapers prior to Best's final departure from Old Trafford. This time he told the popular Willie Morgan that he was welcome to miss the tour in order to rest fully in preparation for the new season and spend time with his family. Morgan gratefully accepted the offer, then picked up a newspaper the following week to find Docherty telling the press that Morgan had refused to go.

Apart from his well-known desire for self-publicity, what could Docherty possibly have hoped to achieve by this? Morgan, although no longer at his peak, was a valuable and immensely popular member of the United team. The repercussions of crossing him were long-running and expensive for Docherty. Morgan left United for Burnley and later told a television programme that Docherty was 'the worst manager there has ever been'. Docherty sued Morgan for slander, but faced with Morgan's meticulously prepared case ended up being charged with perjury himself. The Far East tour also saw a bizarre 'clear the air' meeting between Docherty and the squad in a Singapore hotel, an expletive-filled session during which Docherty reportedly consumed an entire bottle of whisky.

Behind the scenes at United, things were changing for the worse. Edwards's meat company was starting to lose money following a scandal which revealed that he was providing local schools with rotten, infected meat yet still winning the contracts through strategically targeted gifts to the decision-makers. Louis's son Martin, who had previously shown little interest in football, suddenly became involved at the club. With the family business struggling, the Edwards family decided that for all the time and money they had ploughed into United, they ought to start seeing some financial reward.

FA rules stated that a dividend of no more than five pence in the pound could be paid out to shareholders each year. The obvious way to increase revenue would be to multiply the number of shares. Thus, in the late '70s, Manchester United's one pound shares were multiplied by 208, earning an extra 208 five pences for every pound of shares originally owned.

And so the Manchester United money machine began. Despite continued relative lack of success on the pitch (Docherty led the club to a 2–1 FA Cup victory over rivals Liverpool, then left the club over his affair with physio Laurie Brown's wife Mary), Martin Edwards's business acumen built Manchester United into the financial giant it has become. Champagne Louis died in 1979 of a heart attack shortly after Granada TV's *World in Action* programme exposed the seedier side of his business empire, and Martin, the rugby-playing ex-public schoolboy, took charge of the club formed by a group of oil-smeared railwaymen a hundred years before. Managers came and went, but not even the stoic Dave Sexton nor the flamboyant Ron Atkinson, who wore more gold and silver about his person than United had won in several years, could emulate the Busby legacy. United replaced Atkinson, who according to United's Dutch international Arnold Muhren used to hold press conferences in his office whilst reclining on a sunbed in a pair of swimming trunks sipping cocktails, with his antithesis, Aberdeen manager Alex Ferguson.

Ferguson finally brought the title to United in 1993, an honour to which they have clung resiliently ever since. If United were one of the best-supported teams in the world before then, continued success has given them an incredible dominance in the domestic and international arena. Wherever they play, from Ipswich to Southampton, from Leicester to Crystal Palace, whenever United score, people leap out of their seats in all parts of the ground, not just the away end.

It's a tribute to a ruthlessly effective marketing operation, one that will reach its zenith when pay-per-view television arrives. For the thousands upon thousands of armchair fans who will never experience the Old Trafford vibe in person, pay-per-view will be their season ticket. United merchandise is available in just about every sports shop in the country, but their marketing is just as aggressive in other areas. As I write this, the front page of my local newspaper on the south-east London/Kent border is given over entirely to the story of a nine-year-old Child of Achievement Award winner from the area who was sent a bundle of United goodies together with a letter signed by Alex Ferguson following his award. The accompanying colour photograph shows the child with three young friends decked out in full United regalia. A fine gesture, of course, and one that generated maximum PR for United 300 miles from Old Trafford. Whilst Charlton dominate the back pages of the paper, not since the Back to The Valley campaign have they been front-page news in their own locality. All over the country, United's PR machine slickly steamrollers the impecunious efforts of smaller clubs desperate to secure the next generation of supporters.

But it wasn't always so. The European Cup which put United up with the greats almost destroyed the club and was the catalyst for their relegation six short years later.

Building the side from youth again, Alex Ferguson has read his history books. United, on and off the field, learned their lessons and will never find themselves in such a position again. And if you can afford it, you can watch them do it in the comfort of your own home, stepping out from behind your United shower curtain, slapping on your United aftershave, tying the cord on your United dressing-gown and tuning in to the United channel. If there's anyone left for them to play against, that is.

Matt Busby's European dream caused the demise of Manchester United, but in the long run he created a monster. We've seen the future, and it includes Manchester United megastores in every high street, and the Manchester United channel playing in every household. The complete leisure experience available in the comfort of your own home. But, hey, they'll still probably never win the European Cup again. At least there's that consolation.

I Get Knocked Down,
But I Get Up Again

THE DEMISE AND RISE OF CHARLTON ATHLETIC

It is May 1987 and I am standing on a windswept terrace in Birmingham crying my eyes out. I have just seen John Sheridan put Leeds United ahead in extra time of the play-off final replay, a goal which has probably just relegated Charlton Athletic to the Second Division. Charlton do not have their own ground; they are playing at Crystal Palace's sterile Selhurst Park stadium to crowds of around 5,000. Somehow the motley crew of ageing veterans on their last hurrah and promising youngsters thrust into the blood and guts of a scrap for survival have hauled themselves into the top flight, but now their status is ebbing away by the second.

The implications of relegation for Charlton are more than just a return to the old crew in the Second Division they had left one season earlier. Sheridan's goal has left Charlton staring at oblivion. If only 5,000 will come and watch the Addicks at Selhurst in the First Division, how many will want to come and see Stoke City and Fulham in the Second? Defeat in the play-off final replay after extra time could conceivably sign Charlton's death warrant. As The Valley grows decrepit with no sign of a return, Charlton have no future at Selhurst. The 1947 FA Cup winners will beome a footnote in football history.

Still, we were used to staring out oblivion in those days. So when I peered through the tears to see Peter Shirtliff bury the ball past Mervyn Day for the equaliser and then, with three minutes left, dip his head towards an Andy Peake free-kick to guide the ball into the bottom corner, I shouldn't have been too surprised. Relegation? Hah! We tweak your nose!

It is now 11 years later, 5.40 p.m. on a humid May Bank Holiday Monday in 1998, and I am standing on a seat at Wembley Stadium crying my eyes out. The play-off final has come a long way since those far-off days of 1987. Instead of a half-deserted cavernous old ground in the Midlands, the players walk out at the national stadium accompanied by thunderous fireworks and the dubious strains of Robbie Williams's 'Let Me Entertain You'. Once again the marketing experts who have joined the football gravy train have got it wrong. They still labour under the impression that football is about enter-tainment, failing to grasp that the 78,000 Charlton and Sunderland fans there that day were turning themselves inside out with fear, not sitting back in their seats, opening picnic hampers and saying to each other, 'Golly, we should be in for some spiffing entertainment this afternoon, eh!' Entertainment never entered the equation. After nearly three hours of the most agonising, surreal tension, goalkeeper Sasa Ilic has just saved Michael Gray's underhit penalty to earn Charlton Athletic a place in the FA Carling Premiership. It's finished 7–6 on penalties following an astonishing 4–4 draw during which Charlton came from behind three times. All around me, Charlton supporters are dancing, whooping and celebrating, flags are waving, strangers are embracing, and I'm in floods of tears.

Charlton now inhabit an excellent stadium at The Valley, games are sold out long in advance, and we have a team capable of touching consistent brilliance who have taken on the big boys and won. Years of hardship, exile, disappointment and suffering have been finally laid to rest. It's been a long road, and one on which the threat of relegation has been a constant companion. As I watched thousands upon thousands of delirious Charlton fans in the throes of ecstasy, the weight of the previous years' struggles was visibly lifted. At last we can be truly proud of the team's and the club's achievements. There's not a dry eye in the place. But it all started so differently.

In 1977, at the age of seven, I was yet to understand what football was all about. *Ball Boy*'s adventures in the *Beano* led me into a weekly world of sports-manship, gentlemanly conduct and playing for fun. The reality of pitched terrace battles, a portly George Best wobbling around various non-League grounds and a World Cup organised to benefit a vicious military dictatorship were not even hinted at in *Ball Boy*'s sun- and fizzy-pop-soaked world.

In the real world, two candidates vied for the football affections of young south-east Londoners: Nottingham Forest, well on their way to winning the Football League and two years of unrivalled European glory in gorgeous, shiny, red v-neck shirts led by the charismatic Brian Clough, and Charlton

Athletic, a struggling Second Division outfit in a vast, crumbling stadium, whose shirts still bore big flappy collars (with which a winger running down the touchline could, and regularly did, take out the first two rows of supporters) and who were managed by the balding, toothsome ex-Ipswich full-back Andy Nelson. Forest were in *Shoot!* every week (Viv Anderson even had a weekly column), whilst Charlton were lucky to get a couple of paragraphs in the Millwall-dominated *South-East London Mercury*. Forest's exploits were on *Football Focus* where their midweek games were shown bathed in the brightness of the latest floodlight technology, whilst Charlton's lights were so dingy that Brian Moore, perched halfway up the East Terrace on a rickety Heath Robinson gantry, once failed to see Derek Hales being sent off in the gloom on the other side of the pitch during a rare showing on *The Big Match*.

Inevitably my allegiance stayed in south London, to a giant sleeping so deeply it was comatose. In those days, the aggressive marketing juggernaut of the big clubs had not crunched into gear and begun its systematic smothering of clubs too poor to resist. In those days it was still possible to support your local team without the risk of being run out of town by a posse of laughing, pointing Manchester United supporters.

And thus relegation started to follow me around. Over the next 20 years or so, I would witness the Addicks tangle with relegation for a couple of seasons, drop into the Third Division (with an emphasis that called to mind Wyle E. Coyote disappearing over the edge of a cliff and vanishing from view until there was a faint 'whump' and a cloud of dust visible hundreds of feet below), return to the Second, struggle again, almost go out of business, actually go out of business, come back into business whilst fighting the drop again, lose their ground, somehow creep into the First Division, struggle on minuscule crowds, be relegated and saved within the space of a few minutes, struggle some more, be relegated, move back to the ground, develop the ground beyond recognition and, finally, reach the top flight they had graced with honour either side of the Second World War and for a brief while in Selhurst exile. And it's all down to *Ball Boy* in the *Beano*. If I'd preferred *Pup Parade*, maybe I'd have led a less stressful life stroking dogs and going to Crufts once a year.

It all started so innocently, too. *Ball Boy* didn't ask for huge signing-on fees. He didn't have an agent, boot deals or his own range of leisure wear. He didn't test positive for cocaine and marijuana, nor did he have to meet corporate sponsors after matches who have as much right to nominate a 'man of the match' as a herring has to pursue a career as a concert harpsichordist. Maybe the innocence of youth shaped my belief that football was an innocent game run by concerned parties who would uphold the well-being of the clubs for the supporters, gazing adoringly at the red-shirted gladiators on the pitch. Charlton are a part of my life; they are also a part of the local community. That's why the campaign to bring the club back to The Valley was so passionate and successful. That's why they are the best-supported team in south London.

Writing about your own club is always dangerous. Incidents and personalities that seem so important, fascinating or hilarious to you may not be so stimulating for someone not quite as *au fait* with the nature of your passion, rather like listening to friends talking about the antics of their new-born baby. You are interested, genuinely so, but there's only a certain amount of cutesy rattle-throwing, nappy-filling anecdotes that you can stand before your eyes glaze over and you want to smother the little sod.

But during my formative years and early adult life the club endured and survived some startling problems, when relegation often seemed to be the least of their worries. As attendances fell, particularly during the disastrous tenancy at Selhurst Park, relegation was a silent ogre waiting to drag the club towards bankruptcy. As money increasingly became the name of the game, so relegation became the fast track to oblivion.

The First Division years of the late 1980s under the talismanic Lennie Lawrence were a bonus, both financially and in football terms, and the four-year spell in the top flight certainly kept the club alive. Charlton stayed up just long enough. However, as the club teetered on the brink of the Third Division and bankruptcy in the early part of that decade, a couple of points less would almost certainly have meant Charlton Athletic going out of business, existing only in the wispy caverns of a few thousand memories. The fact that the club still exists and is actually thriving is mainly thanks to the supporters, certain players and two unassuming but inspirational managers.

Early memories of watching Charlton consist mainly of amazing flowing football and more goals than you knew what to do with: scores of 3–2, 4–3, the philosophy was that we could let in as many as we liked, as long as we scored more at the other end. Charlton in 1977–78 had a reputation for playing some fantastic football, including beating the eventual Second Division champions Bolton 2–1 at The Valley and hammering Spurs 4–1 with an 11-minute Mike Flanagan hat-trick. According to my memory, we never seemed to lose, and the club was a happy one in safe hands. So it came as some surprise to look back over the club's records and find that the late '70s were a time of intense struggle, declining crowds and rampant disillusionment.

By February 1978, manager Andy Nelson was slowly but perceptibly losing his marbles. He'd taken over in 1974 when the club had just been relegated to the Third Division after a dismal period during the early '70s. Coincidentally, this poor run began when I was born. In fact, on the day I was born, the second Saturday of the 1970–71 season, the Addicks were 1–0 up at half-time, during which I appeared, only for Bristol City to equalise soon afterwards. It was another eight games before Charlton recorded their first win of the season, and to this day I can't help feeling responsible.

Nelson took over from Theo Foley after the latter had led Charlton down to the Third Division they had left in 1935, and immediately guided the club back up into the Second. The next campaign saw a respectable mid-table position attained, with Valley legend Derek Hales banging in 31 goals, followed by seventh place in 1976–77. The goals kept flying in, despite the mid-season loss of Hales to Derby County after he'd scored 18 in 19 games, and the Addicks scored four or more goals on seven occasions. The crowds started coming back, Nelson was hailed as a genius of attacking football, and things were looking up for Charlton Athletic.

Then I came along to spoil things. In February 1978, I showed up for the first time to see Charlton play Oldham Athletic. The game 'attracted' what was then Charlton's lowest post-war attendance (although they were to plumb further depths over the next few years), as 5,139 thrill-seekers braved the arctic conditions to watch 22 players career around the frozen pitch with all the grace and elegance of Bernard Bresslaw on roller-skates. Charlton gave away a last-minute equaliser to draw 2–2.

It was around this time that Nelson, whose increasingly garish choice of ties should have provided a hint of his impending lunacy, announced that the club had struck a unique twinning deal with the New England Teamen of the fledgling North American Soccer League. The advantages of this arrangement were lost on most Charlton fans when it transpired that Charlton would lose three key players, Colin Powell, top scorer Mike Flanagan and Laurie Abrahams, to the Teamen at the beginning of April 1978, six weeks before the English season ended. And if the Teamen reached the play-offs the players wouldn't be back until October at the earliest.

Whilst Nelson apparently believed that he could spare three of our most important team members, the rest of the clubs in the division were not so keen, arguing quite justifiably that Charlton would be sending out what effectively constituted a weakened side which could thus affect promotion and relegation issues. Nelson in his arrogance thought that Charlton, part of the promotion race themselves in November, would be safe from relegation. Quite what he hoped to achieve by letting the players go abroad is a mystery. What was in it for Charlton? No players arrived at The Valley in return, and even if they had they would have been next to useless anyway. Each NASL team had to include three US-born players, and Colin Powell later said that the eight non-Americans in the sides spent much of their time trying to keep the Americans out of the game because of their sheer ineptitude.

My baptism of frost at The Valley had come in the middle of a twelve-match run which yielded just four points and saw the club slide down the table at an ear-bleed-inducing rate. By the time Flanagan, Powell and Abrahams left during the first week in April, the club was in grave danger of going down. A 3–0 reverse at Roker Park in the penultimate game of the season meant that Charlton had to avoid defeat at Orient on the last day of the campaign to stay up. A tense, scrappy 0–0 draw was enough to preserve Second Division status, but the fans were becoming restless at Nelson's strange behaviour.

All this was over my head, of course. I just liked seeing goals go in. I certainly didn't realise the gravity of the situation, despite having graduated from *Ball Boy* to the slightly more mature and saucily named *Nobby* in *Shoot!*.

In the days before fanzines, the only avenue of information open to me was the club programme, produced by the Charlton Athletic Ministry of Truth. You may wonder, when you read the banal pleasantries and obfuscation of controversial issues in your club's programme, just who actually believes this propaganda. Well, I did. All of it. I swallowed the lot. Too young by a long way to overhear people in pubs talking about dressing-room fracas and bungs, the *Shoot!*-programme axis was enough to convince me that everything in the football garden was lovely.

During the summer of 1978, whilst Mario Kempes ensured that the artistry of the Dutch was bludgeoned into defeat in Buenos Aires, Nelson, now sporting ties wider than himself and louder than when The Who played at The Valley in 1976, was busy re-signing Derek Hales after unhappy spells with Derby County and West Ham United. The world's hairiest footballer, Hales didn't so much wear his beard as exist somewhere within it. Hales was already a Charlton legend, although Flanagan had developed into a sensational replacement. Flanagan was enjoying a tremendous season in the US, and was given the NASL's 'Most Valuable Player' award for 1978, beating Franz Beckenbauer and Carlos Alberto into second and third place respectively, with future million-pound footballer Trevor Francis languishing somewhere in the chasing pack. Hopes were therefore high for the coming season when Flanagan and Hales would form what should have proved to be a lethal partnership.

An early injury to Hales kept him out for much of the first half of the 1978–79 season, but still the goals flowed, most notably in a 5–5 draw at

Bristol Rovers. When Hales returned at Boundary Park just before the New Year, he and Flanagan shared the three goals which defeated Oldham, whose manager Jimmy Frizzell said of his team's performance 'We might as well have gone to the local dance'. Frizzell, an immensely likeable throwback to the good old days, had obviously allowed the advent of disco to pass him by.

The Hales/Flanagan dream ticket spectacularly combusted at The Valley when Charlton Athletic met Maidstone United in the FA Cup third round in January 1979. In an incident which was to have a long-term detrimental effect on the club's fortunes, Hales and Flanagan were both sent off for fighting. With each other.

Maidstone had taken an early lead; Flanagan had equalised with 13 minutes left. In the 85th minute, Flanagan threaded a pass through the Maidstone defence for Hales to chase, but the bearded maestro felt that he had no chance of reaching it ('Fuck that' was in fact his reaction) and the ball ran out of play. Flanagan aimed a few choice words at Hales, who responded by aiming a few choice blows in the direction of Flanagan's bubble-perm. Flanagan responded in kind, but presumably had trouble locating Hales beneath the beard. Once the players had been separated, referee Brian Martin consulted his linesman in case he'd imagined the whole thing, and sent off both players. As the Maidstone fans fell about laughing, Hales and Flanagan left the field still arguing and jabbing fingers at each other.

Two days later the Charlton board sacked Hales and fined Flanagan £250. Hales appealed to the Football League on the grounds that Charlton had fired him but retained his registration. Southend and Cardiff were interested, with Hales turning down a £75,000 move to Ninian Park. Flanagan then slapped in a transfer request, his indignation at being fined stoked further by the Charlton board's later decision to reinstate Hales under pressure from the League and the PFA. Tampa Bay Rowdies offered £700,000 for Flanagan, who went missing. Despite appeals to Flanagan's family, who denied knowledge of where the permed absentee was, Nelson couldn't find Flanagan anywhere.

The effect of the affair on Charlton saw the club tumble from a comfortable tenth place to nineteenth, with no victories from the beginning of March to the last game of the season. A 2–0 win over Oldham in that game kept Charlton up, but only just. The game saw unrest amongst the Charlton fans, who called for the resignations of Nelson and long-serving chairman Michael Gliksten. Two last-ditch escapes in two seasons were a little much to bear when both campaigns had started promisingly, and the fans identified crass mismanagement as the reason for the club's predicament.

Flanagan, it transpired, was now working as a painter and decorator whilst the New England Teamen and Tampa Bay Rowdies argued over his services. Eventually Crystal Palace forked out £650,000 for the striker to partner Clive Allen up front and unleash a rash of embarrassing Flanagan and Allen photo opportunities involving fedoras, big fur coats and cheroots.

With the Flanagan and Hales issue now resolved, Charlton could look forward to the 1979–80 campaign as a fresh start for a new decade. Nelson made a couple of shrewd signings, including the return of Colin Powell from the US, and there was the traditional air of quiet optimism as the season started. In true Charlton fashion, this was noisily shattered by events on and off the pitch.

The Safety of Sports Grounds Act had come into effect, and the cavernous, crumbling Valley saw its capacity slashed from a notional 66,000 to a rather more alarming 20,000. Still a tall order for Charlton to fill in their less than successful condition on the pitch, but in the event of a lucrative cup draw a possible barrier to vital financial gain. The summer of 1979 saw construction commence on a new cantilever stand at the south end of the ground and the replacement of the old gabled main-stand roof. Grand plans were set out for ground development, which would eventually see The Valley converted into an all-seater stadium, but the quite startling lack of progress on the pitch put those plans on hold, lack of cash preventing vital ground improvements which might have saved the club from moving out of The Valley in 1985.

On the field, the 1979–80 season went from bad to worse and then deteriorated. The Addicks won just six games all season, picking up a pathetic four points away from home.

After a disastrous start to the season, Mike Bailey, the last Charlton player to play for England, was appointed chief coach with Nelson concentrating on the club's business affairs. The side lurched from defeat to defeat, notable ones being a 3–0 tonking by Preston North End at The Valley on the opening day of the season, a 4–0 spanking at Sunderland, a similar thrashing at Queen's Park Rangers and a disastrous FA Cup tie at Wrexham which saw Charlton humbled 6–0. A 1–0 defeat at home to Birmingham in February was notable for a post-match punch-up in the tunnel between Colin Powell and Archie Gemmill (which was apparently broken up by Derek Hales lifting the pugnacious Scot off the ground by the throat) and a long, vociferous protest after the game by Charlton fans unhappy at the way the club was being run. Nelson was put back in charge of the team, much to Bailey's chagrin as he was in the process of buying a house in London and moving his family down from the Midlands. Nelson then left at the end of March and Bailey took over again. Needless to say, these farcical goings-on didn't exactly help team morale.

Meanwhile, Charlton made two international signings during the campaign, bringing in Johnny Ostergaard and Viggo Jacobsen from Kastrup of Denmark. Ostergaard looked like a blond version of Chas out of Chas and Dave and was a Danish ice hockey international. Despite giving his age as 24, he looked about 40, whilst Jacobsen appeared to be the most boring man in the world. His profile in the programme soon after joining the club included the revealing responses 'miscellaneous likes: none; miscellaneous dislikes: none; favourite food: none'. A rare insight into the glamorous world of the jet-setting professional footballer. Makes a change from disliking smoking and insincere people, and wanting to meet Mohammed Ali, I suppose.

Anyway, both of them led short, unsuccessful Valley careers, notable only for Ostergaard scoring one of the best goals I've ever seen, belting one in from over by the touchline somewhere, and the slump continued unabated.

The Birmingham game came as part of a run of 13 games which yielded a solitary point. Only one more was earned after that and the Addicks became the first team to be relegated in the 1980s. I still thought we were brilliant, of course. The programme told me so. We were always about to turn a corner, the players were determined to keep us up and the mood in the camp was still optimistic. We had to keep getting behind the team. Solemnly digesting this advice, I pictured the players before the game, steely in their resolve never to give up, convinced that the good name of Charlton Athletic should not be besmirched by relegation to the Third Division, a morass to which they had been only once since the days when Hitler was no more than a loud-mouthed weirdo in a Munich beer hall and Manchester City were a force to be reckoned with. We'd been unlucky every week, letting in so many goals and not actually scoring any. Our luck would soon change. We just had to keep believing. I believed, and we were relegated by a mile. We were almost lapped, we were that far behind.

The following season saw Bailey lead Charlton straight back up into the Second Division with much the same squad, a campaign notable for the development of a young Paul Walsh. Charlton still tried to blow it: favourites to go up as champions at Easter, they scraped into third place thanks to a win at Carlisle United in the penultimate game after a run of four consecutive defeats. In typical fashion, Charlton's one moment of success was achieved at the other end of the country from their long-suffering fans with only a couple of hundred Addicks making the long trek north. A late Carlisle goal to make the score 2–1 meant that Addicks fans were left to sweat through the final minutes, perspiration levels rising further when a promising youngster called Peter Beardsley hit the crossbar late on.

In the summer of 1981, some characteristic shilly-shallying from the board led to Bailey departing to take over the reins at First Division Brighton and Hove Albion (First Division? Brighton and Hove Albion?) when Charlton failed to offer him an extension to his contract. Coincidentally, Bailey's replacement at The Valley was the man who'd occupied the manager's office at the Goldstone before him, the flamboyant Alan Mullery. On Mullery's first day, an ominous figure strode in and plonked a cheque for £50,000 made out to Charlton Athletic on his desk. Announcing that the club should treat the money as a gift from a supporter, Mark Hulyer turned, flounced back out of the door and started an association with the club that was to lead to its eventual closure.

As usual, the 1981–82 season started well, with Charlton as high as sixth in March, but results fell away towards the end and the club ended the campaign in a respectable mid-table position. Morale was dented when Gliksten refused to stump up the cash for Mullery to sign Archie Gemmill: at the time Charlton were looking a good outside bet for promotion, and Gemmill could have been the man to see them through. Presumably the bruises on his neck had healed.

Chairman Gliksten was becoming increasingly disillusioned with the club his family had run for over 50 years and was not prepared to put any more of his money into Charlton. The now-familiar slide down the table began. Gliksten, with business affairs in Australia taking up an increasing amount of his time, then surprisingly sold all his shares to the erstwhile philanthropist Hulyer who, at 32, became the youngest chairman in the Football League. It was to be a fateful deal and was to lead to the bankruptcy of Charlton Athletic. Gliksten, crucially, retained ownership of The Valley. Hulyer was a lifelong fan and local whizz-kid businessman. He also sported a moustache, which made me instantly suspicious. Six players had worn them in the relegation season. I rest my case.

Mullery didn't trust Hulyer, who had gone from supporter to chairman in just nine months, and resigned to take over at Crystal Palace. His assistant, Ken Craggs, took over as manager, and a former schoolteacher called Lennie Lawrence quietly assumed the stewardship of the reserve team.

Hulyer announced (unspecific) big plans for Charlton, and promptly tried to sign Kevin Keegan from Southampton. Keegan, however, kept a straight face long enough to inform Hulyer that he had just agreed to join Newcastle. Who knows, if Hulyer had been just a fraction quicker, we might have seen

Charlton boss Kevin Keegan wearing a chunky pair of headphones, jabbing his finger at Martin Tyler and saying that he would 'just love it' if Charlton beat Manchester United to the title.

If Hulyer's attempt to sign Keegan caused much chortling around the football world, when he bagged former European Footballer of the Year Allan Simonsen from Barcelona, crockery smashed to the floor from breakfast tables across the land. Charlton had made a disastrous start to the season with four defeats on the trot (one of these was my first away game, at Wolves on a Tuesday night, where we lost 5–0) following a rare opening-day away win, but had managed to lure a world-class player to The Valley. As a PR coup it was a masterstroke, but Hulyer's youthful enthusiasm was to be the club's eventual undoing.

The fee for Simonsen was £300,000, and when he arrived from the throbbing, sultry delights of the Nou Camp stadium he was flown straight to Brunton Park, the home of Carlisle United. A culture-shocked, open-mouthed Simonsen watched as his new team-mates succumbed to a 4–1 thrashing which was capped by Derek Hales being sent off for headbutting a Carlisle defender.

Still in the grip of relentless childish naïveté, I believed Simonsen when he said he'd joined Charlton for a new challenge. You know the sort of thing: a great set-up, a club that's going places, all that stuff. I swallowed the lot. I really believed that Allan Simonsen had traded Barcelona for south-east London because he agreed with me that Charlton were a great club with a big future. If a television interviewer had asked Simonsen 'Why Charlton?' and he'd replied 'Two grand a week for trudging around the lower reaches of the Second Division, thanks very much' I would have been absolutely mortified. A loss of innocence rivalled only by my discovery of a cache of pornographic magazines in some woods in Orpington a few months down the line. If Simonsen had announced a lifelong ambition to drink flat lager in the Watermans Arms and watch the construction of the Thames Barrier from the top of the South Stand, I'd have found that perfectly feasible.

Mind you, as he shivered in the windswept stand at Carlisle and watched Derek Hales lay out an unsuspecting Cumbrian at the end of a 4–1 thumping in front of 4,500 people, few would have forgiven him for leafing instantly through his phrasebook seeking the words for 'taxi' and 'airport'. Fair play to him, he stuck around for a few weeks at least.

Bureaucratic red tape meant that Simonsen couldn't play in Charlton's next home match against Burnley. The ever-shy Hulyer, however, dragged him on to the pitch before the game, microphone in one hand, the other flung fraternally around the bewildered Danish international. The sophisticated chairman of Charlton Athletic then introduced the new signing to the men, women and children in the crowd as, as I remember it, 'the best fucking signing this fucking club has ever made'.

Simonsen finally stepped on to the pitch as a first-team player in a whirl of publicity against Middlesbrough in November 1982. Charlton, of course, fell to the occasion and with half an hour gone were 3–0 down. Simonsen wandered around the midfield with a look on his face that asked 'What am I doing on the same pitch as these tossers?', remembered his bank balance and threaded a few more immaculate passes to where no Charlton journeyman could possibly have anticipated in a million years. The game finished 3–2, with Simonsen marking his debut with a scrappy goal from a deflected free-kick.

The new signing missed the next two games, which included an impressive 5–1 home defeat by Rotherham United that brought to an end Ken Craggs's brief but eventful reign as manager. Hulyer had taken Craggs for a meal after the game and told him his job was safe. Two days later he was fired. His replacement in a caretaker capacity was Lennie Lawrence, a move of rare foresight on Hulyer's part, although the appointment may have had more to do with enforced parsimony than early recognition of Lawrence's potential.

Under Lawrence, Charlton started picking up points, and Simonsen was making a positive contribution. In fact, the 2–0 Valley win over Newcastle in December was beamed live to Simonsen's native Denmark and watched by 60 per cent of the population. The diminutive Dane had failed to capture the imagination of the south London public, however, and the next home game, against Barnsley, saw just 4,942 people squeeze into The Valley.

Hulyer had estimated that Charlton's average attendance would have to at least double to pay for and keep his expensive import. It was apparent that Simonsen couldn't carry the team by himself, and he was a frequent victim of good old-fashioned 'stopper' centre-halves (future Ireland boss Mick McCarthy was sent off during the Barnsley game for a series of 'stiff' challenges on Simonsen). After all, if you stick Eric Clapton in with the band at Stavros's Taverna in Streatham, the drummer still won't be able to keep time. Crowds were actually falling. Performances weren't helping. Charlton were consistent only in their inconsistency: a 7–1 stuffing at Burnley was followed by a sparkling 5–2 win over Chelsea.

It soon became clear that Hulyer couldn't afford to keep Simonsen. Michael Gliksten then quietly pointed out that Hulyer wasn't paying him off for his shares. Leeds United and Aston Villa then chimed in that transfer fees for Carl Harris and Terry Bullivant hadn't been paid either. Simonsen went back to Denmark, the League placed a transfer embargo on Charlton and the club slipped into the bottom three in April. The Addicks looked doomed. In the last game of the season at The Valley against Bolton, both sides needed to win to have any chance of staying up. In a tense encounter, Bolton took the lead on the hour but Charlton somehow banged in four in twelve minutes to stay in the Second Division.

With the club's finances an increasingly vibrant shade of red, attendances falling and a mob of angry creditors gathering outside the tavern with flaming torches ready to assail Castle Hulyer, relegation to the Third Division in 1983 could have conceivably finished off Charlton Athletic for good. If the punters couldn't be won over by Allan Simonsen and the visits of Newcastle and Leeds United, Bournemouth and Hull City were even less likely to lure the discerning south-Londoner from a comfy chair in front of the wrestling and *Metal Mickey*.

With debts mounting, Hulyer suddenly offered Gliksten £1 million to clear his debt and buy The Valley. When Gliksten asked where, exactly, this money would come from, Hulyer replied that he'd hoped Gliksten wouldn't ask him that and went back to the drawing board.

In the summer of 1983, Charlton's problems worsened when Leeds United issued a winding-up order against the club over the non-payment of Carl Harris's £125,000 transfer fee. The Inland Revenue then pointed out that Charlton owed them a trivial £145,000. Eventually, Charlton were given until October to come up with a financial solution. This at least meant that the club would start the 1983–84 season. A seven-match unbeaten run at the start of the season was ended by a narrow 7-0 defeat at Brighton, whilst Hulyer fended off the Inland Revenue with one hand only for the other to close around a £250,000 winding-up order from Gliksten. The next few games were individually poignant for Charlton fans, as each could have been the club's last. A 1–0 win over second-placed Manchester City would at least have been a nice way to finish.

As Charlton leaped from extended deadline to extended deadline like a contestant on *The Crystal Maze*, Hulyer resigned as chairman but remained as a director. Then, in an amazing turnaround, Charlton tried to sue Gliksten. In a move akin to the Faroe Islands launching an invasion of Africa, Charlton alleged that Gliksten had breached the Companies Act. The legal wranglings were adjourned until the New Year at the High Court which at least gave the club a little breathing space. In the meantime, directors were jumping ship all over the place, until Hulyer eventually made up the entire board.

Further problems surfaced when Rotherham United politely asked where the down payment on Ronnie Moore's £30,000 transfer was, and the club's bank account was frozen. In the High Court, the Inland Revenue issued a winding-up order for £100,000, to be paid within two weeks. Hulyer remained optimistic, in the same way that when Melchester Rovers were 3–0 down with five minutes left, you just knew Racey would bang in a hat-trick and Blackie Gray would nick a winner.

However, Roy Race didn't arrive with his chequebook, and on Tuesday, 27 February 1984, Charlton Athletic were pronounced dead. I still remember the news being announced on the television and, at the tender age of 13, going numb with shock. Things like this just didn't happen in football. Charlton couldn't die. The Valley was still there, you could go and see it. The players were still around. The supporters' club had organised coaches for the game on Saturday. I'd got junior discount vouchers until the end of the season. Charlton couldn't go out of existence, it was incomprehensible. Why and how could this happen? Doom merchants on television were even reconstructing the league table to show how things would stand once Charlton's record had been expunged. Not yet having been exposed to bereavement, I had no yardstick for my grief and spent the rest of the week in a daze.

Meanwhile, Hulyer frantically tried to find someone willing to bail out the club. If Charlton failed to fulfil their fixture at Blackburn on the Saturday, they would be officially kicked out of the League. Sound familiar, Middlesbrough fans? You got off lightly.

Rumours began to circulate that a consortium involving Sunley Ltd, a highly successful local business run by an elderly Charlton supporter named John Fryer, were preparing a package to rescue the club. In the meantime, the Official Receiver came down and locked the ground, Lawrence diving in with some nifty footwork at the last minute to remove the kit hamper in case the Blackburn game went ahead.

Club staff were technically out of their jobs, and the administration was moved to the Valley Club, the social club that existed separately from the parent club. Graham Kelly issued a statement that Charlton would have to pay off all their creditors to stay in the League. The judge at the High Court, however, decided that he needed more time to consider the Sunley proposal, and the Friday 5 p.m. deadline was put back yet again. Word came through to the Valley Club that the FA had agreed as a result to postpone the following day's game at Blackburn, on condition that the club's affairs would be settled by 5 p.m. on Thursday 8 March. Hulyer, meanwhile, resigned as chairman.

On Wednesday 7 March Greenwich Council announced that they would be prepared to issue Charlton with a grant of £250,000 if a suitable consortium could be found to save the club. That evening, however, Sunley chairman John Fryer was on the verge of pulling out of the whole thing. A figure of £2 million was required to pay off the creditors and set the club back on its feet. But a struggling team in a cavernous, ageing stadium with a dwindling hardcore of supporters was not really an ideal business into which to plough a couple of million quid. However, Fryer's fellow consortium members Richard Collins, who had originally joined the board during the Hulyer era, and Michael Norris, a Charlton fan whose business connections had led Charlton to Sunley, managed to persuade Fryer to stick with the club.

The hearing began in the High Court at 3 p.m. the next day, with the agreement being sealed 20 minutes later. The papers arrived at Lancaster Gate just half an hour before the League's 5 p.m. final deadline. Seventy-nine years of history, tradition, success, hope and failure had been saved with minutes to spare. As the news was relayed back to the Valley Club, the celebrations began, and as night fell over the vast, shadowy stadium, a few old ghosts sighed with relief.

Two days later, the 11 representatives of the new Charlton Athletic (1984) Ltd took the field against Grimsby Town to a tumultuous reception. The new board walked sheepishly alongside them, and a hastily constructed sign at the top of the East Terrace announced that 'Sunley Ltd Welcome You to Charlton Athletic'. Fryer, apparently a player of some repute in his day, kicked a ball across the field to Derek Hales, a symbolic gesture that seemed to say 'Right, we've done our bit, now it's down to you'. The game was a 3–3 thriller, with a youngster called Robert Lee, forever destined to be known as the player who used to be a turnstile operator at The Valley, marking his debut with a well-taken goal.

For me, a six-year association with the club had meant almost half my young life. As I surveyed the ground and jubilant scenes around me, I nodded sagely to myself and knew that everything was right with the world. Despite losing their last five games of the season, Lawrence's team occupied 13th place at the end of the campaign, a harmless position at last, and a wholly welcome one after the tribulations of the previous months.

The 1984–85 season was another campaign of disappointing inconsistency, with Second Division status only assured with three games to go. Jimmy Hill, ominously, joined the board of directors. Lawrence was, however, assembling a useful side who were to surprise everyone the following season.

On the final day of the 1984–85 season, Charlton travelled to Manchester City. The Addicks were having a torrid time with injuries, whilst a rampant City needed a win to go up to the First Division. The local press reported before the game that the injury crisis was so bad, midfielder Steve Gritt might even have to play in goal. As it was, 16-year-old Lee Harmsworth made his debut, and in front of the country's biggest crowd of the day he picked the ball out of the net five times. Hold-ups on the motorway meant that we Addicks fans daft enough to travel up to this hiding arrived at half-time. As we entered the terrace during the interval to discover our mixture of half-fit first-teamers, reserves and youth-team players were only 2–0 down, across the Pennines a cigarette was being discarded in the main stand at Valley Parade, Bradford. Within minutes, as we were put further to the sword, more than 50 football fans were dead. City's promotion celebrations were muted, and we returned to London in silence as the Bradford death toll continued to rise. For me, football was fast losing its innocence.

The summer of 1985 saw Lawrence honing the skills he was fast acquiring in signing players on the cheap who would flourish at Charlton and be sold on at net gain at a later date. A new backbone to the side was assembled, and the club embarked on the 1985–86 campaign in good heart.

Off the field, however, problems associated with years of neglect and mismanagement were beginning to surface. Within the space of two weeks, the GLC closed the vast East Terrace (capable of holding 20,000 people on its own) for reasons of safety, and former chairman Michael Gliksten announced he was reclaiming land that belonged to him behind the West Stand, a move that would remove all the club's car-parking facilities and its most-frequented turnstiles. Gliksten, it appeared, had agreed with the Charlton board to cordon off the land as part of what he was owed by the club; indeed, he issued a statement that it had been the club's idea in the first place. The GLC in their defence said that they had instructed the club to carry out urgent repair work on the East Terrace as early as 1979 and this had not been done.

The double blow, pincering two sides of the ground, nudged Fryer into making the most horrendous and misguided decision ever taken by a Charlton Athletic board member. He decided that the best way forward was for Charlton to leave The Valley. Barely a month after the GLC action and two weeks after Gliksten's announcement, fans arriving at the home game with Crystal Palace were given a shabby flyer announcing that Charlton would be leaving The Valley and moving in with their arch-rivals, near-neighbours and that day's opponents.

During the middle part of the 1980s, groundsharing was frequently mooted as the future of football. Fryer, perhaps keen to be remembered as some kind of visionary, the man who set the wheels in motion for the preservation of the national game, had certainly acted with undue haste. Within days of the double blow which, although serious, was certainly not fatal to the proud old stadium, he had decided what action he wanted to take, investigated sharing with several clubs and signed the deal with Palace before the fans, and some of the board, had learned anything of the situation.

Fryer's motives remain unclear to this day. Maybe Palace chairman Ron Noades, probably the leading proponent of groundsharing, saw the problems at The Valley and Fryer's inexperience as a football chairman as the ideal opportunity to realise his dream. Maybe Fryer was flattered by the attentions of the high-profile Palace chairman and seduced by the possibility of going down in football history as the man who started the groundsharing revolution. The haste with which the deal was completed and put into practice does hint at a high level of co-operation between the two clubs. Or at least the two chairmen.

The fact that the club's destination was Selhurst Park piled on the humiliation for shell-shocked Addicks fans. Although only a few miles away from The Valley as the crow flies, the journey to Selhurst Park is a tortuous one whatever your chosen mode of transport. The board's postulations that Palace were our nearest neighbours ignored the fact that Charlton's core support comes from the London Borough of Greenwich and throughout north Kent. Travelling to Selhurst by train involves a journey into central London and out again, and the journey by car is a hellish one through the streets of south London. Selhurst Park was also held up by Fryer to be a modern stadium, the sort of place The Valley could never aspire to be. Modern it may have been – and at the time even that was debatable – but Selhurst is renowned for its dead atmosphere. Even when full, there is no buzz. The atmosphere could never match The Valley, even at its most sparsely populated. And, above all, it was the home of Crystal Palace.

The decision appears to have been a unilateral one on Fryer's part. Greenwich Council's representative on the board, Bill Strong, learned of the deal only when he turned up at The Valley and had the club's leaflet thrust into his hand as he entered the ground, underlining the grim reality of the arbitrary power Fryer appeared to wield in the boardroom.

The Charlton fans were stunned. After 66 years, they were being evicted from the place they had built with their hard-earned money at the turnstiles, an investment that could hardly have been said to have reaped rewards in terms of success on the pitch. The 3–1 victory over Crystal Palace that followed would normally have been greeted with joy unconfined; instead the Addicks' supporters left the ground silently reading and re-reading the scrap of paper that had to be either some kind of cruel joke or a mistake.

Two weeks later, on 21 September 1985, Charlton played their last game at The Valley, against Stoke City. A capacity crowd of just 8,858 watched the game. With the East Terrace closed, the occasion was a sell-out in more ways than one. The atmosphere was strange: subdued yet emotionally charged, rebellious yet reflective. Wreaths were laid on the centre-circle, a parade of former Valley heroes was presented to the fans and a constant torrent of protest and abuse was directed at the directors' box. The cover of the programme, which cheapened the event still further by labelling itself a 'special souvenir edition', pictured midfielder Alan Curbishley challenging for a high ball; his greatest role for the club was still to come. Inside there were directions to Selhurst Park, and the news pages titled 'Echoes Across The Valley' were renamed, rather less sonorously, 'Echoes Across The Ground'.

Predictably, the first half finished goalless, but as soon as the whistle blew for the interval, fans poured on to the pitch. Once there they appeared unsure what to do next, but soon made for the front of the West Stand and chanted at the empty directors' box. 'We're not going to Selhurst Park!' they sang. 'We hate Fryer!' they spat through clenched teeth, showing a passion so rarely observed on The Valley turf in the preceding years. A group made for the goalmouth at the home end. From the pack an arm reached up and grabbed the crossbar, pulling on it to bring it down and force the abandonment of the game. The roar of protest that greeted this action soon dissuaded the errant fan and he retreated sheepishly and anonymously into the throng.

Eventually a semblance of calm was restored and the game continued. Late goals from Mark Stuart and Robert Lee brought the final curtain down on football at The Valley. The East Terrace, on which 40,000 had often swayed, sung and surged, looked on empty and forlorn. The undulations and cracks along the vast expanse made the scene all the more poignant and tragic: the crowd's absence on this emotional day left it naked and humiliated. At the top of the terrace, perched gaily like a bright floral garland on the head of a doomed bull about to be run to death through the streets of a provincial Spanish town, stood the garish yellow sign that so many had welcomed a few months before: 'Sunley Ltd Welcome You to Charlton Athletic.' The words rang hollow as Fryer the saviour became Fryer the traitor.

At the final whistle, as the players sprinted for the dressing-room, the crowd swarmed on to the pitch. Once again, the mass movement of fans had little idea of what to do next. Many just milled around for a couple of hours, digging up sods of earth to plant in hundreds of suburban backyards so at least The Valley would live on in the lawns of south London. Many wandered on to the vast East Terrace, gazing for the last time across the dramatic metropolitan panorama the banking afforded. Eventually, everyone drifted away and the sun set behind the West Stand. An eerie silence descended, a deafening void that would not be lifted for many years.

And so Charlton Athletic moved house. From the biggest stadium in the country, they moved their suitcases into a couple of portacabins round the back of someone else's football ground which is, in turn, attached to a supermarket.

Many, if not most, supporters vowed never to go to Selhurst Park as long as it purported to be the home of Charlton Athletic. A football club is, by definition, somewhere, not something. Players come and go, directors come and go. The only constants, the things that define a football club, are the ground and the supporters. Take away one of those components and you have nothing. The fans support a club, not a team, not a group of businessmen. The 11 players who pull on the shirts and the suits in the boardroom may represent the club, but they are merely custodians, guardians of the legacy provided by the stadium and the fans. You cannot change your allegiance the way players sign for other clubs. Supporting your team is about waking up on the morning of a match with butterflies, the regular journey to the ground, the familiar faces, the build-up to the kick-off, the tension, excitement, boredom, frustration, delight and disappointment of the events on the pitch. The players may be heroes but they are temporary. Leave your own ground and your club dies. The team might have borne the name, but Charlton Athletic died on 21 September 1985 on the whim of a chairman whose support for the club was supposed to have been almost as old as The Valley itself.

Despite being near the top of the division, Lawrence's cheaply assembled side was rarely watched by more than 6,000 people at Selhurst. Although this was comparable with Valley crowds over the preceding couple of years, it is certain that the team's good form would have led to much higher attendances in SE7. Photographs of matches from this period froze the moments of glory on the field in front of a backdrop of hundreds upon hundreds of empty seats.

Miraculously, just when events off the field should have sent the side tumbling down the table towards the Third Division, Charlton clinched promotion to the First with a 3–2 win at Carlisle United, coming back from 2–0 down and helped by a remarkable 30-yard own goal. Brunton Park was proving to be a happy hunting ground for the Addicks.

In the meantime, it had been announced that Greenwich Council would reject any planning applications to build on The Valley as the ground was designated for use as a community leisure space only. Arsonists and vandals took this as a great opportunity and set about destroying the facilities at their leisure. Such was the club's rush to leave their spiritual home that piles of programmes and club records were mulched by the elements outside the back of the West Stand.

If promotion had been a surprise, Charlton's 1986–87 relegation battle in the top flight was anything but. Lawrence strengthened the side but saw most of the club's cash haemorrhaging into the Selhurst coffers. Save for a remarkable 1–0 win at Old Trafford, Charlton were unable to register a victory in their first eight games and failed to win at home until mid-October. Off the field, supporters were becoming more organised: when local newspaper the *South-East London Mercury* printed a petition titled 'The Valley is our home', 15,000 signatures arrived at the newspaper's office. This can be compared with the attendances for Charlton's Selhurst matches in the first two rounds of the Full Members Cup at around the same time: 821 and 817. Ironically, the competition was the brainchild of Charlton's landlord, Palace chairman Ron Noades. By Boxing Day, homeless, friendless Charlton occupied bottom place in the First Division and seemed certain to go down.

The 1986–87 season heralded the inception of the play-offs. In a bid to reduce the size of the First Division to 20 clubs, something always mooted as A Good Thing to reduce the number of matches (despite the fact that clubs were obliged to participate in the supremely irrelevant Noades white elephant that was the aforementioned Full Members Cup), it was decreed that the club finishing 19th in the First Division would join the teams that finished third, fourth and fifth in the Second Division in a knockout competition to decide who would compete in the top flight the following season.

A 3–0 win at Newcastle United and a hard-fought 2–1 'home' win over Queen's Park Rangers in the last two matches of the regular league programme were enough to heave Charlton into 19th place above relegated Leicester City, Manchester City and Aston Villa. The Addicks joined Oldham, Leeds and Ipswich in the play-off semi-finals.

In those days, the twin towers of Wembley were a world away from the play-off contenders (although Charlton had been there a few weeks earlier to lose the Full Members Cup final to Blackburn Rovers, then a mid-table Second Division side, a 40,000 crowd including barely 15,000 from south-east London), with all the matches played over two legs. Charlton travelled to Portman Road to face Ipswich Town in the first leg of their semi-final. Colin Walsh missed a penalty for the visitors, but Charlton still managed to grind out a goalless draw to bring Ipswich back to Selhurst Park on level terms. Just over 11,000 watched Jim Melrose head two goals in quick succession midway through the first half and, despite Steve McCall's late goal for the Suffolk side, Charlton went through to face two ties with Leeds United.

In a classic example of the nature of Charlton's tenancy, the first leg of the Addicks' most important encounter since the 1947 FA Cup final was switched from the Friday night to the Saturday afternoon because of late-night shopping at the Sainsbury's supermarket to which the Palace ground is attached. Despite this concession to suburbia, 16,000 watched a closely fought game drift towards a goalless conclusion until Melrose arrived with a priceless goal three minutes from time. It was a vital lifeline for the Addicks to take to the always-welcoming and hospitable Elland Road for the second leg. A crowd of 31,000 saw Peter Shirtliff hit the crossbar early in the game for Charlton, but the only goal came seven minutes into the second half from Brendan Ormsby for the home side. Three hours of high-velocity, supremely tense football at the end of a long, hard season had failed to produce a winner, failed to throw up the final member of the top flight. The two clubs would meet again.

The play-off final replay would take place at St Andrews, Birmingham, a city not known for its affection for Leeds United. So it was that Charlton fans found themselves joined by locals as part of the 18,000 crowd, a low figure due to the all-ticket restrictions imposed on the Yorkshire club following misbehaviour by their followers.

The tension was unbearable as both sides jabbed cautiously at each other. At stake for Leeds was a return to the division where they had made their reputation under Don Revie. For Charlton, relegation could have meant the end. Already financially crippled, playing at the lower level would have meant drastic cutbacks, non-existent crowds and a mass exodus of players already murmuring about low bonus levels. Once again, Charlton's very existence hung upon the last game of the season. The game at St Andrews was not a classic and despite scrappy chances at both ends the physical encounter finished goalless at the end of 90 minutes. The agony was to be prolonged for another half-hour.

Midway through the first period of extra time, Paul Miller was harshly adjudged to have handled 25 yards from the Charlton goal. Bob Bolder set his wall carefully, but John Sheridan curled the ball past wall and goalkeeper and into the bottom corner of the net. A big hole opened up under Charlton: a one-way journey to who-knows-where. Lawrence tried to cajole some life from his exhausted players for the second period, but the pessimism honed from years of experience supporting Charlton engendered a feeling of utter despair amongst the travelling Addicks, who hoped against hope for a miracle.

Charlton had been up against it for an entire season, and now it appeared that the lack of depth in the squad, that shortage of one or two quality players, was about to prove crucial. More than four and a half hours of football between the two sides had produced just three goals; Charlton now needed to score twice in fifteen minutes.

The seconds ticked away, and the life was visibly ebbing out of Charlton. Seven minutes remained when the veteran Steve Gritt crossed the ball into the Leeds area, Stuart controlled and laid the ball off to Shirtliff, who sidefooted the ball past Mervyn Day for the equaliser. It was a lifeline that Charlton grabbed with both hands, sensing victory. Four minutes later the Londoners won a free-kick wide on the right. Gritt ran over the ball and Andy Peake curled an outswinging cross towards the penalty spot, where Shirtliff arrived fractionally ahead of ex-Addick Mark Aizlewood, stooping to bury a low header into the bottom corner. Charlton had survived against the odds. It was to become a recurring theme.

The play-off victory saved Charlton in more ways than one. Indeed, it was such a momentous occasion for the club that in 1997 it threw a tenth anniversary reunion, appropriately enough for such a hard-fought victory at a pub called the Trafalgar Tavern, where the team and even the referee gathered to remember that incredible night.

The following season saw increased coherence amongst those fighting for a return to The Valley with the launch of the *Voice of The Valley* fanzine. The brainchild of Rick Everitt, now the club's communications manager, and Steve Dixon, now Charlton's marketing manager, *Voice of The Valley* provided fans with a much-needed forum for debate as well as a vital source of information not vetted by the club. Through the pages of the *Voice*, a boycott was planned for the game against Oxford United, with fans due to gather at The Valley rather than Selhurst, when it emerged that director Michael Norris had acquired Adelong Ltd, Gliksten's company, and thus effectively bought back the disputed land behind the West Stand at The Valley. Light was glimpsed at the end of a long, dark tunnel, and the boycott was abandoned. 'Back to The Valley' chants rang around the Baseball Ground as the fans celebrated the news in early March at Derby County. It was to become a regular refrain.

The 1987–88 season saw some improvement on the field, particularly following the encouraging news about The Valley. A five-game unbeaten run saw the Addicks go into the last game of the season at Chelsea knowing that a point would save them from another play-off sentence and condemn Chelsea in turn to the knockout lottery.

Over 30,000 people created a frightening atmosphere at Stamford Bridge. After a quarter of an hour, the crowd intimidated the referee into giving a penalty to Chelsea when John Humphrey clearly brought down Gordon Durie outside the box. Durie himself converted the spot-kick and Charlton were left staring into the abyss again. With just over 20 minutes remaining, however, Paul Miller received the ball from a throw-in, hit the ball goalwards and saw it cannon off both Joe McLaughlin and Steve Wicks before dropping over Kevin Hitchcock into the net. Charlton were back in it. The tension of the final minutes was unbearable. Things threatened to spill over into violence on and off the field, particularly when Leaburn was knocked out cold by an unpunished punch, but Charlton got the draw and Chelsea went into the play-offs and, ultimately, the Second Division. The Addicks had defied the odds again.

The following season, 1988–89, saw Charlton in the rare position of mid-table security. For once the last game of the season, a 4–0 drubbing at Nottingham Forest, was purely academic.

Meanwhile, Michael Norris and fellow director Roger Alwen each acquired a 50 per cent stake in the club, and Fryer was now out of the picture. Having been diagnosed with cancer, the elderly former chairman was to die a few months later in the USA. The new regime continued to look for alternative sites to The Valley, and there were constant rumours of men in suits appearing at patches of waste ground throughout the borough. Although the fans dreamt of a return to Floyd Road, there was a growing acceptance that anywhere in Greenwich would do.

Alwen was a man with a mission, however, and when he took over as chairman in early March 1989, it was announced that the club would return to The Valley. At an emotional public meeting at Woolwich Town Hall on 23 March, Alwen said, 'We have been given favourable indications from the council that planning consent may shortly be given to part of The Valley and we are therefore very happy to put in hand a major refurbishment programme which will enable Charlton Athletic Football Club to once again play football at The Valley.' The fans could hardly believe their ears. Years before Baddiel and Skinner hijacked the phrase, football was coming home to SE7.

On the first Sunday in April, an army of fans arrived at the old stadium to begin the huge clear-up process. Years of neglect had left the pitch a wilderness, whilst the stands had been rendered derelict by vandals, arsonists and the hurricane of 1987. A huge bonfire raged on the pitch, piled high with the weeds and trees accumulated by nearly five years of neglect. The glow from the flames lit the three old stands, bathing the ground in warmth. Life had returned to the old place. Fans returned to their seats and places on the terraces to look down upon the pitch from familiar vantage points. The scene was unfamiliar, the huge bonfire raging on the once-lush turf, but a group of youngsters kicking a football around amongst the weeds reminded fans why they had fought so hard for the moment. Surely it wouldn't be long before a Charlton team took the field here once again?

However, the residents living in the streets surrounding The Valley, many of whom had moved in after the club had left the area, began to voice their disquiet, particularly when plans were unveiled for a 25,000 all-seater stadium incorporating a bowling alley and office facilities to be ready by October 1990. It was not to be plain sailing for Charlton by any means. The hard part seemed to be over; in truth, it hadn't even begun. With the leader of Greenwich Council, Quentin Marsh, and the chair of the planning committee, Simon Oelman, siding with the residents and opposing the scheme, things suddenly looked ominous for Charlton. The council fended off the club at every turn, a far cry from the support the Addicks had received from the borough over the departure from the ground, eventually conceding to a meeting of the planning committee on 31 January 1990, just nine months before the ground was supposed to be ready. It was the first of many delays that were to obstruct a swift return to the old ground.

The meeting was open to the public and Charlton fans packed Woolwich Town Hall, desperate for good news. However, it was obvious that the committee had reached their decision prior to the meeting and Charlton's application was thrown out by ten votes to two. Addicks fans stormed out long before the end; it appeared to be back to square one in SE25.

Meanwhile, on the pitch Charlton's four-season excursion in the top flight was coming to an end. Despite a promising start, including a memorable 3–0 win over the then leaders Chelsea in which Paul Williams, a £10,000 signing from Woodford Town, truly established himself on the big stage, the Addicks spent most of the campaign in the bottom two. A 3–2 defeat at Southampton in April all but sealed Charlton's demise, and they rejoined the Second Division.

Luckily, the Addicks had stayed in the First Division just long enough to avoid bankruptcy. Although in those not-so-far-off days there wasn't the enormous TV revenue available today, it was infinitely preferable to be in the top flight. Relegation in either of the first two seasons could have been disastrous. But now, with a return to The Valley apparently imminent and a new regime in the boardroom, the drop wasn't as calamitous as it could have been. If Charlton had been relegated to the Second Division with no prospect of an end to their tenancy at Selhurst, the mood would have been quite different. But the impending return to the converted chalk pit close to the Thames left the fans with definite hope for the future.

The supporters were about to undertake the greatest piece of organised protest ever orchestrated by a group of fans. The formation of The Valley Party to stand in the local borough elections was a stroke of tactical genius not seen at The Valley since the '30s when someone said 'That lad Bartram's all right as a centre-forward, but let's give him a try in goal'. For one thing, the election would provide maximum publicity for the campaign to return to The Valley, and, secondly, it put Charlton fans in a direct head-to-head contest with their adversaries at the council, where the adjudicators were the public themselves at the polling booths. Democracy would win out.

The Valley Party was unquestionably a gamble. Single-issue parties rarely succeed in winning many votes at the ballot box and the campaign could have backfired spectacularly on the protestors, but the campaign was superbly executed. A total of 60 Valley Party candidates stood in most of the wards in Greenwich, and an excellent series of posters, which evoked both Charlton's past and their uncertain future, outdid the other parties by a mile and deservedly won an advertising industry award.

Initially the main parties did not see their football adversaries as any kind of threat. However, the professional way in which The Valley Party con-ducted their campaign caused panic to spread slowly through Greenwich's established political order. Indeed, a smear leaflet appeared a couple of days before polling day: whilst its origin could not be proved, Labour Party workers were seen delivering them. It was the best compliment anyone could have paid The Valley campaign.

As the polls closed, Woolwich Town Hall was packed with Charlton fans as the count began. As results came in, The Valley vote was larger than even party organisers had hoped. By morning, The Valley Party had polled an incredible 14,838 votes. Whilst not actually winning a seat, which nobody had envisaged anyway, this represented over 10 per cent of the total votes cast: a magnificent achievement and as powerful an indication that the people of Greenwich wanted Charlton back in the borough as anyone could have wished for. Bearing in mind that much, if not most, of Charlton's support comes from outside the borough and were thus ineligible to vote, the figure becomes even more astounding.

One particularly bright spot for Charlton fans was that The Valley Party vote succeeded in unseating Simon Oelman, the chair of the planning committee which had thrown out Charlton's initial application. Oelman's 450 majority turned into a shortfall of some 300 votes, and the defeated councillor compounded his indignity by attacking a Charlton fan outside the hall and getting himself arrested. The leader of the council, Quentin Marsh, came within 300 votes of being defeated thanks to The Valley Party's Kevin Fox, despite going into the poll with one of the safest seats in the borough.

Two days later Charlton said goodbye to the top flight with a high-spirited trip to Manchester United. With the return to The Valley surely back on the cards, it was the happiest relegation ever. The 1–0 defeat was almost incidental to the celebration of the election results, and the game took place in an atmosphere of mutual respect between the two sets of fans.

In the close season, reality brought Charlton back to earth. The club, in the aftermath of the Hillsborough disaster, had to fund half of the redevelopment and installation of seats in the Arthur Wait enclosure at Selhurst Park. Income at the gate would inevitably reduce for the lesser opposition in the Second Division. As a result, Lawrence was forced to sell three-times player of the year John Humphrey, top scorer Paul Williams and record signing Joe McLaughlin. The threat of a second successive relegation loomed on the horizon.

Despite the return of Alan Curbishley, as well as the signing of two defenders, Simon Webster and Stuart Balmer, Charlton were bottom of the Second Division in October, Balmer marking his debut with an own goal in the home defeat by struggling Leicester City. For the first time in his seven years in charge, the threat of the sack hung over Lennie Lawrence. The quietly spoken, agreeable manager had weathered the worst storms in the club's history, but now, with the team looking set to crash through the Second Division and into the Third, the crowd began to turn on him. On more than one occasion as he ran the gauntlet of the fans' feelings on the long walk between dug-out and dressing-room, Lawrence lost his hitherto impenetrable cool and was drawn into undignified slanging matches. Fortunately, the team pulled together, results improved and Charlton finished in 16th place.

Meanwhile, in a move which showed the club's determination to return to The Valley, the new club shop and administration offices opened at the old ground. However, strike action by NALGO, the local government officers' union, delayed the progress of Charlton's revised planning application. Eventually, finally, belatedly, the meeting was called, and once again Charlton fans packed Woolwich Town Hall to witness the application go through by seventeen votes to one.

With Second Division status ensured, there was the rare example of a meaningless last-day match for Charlton in their final game at Selhurst Park, a 1–1 draw with West Ham United in a game notable for the complete absence of emotion. In sharp contrast to the final game at The Valley, the game was

Peter Shirtliff seals Charlton's remarkable comeback in the 1987 play-off final replay against Leeds United, preserving the Addicks' First Division status and, arguably, their very existence (© Tom Morris)

Whilst Charlton fans celebrated the club's survival at St Andrews, The Valley fell further into disrepair (© Tom Morris)

Manchester United supporters rush to congratulate Denis Law on his late goal for Manchester City in the Old Trafford derby match on 27 April 1974, the day United were relegated to the Second Division (© Colorsport)

To help celebrate Swindon's victory in the 1990 play-off final, Ossie Ardiles brought along one of his darts trophies. Ten days later, Swindon found themselves in Division Three (© Colorsport)

Barry Horne's wonder goal against Wimbledon helps to preserve Everton's Premier League status, 7 May 1994 (© Allsport)

Everton fans celebrate at the final whistle, safe in the knowledge that the Toffees would never allow themselves to be in such a position again. Whoops . . . (© Allsport)

Hereford captain David Norton (centre) clears a Brighton attack in the
crucial match at Edgar Street, 3 May 1997
(© David Griffiths/*Hereford Times*)

David Norton (right, on ground) is powerless to prevent Robbie Reinelt
scoring the goal which condemned Hereford to non-League football
(© *Evening Argus*, Brighton)

Hereford's Trevor Matthewson is inconsolable as Brighton's players and supporters celebrate the south-coast club's survival at the Bulls' expense
(© David Griffiths/*Hereford Times*)

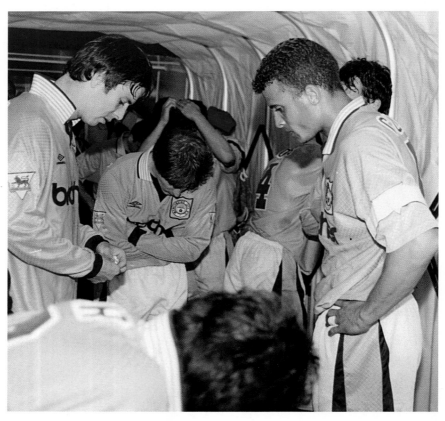

Following their relegation from the Premier League on 5 May 1996,
Manchester City players console themselves with the knowledge that at
least things can't get any worse . . . (© Colorsport)

These Manchester City fans look forward to the reception they'll receive at school on Monday morning following their club's relegation to the Second Division, May 1998 (© Allsport)

Before the start of City's 1997–98 campaign, these fans had full heads of hair . . . (© Allsport)

Juninho collapses to the turf, having learned that Middlesbrough's 1–1 draw at Leeds has not been enough to keep them in the Premiership, 11 May 1997 (© Colorsport)

Paper-hanky salesmen on Teesside reported a record month in May 1997 (© Colorsport)

played out like the sterile affair it was, and at the close the crowd left with ne'er a glance back at the ground where Charlton had spent six years of struggle.

In July, the club was rocked by the announcement that Lennie Lawrence was leaving Charlton to take over the reins at Middlesbrough. Lawrence had weathered the poor results at the beginning of the season and seemed set to lead the club back to The Valley, so his decision came as a complete surprise. Charlton expressed disquiet over the manner of Lawrence's departure, which came about as a result of transfer negotiations surrounding Boro defender Alan Kernaghan, who was at Charlton on loan. It became clear that Lawrence thought it was time to move on, foreseeing that any available finances would go into redeveloping The Valley rather than strengthening the team. Lawrence recognised that the squad in its current form was in no position to challenge for a return to the top flight and could not envisage being allowed to sign any quality players. Middlesbrough, despite having comparable attendances to Charlton at the time and despite having a playing record inferior to that of the Addicks over many years, were perceived as a 'big club', and managed to lure Lawrence away from Charlton.

No one could blame the beleaguered manager: Charlton's impecuniosity and seemingly endless troubles certainly couldn't guarantee job satisfaction. At Middlesbrough, with money to spend, Lawrence could fulfil the potential he had shown on a shoestring budget at The Valley and Selhurst.

Despite much lobbying from the fans that Lawrence's successor should be former midfielder of nearly 600 games standing Keith Peacock, recently fired by doomed Maidstone United, Charlton announced that the reins would be taken up jointly by senior professionals Steve Gritt and Alan Curbishley. It was an appointment that perplexed the Charlton supporters, who then discovered that the return to The Valley was not to be as straightforward, or as imminent, as they had expected. Plans were revised and revised, and huge hikes in ticket prices were announced. It also became clear that the club would not start the 1991–92 season at The Valley, thanks to the constant revisions of the stadium plans.

The construction of an expensive but temporary West Stand commenced, and seats were bolted on to the lower half of the East Terrace. Once again, just as things seemed to be on track the building work was halted as the contractors entrusted with the work went into receivership. Charlton subsequently announced that they would play their first three home matches at Upton Park, where they would eventually remain for the rest of the season. Building work stopped when the new contractors weren't paid, and the situation grew ever more farcical. As their hopes were put on hold for the umpteenth time, the fans began to doubt whether they would ever see a return to The Valley

In the meantime, Upton Park was a definite improvement on Selhurst. The covered North Bank enabled Addicks fans to recreate the atmosphere of the old Valley Covered End, and the proximity to the pitch created a far better atmosphere than had ever been achieved at Selhurst, especially when the team roared into contention for promotion. The Gritt/Curbishley partnership flourished despite there being no money available for players, but the shoestring squad fell victim to injuries, and a 1–0 defeat to a defensive Tranmere Rovers in April put paid to Charlton's play-off prospects.

Eventually the club announced a definite date for the return to The Valley. The 1992–93 season would see Charlton start the season at West Ham, but fans could finally ring a date on their calendars to mark the day their dreams would become reality. The ground would be a three-sided affair to start with, the East Terrace remaining closed save for a walkway to enable fans to enter the South Stand, but the visit of Portsmouth on 5 December 1992 would be the day every Charlton fan's long-drawn-out dream would come true.

Unable to get a ticket for the historic day, or even get close to the old ground thanks to police restrictions in the surrounding streets, this writer stood on Charlton Heights overlooking the ground with a handful of other ticketless fans. As the teams ran out, thousands of red and white balloons were released into the south London sky and the familiar strains of the 'Red Red Robin', the idiosyncratic anthem that had continued to keep the flame alive at Selhurst and Upton Parks, was carried to us on the breeze. In the gap between the South Stand and the East Terrace walls, we witnessed Colin Walsh receive the ball on the edge of the penalty area and crash the ball past Alan Knight into the bottom corner of the net. Seven minutes had been played, one for every year of enforced exile. The roar reached us way up above the ground, the emotion of the hardships endured by the fans, the delays and disappointments, the battles and demonstrations, all released in a roof-rattling, full-throated yell. Charlton were truly back at The Valley. It was a defining moment, the fulfilment of thousands of hopes and dreams, the culmination of seven years of lobbying and campaigning. Nothing could spoil The Valley party.

Since the return, relegation has never been an issue. As the ground has grown into a superb modern stadium, so the team under Alan Curbishley has developed with it. As I write this, exactly one week after the tortuous play-off victory over Sunderland at Wembley, Charlton are a Premiership side. The perennially skint also-rans matched the pecunious Wearsiders in every department, and the only way to separate the two sides was the lottery of the penalty shoot-out. Charlton won 7–6, the same score as in the Addicks' most famous game when they turned around a 5–1 deficit to defeat Huddersfield at The Valley in the '50s. For once, luck smiled on Charlton. But what the hell, no one deserves it more after what we've been through in the last two decades.

That day at Wembley was more than just a football match. Although memorable for the extraordinary events on the field alone, when Sasa Ilic dived to his left to save Michael Gray's penalty, he laid to rest the ghosts of desperate times: the windswept nights at a near-empty Selhurst Park, the frustration of the battles with the council, The Valley Party campaign. The presence on the pitch of Clive Mendonca, the first striker capable of emulating the exploits of Derek Hales, and the presence of thousands of Charlton fans at Wembley showed how far we had come. Unlike at the Full Members Cup final of 1987, when a few thousand sorry-looking fans huddled at the tunnel end, Charlton easily oversubscribed their allocation and could have filled the national stadium with their own fans.

We can live with the 'Happy Valley' headlines. Anything's better than the 'Valley of Doom' and 'Valley of Despair' ones we've put up with up until now. Okay, next season will undoubtedly be a relegation battle from day one, but this time, for once, we'll have a bloody good time.

A Kick up the '80s

THE FALL OF BRISTOL CITY

On 26 August 1978, as Bristol City occupied fifth place in the First Division, their more optimistic fans had half an eye on the League title and a place in Europe the following season. A little over four years later, those same supporters saw their club go bottom of the Fourth Division following a 7–1 hammering at Northampton Town.

City's 87-place plummet happened so quickly that it made your ears bleed. From European challengers to being turned over by the likes of Rochdale, City had in the interim all but gone out of business, almost paying the ultimate price for overstretching themselves off the field in the quest for success and status.

Bristol City had, apart from a brief spell in the top flight in the first decade of the twentieth century, spent most of their history flitting between the Second and Third Divisions. The odd cup run and the derby matches with Rovers kept the Ashton Gate faithful happy, but on the whole City's history could be summed up in terms of mediocrity rather than the spectacular.

In September 1967 City appointed Jimmy Hill's assistant from Coventry, Alan Dicks, as their new manager following a disastrous start to the 1967–68 campaign, but apart from a good FA Cup run in 1974, when a Don Gillies goal was enough to beat Leeds United and put the Robins into the quarter-finals for the first time since 1920, City achieved little of note, hovering around the lower-middle reaches of the Second Division. The name of Alan Dicks was, despite his hitherto unspectacular reign, destined to be written large in the annals of Bristol City.

Dicks received an unusual vote of confidence shortly after the cup run when he became possibly the first and only manager to unseat his club chairman. Harry Dolman, Bristol City's chairman since 1949, was not a big fan of Dicks (stop sniggering at the back there), and when he left for a business trip to the Caribbean he announced that if the manager was offered a new contract by the board in his absence, he would resign. He returned to find that the board had more faith in Dicks than the chairman, and the manager kept his job.

The board's faith was repaid when he unexpectedly guided a predominantly home-grown team into the First Division. Playing to the team's strengths rather than imposing a style on the squad, Dicks motivated the side into a major force. A crowd of 27,394 gathered at Ashton Gate on 20 April 1976 to see Clive Whitehead net the only goal of the game against Portsmouth, the goal that regained the First Division status City had lost 65 years earlier. Let the good times roll, said the fans as they waved two fingers at their blue and white rivals on the way past. The Robins made an excellent start to their First Division career, going top in August and occupying second place in September, but their form soon deserted them and they ended the season fighting relegation. Despite Dicks's attempts to strengthen the side by signing Norman Hunter from Leeds United and Peter Cormack from Liverpool, City found themselves in desperate trouble with two games remaining, at home to Liverpool and away at Coventry City. In their penultimate match, City beat Liverpool 2–1 to set up an intriguing finale.

Tottenham Hotspur and Stoke City were already relegated, which left the final relegation place to be contested between Bristol City, Coventry City and Sunderland, with the Robins facing Coventry at Highfield Road, Dicks's old stamping ground. All three clubs had the same number of points, but Coventry had the worst goal difference. Sunderland, whose goal difference was the best, travelled to Everton.

Conveniently for the two clubs meeting at Highfield Road, the kick-off was delayed for five minutes to allow the crowd of nearly 37,000 into the ground. This, of course, meant that the Sunderland game would be over before the end of the Bristol City v. Coventry match, leaving both sides at Ashton Gate with full knowledge of what they'd need to do to stay up whilst the game was still in progress. A five-minute delay wouldn't really have made much difference to the fans entering the ground and call me cynical, but the crowd wasn't even up to capacity that night.

Coventry took the lead on 15 minutes when Robins keeper John Shaw flapped at a cross which fell kindly for Tommy Hutchison to rifle the ball into the bottom corner of the net. Bristol City hit back immediately, had a shot cleared off the line by Bobby McDonald and saw a Tainton shot fumbled by Les Sealey bounce agonisingly the wrong side of the post. It looked like it was going to be one of those days.

Seven minutes into the second half, Steve Powell's shot beat Shaw but came back off the woodwork. Hutchison was nearest the rebound and thumped a shot into the net off the underside of the crossbar with the goalkeeper floundering helplessly in the goalmouth. It looked as though Bristol City's First Division adventure was over after one season. Within a minute, however, Gerry Gow played a one-two with Gillies and buried the ball past Sealey to put the Bristol club back in contention. As things stood, however, the Robins were down, whatever the result at Sunderland. They were ten minutes from relegation when Gillies somehow squeezed a shot between Sealey and the near post to make it 2–2.

With the Sunderland score still not known, Coventry were now the club in danger. If the Wearsiders were winning or drawing, the Sky Blues would be relegated. Suddenly, with five minutes left, the electronic scoreboard at Highfield Road announced that Everton had beaten Sunderland 2–0, meaning that a draw would be enough to keep both Coventry and Bristol City in the First Division. Unsurprisingly, the game suddenly died a death. Bristol City kept the ball in their half of the field, knocking it around between them as if it were a pre-match warm-up. Coventry made little attempt to take the ball from them, and this travesty of a finale ensured that Sunderland went down. The Roker Park side later lodged an unsuccessful appeal to the Football League, and the post-match photographs of Dicks and Coventry manager Gordon Milne sharing a bottle of champagne contained an irony not lost on Sunderland followers.

When the celebrations had subsided, City chairman Robert Holder realised that unless funds were made available for team strengthening, Bristol City could aspire to nothing more than a perennial struggle at the foot of the First Division. Despite the increase in attendances over the previous seasons, as things stood there was no spare cash to allow Alan Dicks to build a side capable of challenging for honours. Holder then made the remarkable announcement that anyone could purchase a seat on the board for the sum of £25,000.

Piqued at not being consulted over the announcement, and certainly not happy with the terms of the proposal which could allow any old Tom, Dick or Maxwell into the boardroom, the rest of the Ashton Gate board ousted Holder and installed Stephen Kew as the new chairman. Holder launched legal proceedings, the long-drawn-out nature and expense of which served only to worsen the club's financial problems over the next two or three years.

Following their narrow squeak in 1977, City improved slightly the following season despite going out of both domestic cups to lowly Wrexham, and by 1979 they had achieved a respectable mid-table position. The experienced Joe Royle had been signed, marking his debut for the club in spectacular fashion by scoring all four goals in a 4–1 defeat of Middlesbrough, whilst in the close season Tony Fitzpatrick joined from St Mirren for a quarter of a million pounds.

Meanwhile, however, in a move that was to have grave repercussions for the Ashton Gate side, Gary Collier, with over 200 games for City behind him, exercised the newly acquired right to freedom of contract and suddenly left the club to join Coventry City. Dicks, who had assumed that Collier, a vital part of his plans, would sign a new contract and remain at Ashton Gate, was stunned.

City, realising the implications, were determined not to let such a situation recur and offered many of the remaining players unprecedented ten-year contracts with highly lucrative wages. At least then, even if the players didn't want to spend the remainder of their careers at Ashton Gate, the club were assured of a fee once they moved on. Equally, the club had ensured that their best players were committed to the club. It was seen at the time as a wise investment in the future of Bristol City.

Despite this, 1979–80 proved to be a disaster for the club. Having lost first Collier and then Norman Hunter from the defence, City haemorrhaged goals and didn't rise above the bottom three after Boxing Day 1979. Their brief flirtation with the top flight was over and the financial implications soon made themselves apparent.

When City immediately went to the bottom of the Second Division in September 1980, Alan Dicks, the longest-serving manager in the country at the time, was sacked and replaced with Bob Houghton. Great things were expected from Houghton, who had taken the Swedish side Malmo to the European Cup final the previous year. The appointment was seen as a major coup for the West Country club, as no one else had succeeded in tempting Houghton back from Scandinavia. Surely Houghton and his assistant Roy Hodgson would turn the club around and steer them back into the top flight? However, the duo found little cash available and City were relegated again. The recently proud and ambitious club found itself back from whence it had come. Houghton discovered that he had inherited an ageing team, many of whom had been with the club since the mid-'60s, and without a financial injection for new players, he found preserving even Second Division status an impossible task.

Matters were exacerbated by bizarre goings-on in the boardroom. The existing board found themselves fighting an attempted coup by a group of supporters concerned at where the club was heading – which seemed to be unrelentingly downwards. Although the existing board resisted, Archie Gooch, a lifelong fan who had been a director for only a year, became the new chairman.

Gooch inherited a club in total financial disarray. Back in the Third Division for the first time in 16 years, City needed at least one season of stability to allow the new board to take stock and give the supporters some respite from the seemingly endless string of defeats. The club that barely three years earlier had been furtively eyeing a place in Europe now found itself praying for a mid-table position in the Third Division. It was not to be, however, and Bristol City became the first club ever to tumble from the First Division to the Fourth in consecutive seasons.

It was in the autumn of 1981, as the team struggled in the Third Division, that the club's perilous financial situation first came to light. In October it was announced that Bristol City was over £700,000 in debt as a result of the team's downward spiral and was losing money at the rate of around £3,000 every week. The club's assets were deemed to be worth just £78,000, and the visits of Rochdale and Crewe Alexandra were hardly likely to bring the punters, who had quickly grown accustomed to the visits of Liverpool and Nottingham Forest, flocking through the turnstiles and enthusiastically handing over their cash. In December two directors resigned to allow Deryn Coller and Ken Sage, two local businessmen, to join the board with a reported investment of half a million pounds. In January manager Bob Houghton resigned, with his assistant, the future Switzerland and Blackburn Rovers supremo Roy Hodgson, taking over. In the new year, Gooch and his associates formed a new company, Bristol City (1982). There was now the bizarre situation of the club being run by two different boards. The old administration had the task of selling off assets to satisfy the club's creditors, whilst the new sought to establish a sound financial base and to secure the future of the club. Two players, Kevin Mabbutt and Clive Whitehead, the latter having been at City on an 11-year contract, had already been sold, but this wasn't enough to appease the creditors.

The club brought in a firm of accountants to try and unpick the financial knots in which the club had become entangled. They found eight players on long-term contracts worth a total of £290,000 and their first move was to attempt to cancel them. The players were summoned to the ground and were stunned to be told that the new company would not be honouring their contracts. The players, destined to go down in history as the Ashton Gate Eight, found themselves in a dreadful position. Geoff Merrick had supported City as a small boy and risen through the ranks to become club captain. Chris Garland, in his second spell with the club, had first joined City in 1966, whilst David Rodgers had turned professional with City in 1969. Trevor Tainton had been with the club since 1965, whilst the other players, Gerry Sweeney, who'd been at Ashton Gate since 1971, Peter Aitken, Jimmy Mann and Julian Marshall, suddenly found their job security in danger. Despite the six-figure worth of their contracts, the eight players were offered just £58,000 redundancy between them. They immediately turned to the PFA, where Gordon Taylor had just taken over as secretary.

On 26 January, chairman Gooch announced that Bristol City would go out of business within a fortnight if the players didn't agree to the redundancy package. It was a terrible situation, particularly for the players who had been with the club since their youth. On the one hand their livelihoods and careers were under threat, whilst on the other they had the emotional trauma of the club that had nurtured them and which was followed by the supporters that had encouraged them through those careers going out of business if they didn't agree to accept the unimpressive terms. The club set a deadline of noon on 2 February 1981.

With an hour to go, the players reached their decision and agreed to leave the club. A visibly upset Geoff Merrick told television reporters, 'I am heartbroken. I even took my boots to the ground this morning in the hope that things would not turn out the way they have, but I will still be there to support the team on Saturday.' Mann went to Barnsley, Marshall to Blackburn Rovers, Tainton and Rodgers to Torquay United and Sweeney and Aitken to York City. Geoff Merrick and Chris Garland joined clubs in Hong Kong, with Garland returning to Ashton Gate the following season on a match-to-match basis.

Feeling guilty about the way they were forced to treat some of the club's most loyal players, Bristol City arranged a benefit match at Ashton Gate between Ipswich Town, the UEFA Cup holders, and Southampton, which raised over £80,000 for the eight. It's notable that the organisers didn't consider that the home club, Bristol City, would be enough of a draw to make the benefit game worthwhile, even against such attractive opposition as Ipswich Town.

The departure of the Ashton Gate Eight eased some of the financial burden on the club, but the team was now deprived of eight key players, virtually an entire team. Roy Hodgson assembled a squad of sorts, signing a number of players on one-month contracts, whilst other players left the club altogether. Aidan McCaffrey from Bristol Rovers, Les Carter from Crystal Palace and Ray Gooding from Coventry were all signed, but when the first month was up the League refused to allow the contracts to be renewed.

The club, although saved from extinction in the short term, was still in a dire financial position. Gates had dropped from an average of 23,500 to 6,500 in the space of three years and, in April 1982, a share issue designed to raise much-needed funds was poorly supported by the public. Things looked grim until four local businessmen, Bob Boyd, Bob Marshall, John Pontin and David Russe, stepped in and ensured the launch of Bristol City (1982) plc on 30 April. Their first move was to buy Ashton Gate from the old Bristol City company for just over half a million pounds.

On 4 December, City hit the bottom of the Football League. But with a new squad being assembled by new boss Terry Cooper including the superbly named former Southampton and Plymouth defender Forbes Phillipson-Masters, they were able to achieve, for the first time in five years, a comfortable, uneventful mid-table position.

With stability attained both on and off the pitch, Bristol City won promotion from the Fourth Division in 1983–84. Two years later they were at Wembley, beating Bolton Wanderers 3–0 in the Freight Rover Trophy final, and a year later they were back again, this time losing to Mansfield Town on penalties. In both seasons City finished well placed in the Third Division, but they didn't win promotion until 1990 under Joe Jordan.

When Jordan left soon afterwards to take over the hot-seat at Heart of Midlothian, his assistant Jimmy Lumsden took over at Ashton Gate. Good results under his caretaker-managership led to the offer of a full-time contract. No sooner had the ink dried than City crashed to a 6–1 home defeat by Sunderland. Lumsden lasted until February 1992, with City in danger of relegation. Denis Smith took over, and immediately steered the club out of trouble. Astute transfer dealings brought no less a player than Andy Cole to Ashton Gate from Arsenal. Following Smith's replacement by former Ipswich Town defender Russell Osman, City proved again that events at Ashton Gate were often more interesting in the boardroom than on the pitch.

It had been a topsy-turvy few years for Bristol City. Maybe if they hadn't contrived that 2–2 draw with Coventry they would have gone down, regrouped and re-emerged a stronger, financially viable club instead of crippling themselves in the quest to keep up with the big-spending giants of the First Division.

Of the Ashton Gate Eight, Peter Aitken and Julian Marshall eventually slipped into non-League football (Aitken now works for Rolls-Royce in Bristol), Geoff Merrick is a self-employed builder, Chris Garland now suffers from Parkinson's Disease and received the proceeds of a benefit match with Manchester United in 1993, Jimmy Mann went on to be a security officer, a milkman and is now a machine operator in Goole, David Rodgers is the groundsman at Clifton College, Trevor Tainton works as a security guard and Gerry Sweeney recently returned to the club as assistant manager. Those players were all sacrificed in order to ensure that Bristol City survived. The club thought that it could keep up with the big boys, but even then, in the less financially top-heavy structure of English football, they couldn't do so and nearly paid for their ambition with their very existence.

Today, as the gulf between the Premiership and the First Division widens by the season, promoted clubs should take note of the events at Ashton Gate in the early '80s. Spending beyond their means could prove fatal for success-hungry 'smaller' clubs. Bristol City had the potential to build on their success in reaching the First Division: the support was excellent with potential for growth, as Bristol has a wide catchment area. However, they couldn't capitalise on their top-flight status, overstretched themselves financially and plummeted down the League until they reached the hitherto unthinkable depths of having seven goals put past them by Northampton Town.

Today the stakes are much higher. Bristol City have just been promoted to the First Division. No doubt plans to progress higher will be made with the fate of the Ashton Gate Eight in mind. In the meantime, City recently celebrated a centenary that they looked unlikely to reach in the dark days of the early '80s.

Lincoln Blue

BATTLING BURNLEY AND BRYN
THE POLICE DOG

To the ageing hacks of Fleet Street, Burnley were still a big club in 1987. They knew their history: the Clarets were founder members of the Football League in 1888, finishing ninth out of 12. King George V turned up at the 1914 FA Cup final at Crystal Palace to see Bertie Freeman lash a stinging volley past the Liverpool goalkeeper on the hour to take the cup back to Lancashire. Legend has it that when the team arrived back in Burnley bearing the trophy, a curious local commented, 'Is that t'coop? Why, it looks more like a tea kettle.' They had very ornate kettles in those days. Mind you, I'm sure Russell Hobbs could make a better fist of modern trophies than the designers of the crop of contemporary silverware, given the chance.

In 1920–21, Burnley's 30-match mid-season unbeaten run ensured the League title went to Turf Moor. Burnley failed to win any of their last half-dozen games and still finished five points clear of Manchester City. Forty years later, the Clarets scooped the title from Wolves, going top for the first time on the last day of the season with a 2–1 win at Manchester City. By 1976, remarkably for such a small town, Burnley had spent all but two postwar seasons in the top flight.

They were a television producer's dream, too, with ample opportunities for wide-angle shots of mills and rows of little redbrick terraced houses which would pan back to show the cavernous Turf Moor, keeping some brass band busy in the soundtrack business. Burnley, you see, were what football is all about. The grass-roots and the glory all rolled into one.

So when, on the last day of the 1986–87 football season, Burnley, Lincoln City and Torquay United were involved in a three-way scrap to decide who would be the first Football League club to be relegated automatically to the GM Vauxhall Conference, the press pack unsurprisingly headed for Turf Moor. That's where the story was: a once-great club fallen on hard times. What a tragedy it would be if Burnley were to tumble out of the League to visit the likes of Runcorn and Fisher Athletic. They didn't deserve this at all. Lincoln and Torquay we could spare. We wouldn't really miss them; it's not like they'd actually achieved anything, after all.

Football is about results, first and foremost. Whether you deserve to go down or not, if you clock up fewer points than everyone else you come last. In the misty-eyed eulogies to packed Lancashire terraces and Wembley visits, no one thought to ask how Burnley Football Club had ended up in the Fourth Division watched by crowds of 3,000. What had gone wrong? Where had the loyal fans of the past disappeared to? The wishy-washy nostalgia failed to scratch beneath the surface of the sleeping giant to find the malaise that had crippled the club. Certainly no one asked about Torquay and Lincoln. They're just names on the pools coupon, names you skip by whilst waiting for James Alexander-Gordon to attempt, unsuccessfully, to say the word 'Wanderers' again (he says 'Wanderererers', pronunciation fans).

But for Lincoln City in particular, the final day of the 1986–87 season was to be the dénouement of a chain of events that make the use of the word 'tragedy' unusually excusable in a football sense. For Lincoln City were the forgotten club in two very real football tragedies and very nearly underwent one of their own. Relegation from the Football League gave Lincoln City the chance to wipe the slate clean and begin afresh. For Lincoln City, a visit to the GM Vauxhall Conference cleansed them of the trauma of the previous years.

Torquay United had had their problems too. Between 1972 and 1984, they were the champions of mediocrity. In those 12 seasons following their relegation from the Third Division in 1972, Torquay finished no higher than ninth and no lower than 18th. Then, in 1984, manager Bruce Rioch woke the sleeping Plainmoor fans when he thumped right back Colin Anderson as the culmination of a training-ground disagreement and departed for Middlesbrough. A new club ownership then appointed David Webb as manager, and Torquay's troubles really began.

Webb, still embroiled in legal wranglings stemming from an unfair-dismissal claim at Bournemouth, was appointed team manager and also became managing director of the club. His chirpy cockney characteristics were reinforced by rumours that comedian Jim Davidson would also be joining the board. The tacky showbiz theme continued when Webb brought in his own people to take over the running of the Torquay United Social Club. Thus fans arriving for a leisurely pint were suddenly confronted with strip acts and dubious comedians who made Jim Davidson sound like Ben Elton.

A section of terracing was dismantled to make way for lucrative car-boot sales, whilst on the playing side the club's best players were released, ostensibly, according to the manager, to give youth an opportunity. Cynics observed that such a move reduced the wage bill considerably, freeing up cash to plough into shenanigans off the field.

In 1984–85, Torquay United finished bottom of the Fourth Division, six points adrift of the rest of the Football League. The playing staff was in disarray, with players arriving and leaving at an alarming rate. Mario Walsh topped the goalscoring charts with a less than impressive five. Webb himself, despite pushing 40, suddenly appeared in the side, even scoring the winner in a match at Chester. Revealingly, despite finishing bottom with an average attendance of 1,300 (only Halifax had a worse record in the entire League), the club announced a profit. This was helped by an insurance dividend reaped from a fire in the main stand at Plainmoor, six days after Bradford and 12 hours after being passed as safe by the fire brigade.

The following season Webb stood down as manager, appointing player John Sims in his stead. Sims lasted four weeks, when Stuart Morgan arrived to take over the reins. Torquay finished bottom again, and things looked ominous for the Gulls when the League announced the introduction of direct promotion and relegation between the Fourth Division and the GM Vauxhall Conference, the snazzy name for the old Alliance Premier League, for the following season. Torquay were heading for an unwanted hat-trick, and the reward was a trip to Park View Road, Welling.

Torquay were in trouble. David Webb, universally unpopular with Gulls fans, wielded more power over one club than any individual in the Football League. He eventually left midway through the season, his leading of the club to the foot of the Fourth Division deemed worthy of a £46,000 pay-off.

Supporters trace the decline that led to Lincoln City's exit from the Football League back to 1982. 'Some might look back to the parsimonious operation of the club in the early 1960s which could have resulted in the loss of League status or, worse, bankruptcy through mismanagement,' says Simon Edwards, a Lincoln fan now based in Newcastle. 'In the summer of 1982 City's precarious financial situation manifested itself with the sale of the ground to Lincoln City Council. The squad was small and Colin Murphy wanted to buy Norwich's Ross Jack and Chester's unfortunately named John

Thomas for what would now be considered peanuts. He was turned down by the board, and problems with players' bonuses led to a high-profile strike and boardroom crisis.'

'The demise can probably be traced to 28 December 1982,' says the former editor of Lincoln fanzine *The Deranged Ferret*, Gary Parle. 'On that day we sat at the top of the old Third Division and were seemingly well on course for promotion to Division Two. We were pretty much invincible, especially at Sincil Bank, where we'd won all ten of our home games, scoring 35 goals in the process. Despite this, manager Colin Murphy was continually warning the club that the squad just wasn't big enough to sustain a promotion challenge, and on this particular day Huddersfield Town won 2–1 at Sincil Bank in front of just under 12,000 people.

'Only three of the next eleven games were won and the board refused to let Murphy buy two new players, leading to death threats by fans against the chairman, who, along with the whole board, resigned. By the time the mess was sorted out the chance of promotion had faded and just 2,241 watched the last game of the season at home to Gillingham.'

The decline continued, despite the eventual signings of Jack and Thomas, and the lack of success on the field was reflected in the numbers coming through the turnstiles, with attendances dropping well below 2,000. The last day of the season, safe from relegation but only just, saw the Imps visit Valley Parade as the fall guys for Bradford City's promotion party. Paul Rumbles, a 34-year-old Lincoln fan ('for me Lincoln City mean absolutely everything') living in Wrexham, takes up the story of one of football's most tragic days.

'On 11 May 1985 we all went over to Valley Parade to enjoy the summer sun and the end of another season and to witness Bradford being crowned as champions, dreaming that it could soon be our turn. A crowd of 11,076 went to the game, and, as we all know, only 11,020 left it alive.

'I was on the away terrace, across from Bradford's old main stand, and just before half-time a commotion seemed to be starting in the right-hand side of the stand. Hello, a bit of aggro over there was the first reaction, but then smoke started to emerge from the stand. In a very short time fire swept right across it, lapping around the old roofing struts and boards. All the supporters were now battling their way to the front and tumbling over the barrier to the pitchside. It was an unbelievable sight.

'The tragedy was and always will be Bradford's, but many people are unaware that we lost two of our fans as well: Bill Stacey and Jim West. Quite a few of our other more elderly fans who had been in the seats narrowly escaped death.'

Tony Smith, an Imps fan from Welwyn Garden City, adds, 'I wasn't there that day, but I remember Valley Parade as a typical lower-division ground and I had on previous visits sat in the stand where Bill Stacey and Jim West died. Bill was a slightly grumpy but dedicated, stalwart fan who had organised the Sleaford end of the Official Supporters Club coaches to both home and away games. My brother went to his funeral, and his grandson presents the "Away Supporter of the Year" award every year. Both Bill and Jim are commemorated at Sincil Bank with the Railway End stand named after them.'

'The match stood at 0–0 at the time,' continues Paul Rumbles, 'and we haven't played a competitive match at Valley Parade since. In April 1989 we played a game there in aid of the Hillsborough disaster in view of our own shared experiences of death in football. I, like many other Bradford and Lincoln fans who went, was in tears again as that earlier nightmare vividly came flooding back.'

Simon Edwards reflects further on the events at Valley Parade. 'Of course I can still remember the pictures and John Helm's commentary, and even the pattern of play as the fire started, so I guess it's had an effect on me. It was quite simply a tragedy. Bradford City received a lot of coverage, and thus more indirect counselling. Lincoln were, and I'm afraid this is undoubtedly true, forgotten.'

One month later the Lincoln squad, who had escaped relegation by five points that season, returned to Leeds-Bradford airport from an end-of-season break. The plane overran the runway and crash-landed on the tarmac, and the terrified players were forced to escape the stricken aircraft via safety chutes. One tragedy and a near-death experience in the space of four weeks must have taken its toll on the Lincoln players, and skipper Steve Thompson even commented, 'I felt like locking myself in my house and throwing away the key.'

Unsurprisingly, these events saw Lincoln struggle on the pitch the following season. Manager Colin Murphy departed, and by the end of the season City occupied the top relegation spot in the Third Division and dropped into the Fourth on goal difference. On the last day of the campaign, City needed to beat Wolves by 17 clear goals, but just missed out, losing 3–2. The popular George Kerr had taken over from John Pickering as manager during the season, but a run which yielded just two wins in twelve matches sealed the Imps' fate.

'We were too good to go down that season,' reflects Edwards. 'A 2–0 win at champions Reading suggested what we were capable of when things went right. Kerr had brought in players he knew from his time at Rotherham United, and a number of skilful Scottish players. We looked set for a quick return to Division Three and were clear favourites for promotion.'

The Football League had already announced that the Fourth Division's bottom club would be relegated to the Conference and replaced by the champions of the semi-pro arena's prestige division at the end of the 1986–87 season. Lincoln fans, however, took far less notice of this than the regulars at Plainmoor, who had finished bottom in both previous seasons. 'We were a Third Division club making a brief return to the League's basement, so this rule wouldn't concern us,' says Edwards. 'It was intended for the likes of Torquay, Rochdale and Hartlepool.'

City made a comfortable, confident start. The play-offs were also introduced that season, and the Imps were considered almost certain to achieve at least a place in the fledgling end-of-season knockout tournament. On 21 December 1986, Lincoln visited the County Ground to take on runaway leaders Northampton Town. Manager Kerr confidently expected the Imps to come away with a result. They lost 3–1. The good early-season run had taken Lincoln to the heights of sixth place, but the following weeks saw a horrendous run of results which led to a protracted tumble down the division.

Simon Edwards remembers a match against Cardiff City as being typical of the time. 'We lost to a penalty, having missed one ourselves in the previous move of the game. We hit the woodwork on numerous occasions and a number of simple chances went begging. This type of performance continued into March, with the team generally playing quite well but profligate finishing and unlucky defending preventing us from picking up points. It would be possible to point out endless examples of incidents which, had just one of them not happened, would have meant City retaining their League status, such as Bobby Mitchell slipping over at Orient and letting them in to score the winner.'

The encouraging performances kept Kerr talking of a play-off place right up until mid-March, when the club lay in 14th place. One legacy of Lincoln's traumatic afternoon at Valley Parade was the demolition of the main stand at Sincil Bank, also in March. Edwards points out that out of all the lower-division clubs, it was only the two teams involved that afternoon, Bradford and Lincoln, who took serious steps to redevelop their stadia in the immediate wake of the disaster. A three-sided ground with a building site running down one touchline, as well as dreadful crowds, did little to help lift the increasingly demoralised squad.

Despite Kerr's encouraging words, a run of nine defeats in twelve matches led to his dismissal in mid-March. 'This was the first of many instances of chairman John Reames exhibiting a horrendous lack of patience. Clearly the winless sequence just got too much for him,' says Edwards. 'The sacking of Kerr still annoys me. It was the act of a man frustrated by impatience. Now I, along with every City fan, will admit that Kerr was not the best manager in the club's history, but he was a nice man, knew a decent player when he saw one, and had the team playing attractive football. If he had stayed, City would have got that vital extra point; in fact, we'd probably have finished in a comfortable 17th place or thereabouts.'

Midfielder Peter Daniel was appointed player-manager in a caretaker capacity, his first game in charge drawing just 1,196 to a home match with the seemingly doomed Torquay United, City's lowest ever Football League attendance. April saw a slight improvement in results. Lincoln won 2–1 at Crewe and turned over Northampton 3–1 at Sincil Bank. Even with three games to go, no one seriously considered Lincoln as relegation candidates. 'If I can remember correctly, four teams were still below City at this stage of the season,' recalls Gary Parle. 'Rochdale, Tranmere Rovers, Torquay United and Burnley.'

Lincoln lost their antepenultimate match at Wolves, but still needed just one point from their last two games to make themselves safe. Those games were at home to local rivals Scunthorpe United and away at Swansea City. 'We took the lead and with eight minutes remaining knew we were safe,' remembers Paul Rumbles. 'But then Scunthorpe first went and equalised and then in injury time the bastards scored again. We'd lost and still needed that one point to make absolutely certain.' The trip to the Vetch Field awaited.

Torquay United had also started the season well, with just two defeats in their first eight games despite losing key player Mark Loram to Queen's Park Rangers during the summer. A run of six consecutive defeats in October and November included a visit from Wolverhampton Wanderers which saw a number of their followers causing trouble in the town and on more than one occasion invading the pitch. In a crass overreaction, the police insisted the club introduce an identity-card scheme, something rightly discredited when Margaret Thatcher tried to implement it a few years later, and curtailed Torquay's traditional Saturday-evening kick-offs, bringing Gulls matches forward to 2 p.m. Away fans were banned, and the ground capacity was limited to 4,999 in order to avoid the necessity of local-authority licensing. The worst-supported club in the League now had the smallest capacity to watch arguably the worst team in the country.

Manager Stuart Morgan found his playing resources severely stretched, and a terrible run of injuries forced him to play a rash of inexperienced youngsters. On one occasion, a vital 2–2 draw at Burnley, veteran striker Derek Dawkins had to play with a broken wrist just so Torquay could put out a full team.

In their penultimate game of the season, Torquay went to Leyton Orient desperately hoping for at least a point. With the 90 minutes up, the Gulls looked to have secured an invaluable 2–2 draw, only for O's full-back Terry Howard to score the first goal of his career deep into injury time.

Going into the last game on 9 May 1987, Burnley, who entertained Leyton Orient, were bottom with 46 points, Torquay, at home to Crewe, had 47, whilst Lincoln travelled to Swansea City with 48 points to their credit and the knowledge that only a near-freakish combination of results could relegate them. Tranmere had ensured their safety with a win over Exeter City the previous night. So a point at Swansea would have made Lincoln safe, although if Burnley didn't win and/or Torquay lost, Lincoln would avoid the drop even if they lost themselves.

Most Lincoln fans were confident that the Imps would not be relegated. Gary Parle remembers, 'In the final week of the season relegation was hardly given a second thought. But Rochdale guaranteed their survival with a win in midweek. Then, in a fixture that was, amazingly, given the importance of it, played on the night before, Tranmere beat Exeter to ensure their survival. So 9 May was judgement day for one of three teams.'

Paul Rumbles has mixed memories of May 1987. 'I was living in Coventry at the time, as I was studying at Warwick University. Coventry was alive with sky blue everywhere as the team prepared for their first ever FA Cup final, against Spurs. Lincoln's brilliant ex-captain Trevor Peake would be playing and I had already got my ticket for Wembley, but I still had Lincoln's unresolved fate paramount in my thoughts.'

Mick Hupalowsky, an electrical contractor from Sleaford, awoke early on the Saturday morning. 'My passion for Lincoln City started when my dad took me to Sincil Bank when I was nine years old. My school backed on to the training ground and every dinner time we'd be down by the fence watching players like Graham Taylor training. Lincoln City is in my blood. I wouldn't support another team even if Lincoln packed in tomorrow and they turned the ground into allotments. I've got the Imp tattooed on my arse, and I've even named my house Sincil Bank.

'I woke up at seven o'clock that morning and for some reason turned to my wife and said, "We've got to go to Swansea. I think we're going down."'

Paul Rumbles was an early riser that day as well. 'I'd made my sandwiches and headed for Coventry station for the long train journey to Swansea.'

'*On Football Focus* that lunchtime,' says Simon Edwards, 'Bob Wilson didn't even mention City in his piece about the situation. Most of the country was, of course, focusing on Burnley, former League champions. The media pre-occupation was perhaps understandable, but still out of order. It's something that raised its head again recently with massive coverage of the plight of Brighton at the expense of similar clubs like Hereford and Doncaster Rovers. The media frenzy whipped up support for Burnley with the result that a huge crowd turned up, as did a national radio commentary team, and the kick-off for their game with Orient had to be put back more than 15 minutes to let everyone in.

'It was obvious what was about to happen, yet a belief that football wouldn't be so unkind, so conspiratorial, gave us some glimmer of hope – that classic hopeless optimism of the football fan. It was clear City would lose to Swansea, a routine end-of-season mid-table game – or so it should have been.'

Paul Rumbles had arrived safely from Coventry. 'The match was awful. Our players just didn't seem to be putting in any effort. We were soon 2–0 down and knew that we were going to get nothing out of our own game. All ears turned to the pocket radios in the crowd. Our three-way battle was the main feature on the radio and we soon learned that Torquay were also losing 2–0, whilst Burnley had kicked off late.'

'By half-time City were a goal down and Torquay were 2–0 down,' recalls Gary Parle. 'If it had stayed like that we'd have been safe.'

A crowd of 16,000 people had crammed into Turf Moor, five times their average for that season. The irony of the renditions of 'You'll Never Walk Alone' from the suddenly packed terraces that day was apparently lost on most of the people there. Burnley soon went 2–0 up. Torquay had gone 2–0 down just before half-time to a goal from a promising Crewe youngster called David Platt that was, apparently, well offside. A second goal for Swansea killed off Lincoln's chances of having a hand in their own destiny. However, as Paul Rumbles remembers, City still felt safe. 'We felt some relief. Useless Torquay were getting well beaten. Our result didn't matter now; we would be safe.'

Two minutes into the second half, Jim McNichol hit a 20-yard free-kick into the back of the Crewe net to give Torquay a lifeline. If ever a game was one of the proverbial two halves, it was taking place at Plainmoor that afternoon. Crewe had steamrollered the Gulls in the first half, but McNichol's deflected goal gave Torquay renewed resolve. They bombarded the Crewe goal for the rest of the game.

At the Vetch Field the final whistle went on Lincoln's 2–0 defeat. As things stood at that point, Torquay were bottom, and Lincoln had survived. Gary Parle watched the scenes at the Vetch. 'At the final whistle the City players came over to the travelling fans, not to accept their applause but to hear the latest scores. It was into injury time and Torquay were still losing; Burnley were 2–1 up with 15 minutes left.' Lincoln were still safe.

With seven minutes remaining at Torquay, goalscorer McNichol ran to intercept a wayward Crewe pass on the right flank and cleared the ball up the touchline. At the side of the pitch a police alsatian, Bryn, saw the Torquay player careering towards him and his handler, PC John Harris. Years of intensive training had taught Bryn that, when threatened, he should go for the most vulnerable part of the attacker's anatomy. He sunk his teeth into McNichol's groin some five yards inside the touchline, and the stricken Torquay midfielder collapsed in agony. The game was held up for several minutes while McNichol received treatment. Boss Stuart Morgan gave his players the news that Burnley were winning and Lincoln were losing. The Gulls, minutes away from doom, needed a point.

McNichol, later to have 17 stitches in the wound, eventually struggled to his feet and played on. In the fourth minute of time added on for his injury, Crewe defender Terry Milligan tried to play his way out of trouble in his own penalty area. Torquay striker Paul Dobson pounced on the hapless defender's error, turned and rifled the ball into the bottom corner of the net for the equaliser. Plainmoor erupted.

Back at the Vetch Field, 'The players left the field and as the fans were leaving the ground the news came through that Torquay had equalised,' says Parle. 'A deathly hush descended on us and it was at that point that the nightmare became a reality. Torquay had gone above us on goal difference. The walk back to the car was a long one. Burnley were still playing and winning. One Orient goal would have saved us.'

'That was it,' according to Simon Edwards. 'Morbid disbelief meant I sat stunned, listening to the fawning commentary of Burnley's delayed but oh, so certain victory over Orient.'

Paul Rumbles also felt the cold, dreadful sensation of his club's demise as the minutes ticked away at Turf Moor. 'Those on the coaches to Lincoln set off. I was travelling on my own, of course. I sat on the pavement outside Swansea's ground listening to my radio as the Burnley game went into its final minutes. The fear that had been growing in me now became immense as I realised that we were now bottom of the League. Orient seemed to be making no effort at all. This, coupled with the late kick-off which enabled Burnley to know what they had to do, made it certain in my tortured mind that they must have fixed the game. At around 5.15 p.m. it was all over. Torquay had their point, Burnley all three, and we had none. Alone on a cold kerbside in South Wales, I had just witnessed my club end their Football

League career. For the second season in succession, goal difference had seen us relegated, but this really was a whole new ball game. Going up and down the divisions was something we had always done. You knew that in a season or two you could always go back up again. But this was something else altogether. I felt like my club had just died. I just sat there and cried and cried. As bad as this sounds, at that moment I felt worse than at the Bradford fire.'

Tony Smith walked towards Swansea town centre. 'My chunky '70s-style radio briefly crowed that Burnley had been saved. There was some cock and bull story [an unfortunate choice of phrase, considering where McNichol had sustained his injury] that a police dog had delayed the Torquay game, but Lincoln City were destined for the GM Vauxhall Conference.'

Mick Hupalowsky still can't believe the circumstances surrounding Lincoln's demise. 'It was ridiculous! We were relegated and yet the first time we went bottom of the league all season was actually 15 minutes after our season had ended! As my wife and I drove the 250 miles home, neither of us uttered a word until we were about 30 miles away from Sleaford. We were just stunned. I think my first words were, "Do you want some chips, then, or what?" My wife just grunted.'

Tony White sat in his car and pondered the immediate future. 'On Monday I'd be back at work amongst the heathens. You know the type I mean: never go to a match, "support" a top team, reflect only glory if achieved by local teams, talk rubbish about the issues raised by the media. How could anyone possibly know how I felt just then, supporting a team that had fallen through successive divisions and out of the newly sprung trap door, despite only stepping on it once on the very last day of the season?'

Paul Rumbles, on top of his grief, had transport problems to contend with. 'I still had to catch my train, but realised I had already missed the first one. By now our players were coming out of the ground. They looked awful, dejected and ashamed. I wanted to abuse them for doing this to my club, but I couldn't. They clearly felt as bad as me. One of them, our forward Jimmy Gilligan, came over to me and asked why I was still there. I explained that I had come down from Coventry and couldn't catch a train back for another two hours. Jimmy said that he was driving back to London and could give me a lift as far as Bristol, an offer I gratefully accepted.

'It was a sad journey back. Jimmy couldn't explain what had happened; essentially the players just weren't good enough. Jimmy dropped me at Bristol Parkway. I had another hour to wait, so found the nearest bar and just drank and drank and drank. Naturally I missed the train, eventually catching the last one back to Birmingham New Street. There I had to kip on the platform until I could catch the first train back to Coventry the next day.'

All very different from the scenes at Plainmoor and Turf Moor. Supporters streamed on to the pitch at both venues. Torquay supremo Stuart Morgan said, 'I always said it would go to the last game of the season, but the last minute of the last game is something else. In previous games there was a feeling of, well, there's always the next game, but for the Crewe game there was no tomorrow. It got to the younger players; they were petrified.' Torquay's chairman announced that he was going to buy Bryn 'the biggest steak in Torquay', at which news Hilda the Torquay elephant presumably went into hiding.

Back in Lincoln, the devastated Imps fans, Simon Edwards included, scoured the newspapers. 'The media seemed vaguely surprised at City finishing bottom. You see, they had come from nowhere, and no one, including City themselves, really, could see us finishing last. The *Guardian* on the Monday said we had been "in the wrong place when the music stopped", which I suppose is true really. It was the first time that City had touched the bottom of any division in any season since the mid-'60s.

'Everyone was devastated. Ironically, City had been one of only half a dozen clubs in the lower divisions to make an operating profit over the season, thanks in the main to the Strodder sale. This was added to the irony of the beginnings of the costly redevelopment of the ground and the humiliation of being victims of a rule in keeping with the prevailing business ethos of the time aimed at cutting adrift the dead wood (Halifax, Hartlepool, Rochdale, Torquay), which had resulted in us having to look up Fisher Athletic, Sutton United and, worst of all, Boston United on the map.

'The squad had included some pretty decent players in Lee Butler, Simeon Hodson, Kevin Kilmore, Tony Simmons, Gary Lund, Gary West, Ian McInnes, Jimmy Gilligan, Shane Nicholson and Steve Buckley, but there were only two or three who appeared to really care.'

It was a grim summer for Lincoln supporters. Paul Rumbles remembers, 'As the weeks went by I became more and more dejected. I studied the football history books and discovered that Lincoln's points total was the highest ever attained by a team finishing bottom of any division in the whole history of the League, yet we'd still been turfed out. We hadn't been bottom all season, not even in the bottom four until the last week. It all seemed so unfair. We had more fans and a much better ground than many other clubs in the Fourth Division. When we had won that division in 1975–76 under Graham Taylor, we had set a points record that stands to this day [taking into account the three-points-for-a-win system]. Quite simply, it shouldn't have been us.

However, I also found that Lincoln had left the League on three previous occasions. Every time we had returned at the first attempt.'

The newspapers speculated that as the players' contracts were secured by the Football League, and were printed upon League headed paper, they were no longer valid and the entire playing staff was free to go if they wished. Eight players remained on contract, and they were given until mid-July to find other clubs or they would stay at Sincil Bank. Four players were sold, raising over £200,000 which was made available for team strengthening. Indeed, the club's administration in its first progressive move for many years announced that the club would retain a full-time playing staff and not join the part-timers.

After the removal of Peter Daniel, the board received over 100 applications for the manager's job at Lincoln. Things were looking up. 'Fortune had started to smile on us again,' says Paul Rumbles. 'We were building a new main stand to replace our old wooden one, and then it was announced that our hero Colin Murphy was returning as manager and that he had been given an ultimatum of two years to get us back into the Football League. He only kept three players and brought in a whole new squad on two-year contracts.'

Lincoln's first game in the GM Vauxhall Conference was at Underhill, the home of Barnet, and the new-look Imps went down 4–2. They were not helped by a moment of high comedy from goalkeeper Nigel Batch, who ran out of his area to clear a through ball and, in attempting to punt the ball out of the ground, missed it completely, fell on his backside and let Barnet's Nicky Sansom in for a gift of a goal. The following week Lincoln went down 3–0 at Weymouth and found themselves propping up the table again. 'Surely we were not going to suffer a third and much more ignominious relegation, leaving us lower than Boston and down with the likes of Gainsborough Trinity?' asked Paul Rumbles.

Murphy, however, was slowly building a good side, albeit one that was a little over-physical for many tastes. He signed three players on the first three Saturdays of the season, and the squad gradually began to develop into a tight and effective unit. Lincoln suddenly found themselves as the big team whom everyone wanted to beat. As the season progressed it became clear that the promotion spot would be contested by Lincoln and Barry Fry's Barnet. Crowds were up both home and away, and in April the Imps set a Conference attendance record of 7,542 for the local derby with Boston United which finished 5–1 to the home side. By the end of April, Lincoln had three games to play, all at home. Paul Rumbles takes up the story.

'We drew the first game against Maidstone and then at the end of April beat Stafford Rangers 2–1. Over the tannoy came the news that both Kettering and Barnet had been beaten. Our win had taken us into first place for the first time. All of a sudden our precious Football League place beckoned, and to get it back we needed only to win our final match. For once our fate was in our own hands.

'On Monday, 2 May 1988, a bumper crowd packed into Sincil Bank to see us take on Wycombe Wanderers. Official figures gave the crowd as the police limit of 9,432, but stewards and my own eyes told me that there were really over 13,000 in the ground that day. All we wanted was that vital victory.

'Before long the tension was relieved, as Mark Sertori put us 1–0 up. The Football League loomed nearer. Later little Phil Brown scored a second goal and the ground erupted. When the final whistle went every single Lincoln supporter was over the walls and on the pitch. Murphy's mission had been accomplished: we were back in the Football League at the first time of asking. It was, without doubt, the happiest day of my life. The dark days of Bradford and Swansea were behind us at last. For once the last day of the season had meant joy, not tragedy for the people of Lincoln.'

So, with promotion in the bag and capacity crowds squeezing into the ground, relegation had appeared to be a necessary shot in the arm for the club. 'Was it a blessing in disguise? It certainly led to one of our most exciting seasons and earned a title, but the momentum wasn't carried forward and the club have wasted nearly ten years since then by quickly sacking managers, some undeservedly, and never having a settled team,' opines Gary Parle.

Simon Edwards shares his views. 'The prevailing feeling was that it had done us good, but if that's the case, why has there been no further progress on the pitch? We have yet to appear even in a play-off. The ground has been completely rebuilt, the structure of the club is much better and its community role is well-defined. City still produce fine youngsters – just look at Darren Huckerby – and probably only Crewe have a better record in that respect, but chairman Fred Reames seems to hire and fire managers as panic measures, as if memories of 1987 cannot be erased.'

Tony Smith is convinced that relegation was a necessary boot up the backside for a complacent club administration. 'Have no doubts that it was a close thing, but relegation was actually the beginning of the rebirth of Lincoln City. They may not be much higher in the League than when they carelessly tossed away that status, but they have completely rebuilt the ground and stand a chance of surviving into the next millennium despite the Premier League fat cats creaming off most of the money.'

Paul Rumbles disagrees. 'Winning the Conference was great, but being in it in the first place was dreadful, and all of us were relieved to get out of it so quickly. I never want to go through that torture again and I would rather not have gone through it at all. I am delighted for fans of Halifax, Colchester and Darlington that they have since emulated our feat and made the return trip.'

'On the pitch we have been lacking the killer instinct for a decade now,' continues Edwards. 'The supporters easily become cynical and bemoan their own misfortune, but the point is that they have had absolutely nothing to get excited about. Absolutely nothing. Even when better things are hinted at there is a lack of belief that they can be achieved, not just amongst the supporters but seemingly within the club itself.

'Bad luck and tragedy still dog us. When York City striker David Long-hurst collapsed and died on the pitch during a match in 1990 we were the opposition. The first people at his side were City defenders Grant Brown and Paul Casey. We always seem to be the footballing fall guys.

'In 1997 we went out of the FA Cup to Unibond League village side Emley, possibly the greatest humiliation in our history. No League club has a worse FA Cup record than us: only one appearance in the third round since 1977!

'The events of 1986–87 are still indelibly branded on my mind as they are on those of too many people associated with Lincoln City Football Club. It was, after all, the final component in a quarter-century process that had allowed us to devolve from being a club like Barnsley or Notts County, who could proudly sit with the footballing middle class, to a Rochdale or Colchester, scrapping for survival and respect in the ghetto of football's underclass.

'Ours was the ultimate relegation. It wasn't simply that it was a step into the unknown as the first victims of a new ruling, rather that it took place under freakish circumstances. I am not just referring to the police dog at Torquay but to several months', in fact several years' accumulation of incidents which suggested that our destiny was outside our control. The effects of 1986–87 are still felt now in that there is a culture of fear and pessimism amongst board members and supporters. It's my feeling that despite the kick up the backside that relegation undoubtedly was, it caused a fundamental feeling of insecurity and lack of self-belief which still hinders our progress all these years later.'

Relegation does seem to have benefited Lincoln City in some respects. They were forced to rebuild the side, the ground was redeveloped and the club returned to the Football League at the first attempt in front of bumper crowds. But progress since has been slow. The club seems to have aimed at consolidation rather than progression, although the procession of managers seems to suggest, in some distorted way, that the club does want to succeed. Indeed, at the time of writing Lincoln City occupy a coveted position in the Third Division play-off zone as we near the end of the season, despite the sacking of John Beck in February 1998.

Lincoln City have suffered, literally, more than others. Maybe the legacies of Bradford, Leeds-Bradford airport, relegation and the death of David Longhurst have had longer-lasting effects than even the club realises. Lincoln fans certainly know that football is not more important than life and death. In fact, there's probably not a set of supporters in the land better qualified to refute Bill Shankly's statement, Liverpool fans excepted. But this doesn't stop those fans from being hungry for success. Over a decade has passed since Lincoln City's defeat at the Vetch Field condemned them to non-League football, but little progress has been evident on the pitch.

Lincoln fans deserve better. But will a manager ever be allowed to stay at Sincil Bank long enough to deliver the goods?

Betting, Backhanders and Broken Hearts

SWINDON TOWN'S TEN DAYS OF GLORY

As they left Wembley Stadium on 28 May 1990, the supporters of Swindon Town didn't so much walk out of the ground as float. Their team had just beaten Sunderland in a tense play-off final to win promotion to the First Division in Ossie Ardiles' first season as manager, and they began to look forward to replacing visits to Oakwell, the Victoria Ground and the Den with trips to Anfield, Old Trafford and Highbury. Swindon were in the First Division.

On the steps of Wembley in the shadow of the twin towers, heading down Olympic Way and back to their coaches, minibuses and cars, the thousands of fans who had travelled up from Wiltshire grappled to comprehend the enormity of the occasion. They wouldn't believe it until they saw it, until the fixtures came out and they gathered at the County Ground in August to watch the new dawn of Swindon Town FC.

Alas, it wasn't to happen. Not that season, anyway. Within ten days, the Football League had snatched Swindon's elevation from under them and the club were demoted to the Third Division. Shady goings-on behind the scenes under a previous administration had led to the club admitting 36 separate breaches of League regulations, and the punishment was swift and harsh. Not only were they prevented from taking up their place in the top flight, they were also demoted to the division below that which they had just left through the front door.

The players and supporters had been punished for the actions of a couple of crooks behind the scenes months, even years before. Against the odds the little club had earned the right to play with the big boys, but their ball was taken away before they'd even had a chance to kick it. It was a horrifyingly unjust move, and although the sentence was later commuted to retaining their place in the Second Division, Swindon Town felt justifiably aggrieved. Particularly when, a few years later, Tottenham Hotspur, one of the biggest of the big boys, admitted 34 similar offences and eventually escaped with a fine the size of which Alan Sugar could comfortably drop down the back of the sofa and not worry about retrieving. It was one rule for the rich, another for the poor, and although Swindon eventually joined the top flight, their demotion had set the club back in terms of finance and progress to an incalculable degree.

The progress they had made had been incredible. In 1988–89, Swindon had reached the play-offs under Lou Macari, only to lose in a two-legged semi-final to a Crystal Palace team which spent most of the ensuing seasons yo-yoing between the top two divisions as if they were unable to decide which one they liked best and continuing to labour under the misapprehension that they are Premier League material.

At the end of the season, Macari left the County Ground to take up the reins at West Ham United, and Osvaldo Ardiles was appointed in his stead. Like Macari before him, Ardiles arrived at the club to take up his first ever managerial post. He made an immediate impact on the opening day of the season, coming on as substitute and getting himself booked in a 2–0 home defeat by Sunderland, the club with whom Swindon's fortunes that season were to become heartbreakingly entwined. It was a less than spectacular start to the season, and by the beginning of October, Town occupied a lowly 17th position.

In November, the *Sunday People* printed allegations that were to open not so much a can of worms as an entire tinning plant of the things for Swindon Town. Supporters waking with hangovers induced by the 2–0 victory over Middlesbrough the previous day found their club all over the back page. But there were no eulogies to Swindon's attacking prowess or insurmountable defence. Instead the *People* revealed how Macari and Swindon chairman Brian Hillier had placed a large wager on Swindon losing an FA Cup tie at Newcastle United in 1988. They lost 5–0. Macari and Hillier collected £7,500. The *People* even printed a copy of the cheque Hillier collected from the bookies.

Anna Merriman is a lifelong Swindon supporter and the editor of the club's fanzine *The 69'er*. She wasn't totally surprised at the revelations. 'Lou wasn't what you'd call betting-shop shy. He made no secret of introducing wagers during training sessions, saying that it geed up the players. I don't know how deeply they actually became involved, but I've heard rumours that at least one player left Swindon in the end because he owed goodness knows how many thousands of pounds, and I've even heard that one player was signed primarily to act as Lou's personal stake-man.'

On 4 January, ironically two days before Swindon took on Bristol City in the FA Cup, the Football Association formally charged Macari and Hillier with bringing the game into disrepute and contravening regulations regarding the placing of wagers on football matches. The Hillier regime was already unpopular with supporters. At that year's AGM he'd reduced the size of the board from nine members to five and cancelled the planned and much-trumpeted issue of 250,000 shares in the club. Despite occasionally making the right noises, he'd shown little interest in acting to redevelop the Shrivenham Road stand and the Town End at the County Ground, condemned four years earlier and restricted to a limited capacity. The club were in the ridiculous position of having to call off matches if the wind speed was considered to be a danger to the rickety Shrivenham Road stand, something that had put paid to a match with Bournemouth the previous season.

But these charges were to be the least of Hillier's worries. Two weeks later the *Sunday People* was at it again. This time the tabloid alleged that since Macari had arrived in 1985, a number of unlawful payments had been made to players by the club. 'One of the directors, Lionel Smart, called for Hillier to resign and the sacked former club secretary Dave King threatened to tell all,' reveals Merriman. 'But I hoped that if he felt anything at all for Swindon Town he'd keep his lips sealed.'

On 12 February the FA announced that it had banned Brian Hillier from any involvement in football for six months. Macari escaped a ban but was fined £1,000, and the club were fined £7,500, the total winnings from the ill-advised wager. In his defence Hillier had claimed that he had placed the bet as 'insurance' against Swindon being knocked out of the competition and to cover the club's expenses from the trip to Tyneside, but no one seriously believed him.

The *Guardian* commented, 'Swindon supporters had feared that the club, at present pushing for promotion from the Second Division under Ossie Ardiles, might have points deducted or even suffer relegation, but this was never likely.' Anna Merriman recalls, 'I was comforted by the *Guardian* writing that, but I remember being warned that it didn't encompass any sanctions resulting from the illegal payments. It wasn't over by a long way.'

Swindon's now sadly defunct fanzine *Bring the Noise* distributed leaflets calling for Hillier's resignation at the next two home matches against West Ham United and Portsmouth. The West Ham game should have been the occasion of Lou Macari's first appearance at the County Ground since leaving Swindon to take over at Upton Park, but it was not to be.

'We'd been talking about it for weeks, wondering what sort of a reception he'd get, how he would take it and so on,' says Merriman. 'I'm not certain I would have applauded him after the mess he'd helped get us into, because as someone who has never committed a crime I find it hard to understand people who do. I'm convinced that he must have known what he was getting into, and I had this image in my mind of him creeping along the touchline, hands in pockets and head bowed.

'The reality was quite different. He disappointed everyone by not turning up, with the most popular theory being that he'd chickened out. The truth, we discovered the next day, was that he'd resigned as manager of West Ham United on the day of the game, citing a lack of support from the Hammers' apparent reluctance to back him in the appeal against his fine.' One can only guess at whether his impending weekend appointment at the County Ground had hastened his decision. Was it coincidence that the Hammers' next opponents were Swindon Town?

In the face of vociferous calls for his removal, Hillier announced intentions to appeal against his ban and hinted that once he'd served his six months he'd be back at the helm as if he'd never been away. At the next game, at Portsmouth, the first 'Hillier Out' banner appeared, only to be swiftly removed by the Hampshire Constabulary. The 1–1 draw kept Swindon in third place, and by mid-March a run of just one defeat in thirteen matches had put them into a promising position. The club, in the light of the reduced capacity at their rapidly deteriorating stadium, made the last six matches of the season all-ticket affairs. Thus it was that Hull City found that they were the opponents in an all-ticket game, possibly for the only time in the last 30 years. However, the Tigers left with all three points, and the following Tuesday Swindon went down 1–0 at Ipswich Town. Their promotion challenge was spluttering to a halt. 'I thought we'd thrown in the towel on automatic promotion, because at that stage Sheffield United were seven points ahead in second place. I was increasingly pessimistic about our play-off chances too, as our rivals weren't going to keep doing us favours forever,' says Merriman.

On 3 April, the Football Association rejected Lou Macari's appeal. Hillier was sticking to his story that the bet was placed not for personal gain, but as insurance against Town being knocked out. Merriman couldn't believe it. 'Where did he unearth that hogwash from? And anyway, the FA didn't care why he put the bet on, just that he did it at all. If he'd wanted them to let him off, he should have come up with something a bit more original than that! I had no sympathy for him whatsoever, and hoped that they would throw out his appeal as well as Macari's.'

Such hopes were magnificently fulfilled: not only did the FA reject Hillier's appeal, they increased his ban from six months to three years. 'It was the best news we'd had for a while,' recalls Merriman. 'It meant he had to admit defeat and leave the club.

'By mid-April we were still fourth and looking good for the play-offs, but I was becoming increasingly worried about the consequences of the investigations of our other activities. If we managed to qualify for the play-offs we were worried that the FA would exclude us because of the enquiry into illegal payments.'

A 2–1 defeat at Blackburn Rovers on Easter Monday saw Swindon drop to fifth place, with the chasing pack gaining as the weeks went by. On 28 April the Football League announced that a Special Management Committee Commission would sit at Villa Park on 4 May to rule on the illegal payments situation. The timing couldn't have been worse, as Anna Merriman recalls. 'Twenty-four hours before our last match of the season – the perfect way to make us feel as nervous as possible!' On the day of the announcement, Swindon were held 1–1 by struggling Middlesbrough. Blackburn's defeat at Ipswich, however, meant that Swindon reclaimed fourth place.

On Tuesday 4 May, Swindon's problems off the field were exacerbated when Hillier, Macari, ex-club accountant Vince Farrar and defender Colin Calderwood were picked up in early-morning raids on their homes by the Inland Revenue. 'Why they found it necessary to swoop like that I don't know,' says Merriman. 'It was like *The Sweeney*! Going as far as taking Calderwood in for questioning was a complete joke. When he was picked up he was somewhere in the south-west with the rest of the squad, preparing for the Stoke game on the Saturday. He was, needless to say, released without charge.'

These developments meant that the Football League hearing had to be postponed beyond the end of the regular season. Swindon would not discover their fate until the fat lady had left the building. The implications were not lost on Swindon supporters, Anna Merriman included. 'It was rumoured that if Macari, Farrar and Hillier were prosecuted by the Inland Revenue, the League might not have been able to act until everything had gone through the criminal courts, by which time we'd have safely negotiated the play-offs and made it into the First Division. It would then be too late. But we really hoped that everything would be decided before the Stoke game on the Saturday so we'd know where we were, whether we were in the play-offs or not.'

On the Thursday, Macari, Hillier and Farrar were bailed at Swindon Magistrates Court and forced to hand over their passports. Swindon went into the game at Stoke needing to secure a point to ensure a place in the play-offs. Anna Merriman was there to see Swindon draw 1–1. 'The game wasn't exactly an anti-climax,' she says. 'We played well enough to get the draw, but we were just waiting for it to be over so that we could begin the celebrations and nurse our battered nerves. The police requested our prolonged presence after the final whistle, of course, but we would have stayed anyway. A few hundred home fans remained as well, which showed loyalty to their team when they had finished bottom and knew they were relegated weeks ago. They came marauding on to the pitch and a line of policemen marched across to stop them coming too close to us, but they weren't looking for a fight. We engaged in some mutual appreciation instead. The police hadn't really bargained for that.

'After five minutes of "We want Ossie!" from the supporters, he obliged by leading the team out to a huge roar. It was a fantastic scene. All the players were messing about. Steve White borrowed a policeman's helmet and used it as a codpiece, and Bodin gave one of the fans a can of beer. It could have gone on all night and we wouldn't have minded.'

Swindon would meet Blackburn Rovers in the play-off semi-final, with Newcastle United facing Sunderland in the other game, but the Town fans' celebrations were tempered slightly by the League Management Committee hearing still hanging over the club. Rumours abounded, as Anna Merriman recalls. 'There were unconfirmed reports of unconfirmed punishments. One rumour was that if we'd finished in the top two they'd have made us take part in the play-offs, if we'd finished in a play-off place they'd exclude us altogether, and if we'd finished below that, it didn't bear thinking about.'

Merriman and just under 5,000 Swindonians travelled to the pre-Walker Ewood Park for the first leg. 'We couldn't wait for the game to start, but were grateful for some light relief prior to the kick-off from someone who came out on to the pitch dressed up in what looked like a Wurzel outfit, wearing a red and white rosette and carrying a pitchfork. This Swindon legend, the moonraker, is about trying to find gold, and got us singing even more. There was no break in our singing at any point during the game, and I think our spirit had grown out of the mess we had found ourselves in off the pitch. It was solidarity in adversity, and it was great.'

With the backing of the fans, Swindon left Lancashire with a valuable 2–1 lead to take into the second leg. 'The win gave us that feeling of euphoria which hits you when you have shown nearly complete supremacy,' says Merriman, 'and in such a vital game I like to think our support helped.'

In the return leg, Swindon sealed the result with two first-half goals, while Blackburn could manage only a late deflected goal from Howard Gayle. Cue celebrations. 'I had only been on the pitch once before,' recalls Merriman, 'when we'd won the Fourth Division four years earlier, so I ducked under the crush-barrier, scaled the advertising hoardings and joined the dash across the grass. We stood and waited for the players to come back out, and as the Blackburn fans couldn't leave until we'd gone they had to share our glory too.'

Swindon's day of reckoning dawned on Bank Holiday Monday, 28 May 1990. Merriman fondly recalls the experience of watching her side at Wembley. 'There wasn't a bus, coach, minibus or van left for hire in the whole of the Swindon area that day, and I'd been ready since first light, Swindon shirt on, scarf around my neck and mascot perched precariously on my shoulders. Ossie's red and white army were on their way to Wembley.

'The closer we got to the stadium, the more colour we saw lining the streets and the more supporters we saw gathering outside watering-holes. At first it wasn't easy to tell whether they were our fans or Sunderland's, but the nature of their respective hand signals helped.

'Arriving at Wembley, I had to revise my preference for watching football in a small, packed ground to watching it in a large packed one miles from the pitch. When everyone's so geared up for the game, Wembley really is some-thing else. It was amazing even before the game. So many people were walking around in the sunshine feeling that this could be their day that you couldn't help being carried along by it all. At the time, the only thing worrying me was the thought of losing my ticket! No words could describe the game, because for us it was just like a fairy-tale, the best thing to happen to Swindon ever.'

Sunderland had the best of the opening exchanges, but the Wiltshire side soon took control of the game. Only profligate finishing kept it scoreless until the 26th minute when Alan McLoughlin, a future Republic of Ireland international, hit a shot from 25 yards which took a huge deflection off Gary Bennett and looped over Tony Norman and into the net.

'People were open-mouthed, waving their flags and scarves, jumping about kissing each other and whooping with delight,' recalls Merriman. 'It was like slow motion, an action replay which captured sight and sound perfectly, relaying the triumph with minute precision, echoing the orgy of movement, recording a fragment of history, but no photograph could have captured the feeling.' It was to be the only goal of the game.

'At the end of the game, a few people around me were crying, some were hugging their neighbours, others were just applauding and looking bewildered. The players ran around like headless chickens, dancing around, clapping us, clapping each other, clapping anyone. Ossie bounded on to the pitch and embraced each of them in turn.

'Calderwood went up and lifted the trophy and we exploded again. Then they returned to the pitch clutching the trophy as if they never wanted to be parted from it and danced around in front of us. It was mostly McLoughlin and Ossie who were in demand from the photographers. Finally they did a lap of honour and received applause from those Sunderland supporters who hadn't already left the stadium. Not one of us moved for ages, and when we did it was with great reluctance.'

Ardiles had allayed any concern about his lack of managerial experience. In his first season in charge he had guided a club who had resided in the Fourth Division just four years earlier to the top flight, making the most of a squad of limited ability. 'McLoughlin was a prime example,' says Merriman. 'The previous season he'd played about 13 games, didn't score and was even loaned to Torquay by Lou Macari. In the promotion season, however, he played in every game, scored 15 goals and went to Italy that summer with the Republic of Ireland.

'The journey home was surprisingly subdued. We sat on the coach just trying to take things in. As we approached Swindon itself there were people standing on the bridges over the motorway, waving scarves. There was even a cow in a field with Swindon colours on. The success was a great fillip for the town, and we'd shown the critics that we do merit attention. Now no one would ask "Where's that?" when I said I came from Swindon, or say "They're in the Third Division, aren't they?" any more.

'Waking up the next day was like waking up on Christmas morning. It was like having a new bike and wanting to show everyone, except that there was no one to show because everyone else had one as well. I honestly didn't believe that the FA would punish us now, at least not by anything that would stop us playing First Division football the following season.

'That afternoon we went into town to see Ossie and the players tour the streets in an open-topped bus. The streets were heaving with thousands of people. The day before we'd seen the triumph itself, now we were just inhaling it deep into our lungs. It was brilliant. What a day, what a team, what a town. Things were looking very rosy indeed.'

The Football League Management Commission sat at 11 a.m. on Thursday 7 June, ten days after Swindon's Wembley triumph. The open-topped bus was back in the garage, the players had dispersed for the summer, and the club settled into planning for the new season. Fans were budgeting for season tickets, many of them feeling that it would be the only way of ensuring they would get into the games, and atlases were consulted for the best routes to Manchester, Coventry and Southampton. The whole town of Swindon eagerly awaited the publication of the fixture list to see who'd be the first visitors to the County Ground. Liverpool? Spurs? Arsenal?

It was a success almost impossible to comprehend. Although they expected some punishment, it was sure to be fiscal rather than anything else. Surely the League wouldn't be so crass as to deny the club its hard-earned place in the First Division? Surely they wouldn't shatter the hopes and dreams of the thousands of supporters who'd travelled to Wembley and lined the streets of the town in celebration?

Shortly before 11 a.m. a tray of tea and biscuits was placed on the dark oak table in the sumptuous Villa Park boardroom, the door swung closed and the meeting began. Doug Ellis, John Smith and Arthur Sandford sipped their tea and began to determine the fate of Swindon Town. The club had admitted 36 counts of illegal payments to players dating back to 1985, each of which would be dealt with in turn. It was to be a long meeting.

'We had to be optimistic, even though we knew that the charges against us were pretty serious,' laments Merriman. 'Most of the players who'd apparently received these undeclared sums had since left the club, although a few were still there. The amounts were apparently insubstantial, but it was reported that the payments had continued during the promotion season, something Ardiles fervently denied.

'I spent all day unable to concentrate on anything else, interested only in catching every radio news bulletin. The first thing I heard was at midday, when they reported that the meeting was well under way. At two I telephoned the club, at three, four and five I telephoned the Clubcall line. They were certainly prolonging the agony, and there was still nothing on the six o'clock news. Maybe it was a case of no news being good news, I told myself. Then at 7.30 p.m. I heard it. The Football League had demoted us to Division Three.'

The commission had sat all day to decide that Swindon would be demoted to the Third Division with Sunderland going up in their place. Tranmere would go up to Division Two. Each director was individually censured by the League, who issued a statement that 'The present directors freely admit that they had failed in their duties and responsibilities as directors of a Football League club'.

Anna Merriman was furious. 'I wanted to know how they could do this to us after letting us go through the play-offs and begin preparations for the following season. Why didn't they punish us before? Believing for ten days that we would be playing in the First Division and then having it taken away was like being kicked in the teeth when you've just got back from the dentist.

'It represented the total waste of a whole season of graft, brilliant football and great victories; all that had been for nothing. And being demoted two divisions didn't undo just two years' work, but about ten. It cost us millions of pounds in lost revenue from sponsorship, gate receipts, television and pools money, but that was nothing compared to the fact that we wouldn't be going to Liverpool, or even Bristol City, for that matter, the following season. Most of the players would leave, and there wasn't a chance in hell that Ossie would stay. I don't think the League had really thought through all of the consequences.'

The next day the newspapers were full of the story of Swindon's ten days at the top. Chairman Gary Herbert announced that the club would definitely appeal against the decision. The streets of Swindon, just over a week earlier packed with thousands of noisy promotion-drunk fans, were suddenly eerily quiet.

'Swindon was like a morgue,' says Merriman. 'The flag on the town hall flew at half-mast, everyone was depressed and even my brother had been crying. We hadn't given up hope, though, despite the depression. Although a 40,000-signature petition had been ignored before the hearing, we were planning protest marches, and local MP Simon Coombs promised to raise the issue in the Commons. None of the players had talked about leaving. Colin Calderwood made a statement which said the players would back any action taken by the club towards reinstatement and Gordon Taylor of the PFA also backed us. A local lawyer urged the fans who'd gone to Wembley to write to the Office of Fair Trading, claiming that we'd all been lured there under false pretences.'

The issue had wide-ranging repercussions throughout the game. Newcastle United challenged Sunderland's right to take Swindon's place, saying that they had finished third, above the Rokerites, and therefore the place should be theirs. Sunderland pointed out in return that they'd beaten Newcastle over two legs to reach the play-off final in the first place. Sheffield Wednesday entered the fray; they'd finished in the highest relegation place and argued that they should be allowed to stay in the First Division. West Ham United, meanwhile, would have had a play-off place if Swindon had been excluded from the knockout tournament.

It was the same in the Third Division. Tranmere had been beaten in the play-off final by Notts County, and agreed that they should be the ones to go up to the Second and fill the place left open by Swindon. Bournemouth, in a similar position to Sheffield Wednesday in the First, argued that they should stay up. There was even talk that Cambridge United, who'd beaten Chesterfield in the Fourth Division play-off, would be denied a place in the Third. The implications were seemingly endless, and the affair was threatening to turn into a fiasco.

On Tuesday 12 June, as the World Cup got under way in Italy, Swindon announced they would be going to the High Court to overturn the League's decision. 'The club weren't denying the charges, but argued that the sanctions should have been more equitable: fines for the individuals involved instead of the collective punishment of tens of thousands of innocent people, each of whom had spent a lot of money on a season that might as well have not taken place,' says Merriman.

The following day the League confirmed that Sunderland would go into the First Division and Tranmere into the Second. Anna Merriman watched the Sunderland reaction to the announcement with incredulity. 'I was livid. Denis Smith had the nerve to go on television drinking champagne. Sheffield Wednesday and Bournemouth declared they'd appeal and would go to the High Court if necessary, whilst our appeal was set for the following Monday.'

The supporters of Swindon took to the streets again on Sunday 17 June, almost three weeks after their celebrations. This time the mood was fuelled by anger rather than joy as 20,000 fans marched through the streets in a protest labelled 'First Aid'. Thousands of 'First Not Third' stickers were produced. The following day the High Court hearing was adjourned until the beginning of July.

The media appeared to back the original decision. Jimmy Hill, not usually known as a voice of the fans (nor of anyone except Jimmy Hill), agreed with the decision, making the startling assertion that the Swindon fans shouldn't complain; after all, they had had a fantastic day out at Wembley and now held some terrific memories. How this man continues to find work as a football pundit is absolutely bamboozling. Colin Gibson in the *Daily Telegraph* opined that Swindon were nothing more than cheats, and should consider themselves lucky not to go down to the Fourth or even be kicked out of the League altogether.

Anna Merriman was outraged. 'How the media can let people pontificate about football when they apparently know, and more importantly feel, nothing about it is absolutely beyond me,' she says. 'The journalists also knew that there was no way action like this would be taken against big clubs, as the Spurs farce proved a few years later. For years the clique of the big clubs had walked all over the smaller ones and we'd allowed it to happen. The advent of the Premier League proves that. And it was probably no coincidence that of the three men who decided our fate, two were the chairmen of big clubs: Doug Ellis of Aston Villa and John Smith of Liverpool. I believe that they knew what they were going to do before they even arrived at Villa Park that morning.' Was it just coincidence that Sunderland, promoted in place of Swindon, were perceived as a big club, with much larger gates than Swindon could hope to achieve at the crumbling County Ground?

In the meantime the club had decided against taking their case to the High Court, perhaps nervous of the implications that, on appeal, Hillier's ban had been extended six-fold. The cost of losing the case would also have been astronomical for a club now budgeting for the Third Division rather than the First. Instead they would settle for appealing directly to the Football Association.

The appeal hearing took place at Lancaster Gate on Monday 2 July. Once again, Anna Merriman and the rest of the Swindon fans spent the day on tenterhooks. 'It felt like judgement day: our life in the hands of the FA. We waited in the same state of apprehension which we had a month earlier, and the decision wasn't reached any quicker that day. The six o'clock news had a report about the hearing and said that no decision had been made, but just as the programme was about to close they flashed up our club badge and said, "The Football Association has just announced that Swindon Town will play in the Second Division next season." I smiled and said one word. "Brilliant."'

After all they had been through, the Swindon supporters decided that anything was better than the Third Division, especially as Bristol City and Bristol Rovers had been promoted together from the Third and would have played at a higher level than their rivals from Wiltshire. There was a half-hearted campaign for reinstatement to the First Division, but most fans had had enough of the whole business.

Hillier, Macari and Farrar were sent for trial at Winchester High Court. The case lasted five weeks, and culminated with Macari, by then the manager of Stoke City, being acquitted. Hillier was convicted of conspiracy to defraud the Inland Revenue and Farrar of conspiracy and false accounting. Farrar received a six-month suspended prison sentence whilst Hillier was sent to prison for a year, a sentence later halved on appeal.

The following season Swindon struggled in the Second Division. The club was forced to sell a number of key players to pay off debts that included the

£500,000 bill from the appeal hearing, and was hit by a rash of injuries. 'There was more anger directed at the remaining members of the board as well,' recalls Merriman. 'Gary Herbert stepped down as chairman and was replaced by Ken Chapman, and a fans' representative was elected to the board. I think Chapman did a good job really, all things considered. Some idiots started "sack the board" chants when Ossie deserted us for Newcastle with nine games of the 1990–91 season remaining, but they were a definite minority. We'd beaten Newcastle 3–2 at the County Ground that night and I wondered whether he'd have joined anyone at that point. He said that everyone knew he'd wanted to leave the previous summer and I'd have preferred it if he had done, and left us to commence the rebuilding instead of wasting a whole season of no one knowing whether they were coming or going.

'Today we still talk about that season and still feel bitter about those individuals that did it to us. I remember everything as if it were yesterday, but, hey, life's gone on. It's a shame that the 30,000 who went to Wembley never came back, but we are not just anybody, we are the mob, the ones who light up the Bank with our laughter and travel to away games with smiles on our faces and Town in our hearts.

'Jimmy Hill was right in one way, we did have a good day out at Wembley. We had an excellent year and we have fantastic memories of a season that for all intents and purposes might never have happened; a season that never was but one which saw us make a lot of people smile and rub a few noses in the dirt. That can't be all bad.'

In December 1990, the FA announced that the case against Swindon Town had been closed and so, apparently, was the door to the top flight, as the team struggled to emulate the promotion season that wasn't. However, under the management team of Glenn Hoddle and John Gorman, Swindon did make it into the Premier League in 1993. Their season ended in comprehensive relegation, ten points adrift at the bottom, but at least they'd been there and laid a few ghosts to rest. Who knows what would have happened if Swindon had gone up that year? The fact that their long-suffering fans were denied finding out by behind-the-scenes corruption speaks volumes for how big business can ruin football. And that was before Italia 90, before the new football businessmen jumped aboard, shovelling cash into the furnace to keep the gravy train up to speed whilst they laundered the money handed over at the turnstiles, the supporters' investments in their dreams.

The club had played with the dreams of the fans, the lifeblood of the game, and it was the fans who paid the ultimate price. The criminally convicted could serve their time, pay their fines and start afresh. Supporters have longer memories, hopes piled high that are easily dashed. Hoddle and Gorman got Swindon to the promised land; perhaps they would have already been there.

That season was also marked by the Tottenham Hotspur fiasco. The long-running feud between Terry Venables and Alan Sugar, the one-time 'dream ticket' at White Hart Lane, caused evidence to be made public of financial misdemeanours. Spurs reported themselves to the FA, disclosing that undeclared loans had been made that were never to be repaid, and that a number of illegal payments had been made to players. Just like Swindon.

As a result of admitting 34 charges of breaches of League regulations, the inquiry announced that Tottenham would be fined £600,000, banned from the FA Cup for one year and docked 12 points from the forthcoming season. Supporters across the land rejoiced.

Alan Sugar made precisely the same argument on appeal as the Swindon administration had done: that the people responsible had left the club, and that the points deduction and FA Cup ban would just make the fans suffer. Because he cares for the fans, does Alan Sugar. As a result, the FA Cup ban was lifted, the points penalty halved and the fine increased to £1.5 million. A heck of a lot of money to most clubs, but not to Spurs. Within 48 hours of the appeal, Spurs laughed in the face of the FA, announcing the signings of Ilie Dumitrescu for £2.6 million and Jurgen Klinsmann for £2 million, spending three times the amount of their fine on just two players.

Not only had Spurs kept their place in the Premiership, they had also paid their fine with loose change and come out of the affair stronger than when they had gone in. No individuals were called to account, and Spurs, coincidentally managed by Ardiles, got off to a flying start to the season, playing some exhilarating football and raking in cash at the turnstiles.

In the meantime, Swindon now occupy a mid-table position in the First Division and were eliminated from the 1998 FA Cup at home to Stevenage Borough.

It's a funny old game. It's absolutely hilarious.

The Best of Times,
The Worst of Times

EVERTON'S NARROW SQUEAK

Everton FC have been members of the top division for all but four seasons in their distinguished history. The last time they competed in the old Second Division was in the days before rock'n'roll. At the end of the 1993–94 season, however, the Goodison Park side went into the last game occupying 20th position following a 3–0 defeat at Leeds which saw them drop into the relegation places for the first time all season. A late run of ten games had produced just one victory, which didn't bode well for the Blues as they took on Wimbledon, who were on the back of a tremendous run of seven wins in nine games. With Swindon already relegated and Oldham all but certain to join them, the final relegation spot was between Ipswich Town, away at second-placed Blackburn, Southampton, visiting West Ham, Sheffield United, who travelled to Chelsea, and Everton.

LOUISE KELLY: I still break into a sweat thinking about this one. Rob had gone to a stag party along with a few other Evertonians, and I had no one to go with. So along I went to see his mum and dad and persuaded his mum to come with me. We got to Goodison at noon and couldn't get in. Tragedy! We even tried to get in with the Wimbledon fans.

GUY McEVOY: It had been a strangely non-Everton season for me up to that point. I'd only managed to get to about three home games. The previous season I'd been exiled in Israel and then I'd come home, started at university

138

and fallen in love. My passion for Everton had, I'm ashamed to say, waned a bit in my absence. But on the Friday night I'd had a row with my girlfriend and was feeling a bit down. I flicked on the teletext and looked at the league table. Suddenly the gravity of the situation struck me and I became convinced that this was happening to Everton because I'd stopped caring. Somehow because I'd not been there to add my voice to the chants, the team had lost its spirit. I had to go to the match.

Feeling guilty about the row, the girlfriend grudgingly agreed to come with me. We arrived at Goodison at midday and couldn't believe the queues.

MIKE BERSIKS: I live in South Africa and woke up that morning in a cold sweat and moped around the house until after lunch, occasionally going back to my league table in the local paper until I knew every combination for all of the bottom six teams. This depressed me even further as, sickeningly, the message was drummed home: my beloved Everton team, which had been playing piss-poor football all season, had to win against our bogey team Wimbledon.

I went to play a bit of footie with my mates at 2 p.m. and it took my mind off the impending doom. It even brightened my day as I (of little skill) scored a hat-trick. I took this as being a good omen. Afterwards I walked to my mate's house with a feeling of disaster increasing as kick-off time approached. In South Africa we get English soccer live but on a pay channel, which I don't have, so I had to go to a friend's house to watch the match.

JOHN O BURNS: I'd met Ruth, a South African girl, at about the time Everton appointed Mike Walker as manager following Howard Kendall's resignation. I had grave reservations about this appointment. Mike Walker in his first managerial appointment had run Norwich City for only 18 months, taking a relegation-threatened club to top-six notoriety, but his limited pedigree gave me reservations. I hoped they were unfounded.

As the weeks rolled on towards the season's end, Everton went into a freefall dive down the Premiership. Were these the same players who had topped the table by winning their opening three matches?

After a week or so I discovered that Ruth had an amazing capacity to consume copious amounts of alcohol. Not being a big drinker myself, I found it amazing that someone of such small stature could imbibe such large quantities of fermented grape juice. After constantly slinging Ruth, a lawyer, over my shoulder to put her to bed, her novelty was beginning to wear off. To compound my failing affection, she said that she was 'probably' a Manchester

United fan. Apparently she used to see them quite a lot on South African TV, wearing 'cute little red shirts'. Another example of Murdoch, Manchester United and television influencing the silly, gullible and naïve, of which Ruth was obviously all three. Show it to them long enough and they will suck it in and love it.

The point at which I realised that Everton were in serious danger was Saturday 30 April. I was in a pub in London with Ruth, and after pre-occupation regarding the score at Leeds all afternoon, I persuaded the manager to tune in to Teletext and the football results. I stared at the screen. Leeds United 3 Everton 0. Apart from a miracle, relegation now appeared inevitable. I slowly said to Ruth, 'Everton have just been beaten at Leeds; they may be relegated.' To my surprise she commiserated. What does she know, I asked myself? She doesn't know how I feel, she hasn't got a clue, she doesn't understand. Everton don't play in lower divisions, this is alien to all Evertonians. After about ten minutes Ruth said, 'John, stop staring at the screen. It's not going to change.'

The crucial match was against Wimbledon, the team with the best current form in the Premiership. Even if Everton won they could still go down if other teams around them won. The team that has graced the top flight for more seasons than any other club could be relegated.

My brother, a season-ticket holder, told me he couldn't get me a ticket. He advised me to 'get up here and start queuing by 11.30 or you won't get in'. I inwardly tore my loyalties apart. Rightly or wrongly, I concluded that I would not be there. Listening to the match on Radio Five by myself was the only alternative. I wanted no one else around. I made sure that Ruth was nowhere near my place that afternoon. After all, I was starting to believe that it was all her fault.

MARK WILLIAMS: I had only gone to a couple of games that season, notably the games where we got knocked out of both cup competitions. I'd gone with a mate from university who'd never been to Goodison before. I parked the car half a mile from the ground and trekked towards Goodison in almost complete silence. We just couldn't believe the queues and, having not got there until 12.45 p.m., stood no chance of getting in. We just wandered hopelessly around the ground. I don't know why, we'd given up all hopes of getting a ticket.

PHIL BOWKER: For most of the season I'd been working in Germany. It was great fun but the only way to follow your team there is through the media:

any news was whatever you could get from the papers. Also the Germans don't, or won't, follow English football that closely, so nobody at work really cared one way or the other that I supported Everton and that we were in deep *Scheisse*.

Then, about two months before the end of the season, I got a new job in Ireland. The difference couldn't have been more dramatic: from complete indifference to being surrounded by Liverpool and Manchester United fans slagging me off and making my life hell. Then for my new job I had to go back to Germany for a week: the week prior to the match.

I still had a couple of things to sort out in Nuremburg, where I used to live (my wife was still there, for a start), so I decided to spend the weekend of the match there. I will never forget that Saturday morning, driving down from Bonn, where I'd been for the week. I was so nervous; my insides felt like they stretched from my knees up to my brain, and they were in constant turmoil.

LOUISE WILLIAMS: I was in Cyprus with my dad. We managed to find a bar in the middle of nowhere, one of those with a clichéd English name like the 'Dog and Duck' or something, where the match was being shown live. You can watch Premiership matches live on a Saturday in some countries and we were dead chuffed to find that the bar had the Everton game on. We even got my mum off the sunbed to come and watch. It was 100° F in the shade.

GUY JACKSON: Throughout that season I would often go to a friend's house in London, where I was living, to develop photographs in his darkroom. My mate had a lodger, an 18-year-old Everton fanatic. As things got worse and worse while the season wore on, he often asked me, 'What are the chances of Everton going down?' I would always reply that there are certain teams which will never be relegated, and Everton are one of them. As the final few weeks of the season loomed, this statement took on less and less conviction but I carried on with it regardless. The lad seemed to believe me and it cheered him up whenever I told him.

LOL SCRAGG: I remember queuing up outside the Glad for two hours from midday and I was one of the last few in the ground. After finding a step to sit on, the first thing that struck me was the optimism amongst fellow fans, an optimism that I have to confess I didn't share.

GUY McEVOY: I wanted to be in the Gwladys as normal but suspected we wouldn't get in, so we tagged on the end of the Top Balcony queue and hoped for the best. At 2.55 we finally got in, finding some seats just as 'Z Cars' blurted out. I'd never actually sat in the top tier before and remember trying to work out if the dizziness was due to nerves or vertigo.

As the game kicked off I instantly regretted bringing the other half with me. 'Why did he pass to him?' she would ask as Anders gave the ball away. 'That's a penalty!' she exclaimed audibly as he handballed it, followed by 'You've had it now' as Ablett committed hara-kiri. I felt intense shame that I had deprived a fellow blue of a seat by bringing her along. The relationship was becoming strained, to say the least.

MIKE BERSIKS: The game had hardly started before that ridiculous Limpar handball and penalty. Then the Ablett own goal was like a kick in the crotch. I felt sick and wanted to cry. I was cursing Limpar, Ablett, Walker and Wimbledon and my mate had the good sense to say nothing, as I think I would have taken a swing at him.

JOHN O BURNS: The atmosphere and sheer volume of noise at Goodison Park that afternoon was clearly coming across on the radio. No sooner had the match begun than Anders Limpar handled in the penalty area for no apparent reason. Wimbledon scored from the penalty spot. Near-depression set in. There was a whole match still to go, though, and I convinced myself to be optimistic.

It appeared not too long after that Gary Ablett deflected the ball into his own net. That was it: relegation. I turned off the stereo and walked around the kitchen and outside on to the landing. I thought that they would probably be promoted next season. After all, Mike Walker had about 14 million quid to spend. If ever a club should not go down it's one with that amount of money to add quality to the Premiership, but strange things happen.

OSMO TAPIO E RAIHALA: I watched the game on TV and after just three minutes there was some incident that the Finnish commentator thought would lead to an Everton free-kick. You can guess my fear when it was taken to the penalty spot. Later on, even from TV I could see that the ball was going well wide when Ablett turned it into the net. During the first half the commentator had wondered how Finnish Evertonians were taking it, and to make things worse he even mentioned me by name!

MARK WILLIAMS: We were still wandering around when I heard we'd given away a penalty. I kicked the lamppost by the bus-shelter at the Park End so hard I hurt my foot. I could see the Wimbledon fans from where I was standing and knew they'd scored by their reaction. Kerry and I went into Stanley Park to see if we could see from up a tree, but we couldn't. After about 15 minutes we decided to drive back to Lancaster and listen to the match on the radio.

ROY-KING MIAA: From Norway, I had avidly followed the sports segments on Sky News. What surprised me was how full the ground was two hours before kick-off. I carefully tuned in to the BBC World Service, which of course faded in and out at the wrong moments. When they announced that Wimbledon had taken the lead through a penalty, due to Anders swinging a right hook at the ball, I thought we were finished. During that season Wimbledon had won every game in which they'd scored first. When the news filtered through that Ablett had toe-poked the ball into his own net, I turned the radio off by the simple method of opening the bedroom window and slinging the bloody thing as far as I could. Needless to say, reception was seriously impaired after that.

RUTH GRIMLEY: I was still a student in 1994 and was spending my Saturdays helping on a local radio station's *Saturday Sports Special* programme. For weeks before the match I had been getting more and more stick about Everton's prospects, and when I arrived at the station on the Saturday morning I was offered a box of Kleenex in preparation.

We ran a sports quiz during the first half of the football. I was keeping score on this occasion so I was in the studio itself. Within minutes of starting the quiz, a Liverpool fan let me know through the glass that we were one down. There was a break in the quiz when the second went in and he tried to sound sympathetic saying, 'Relax, it's all over now.'

PHIL BOWKER: I arrived in Nuremburg about an hour before kick-off and had nothing to do except sit on the settee and wait for 5.30 local time, when I would stroll down to the Irish pub and watch the results on Sky.

STAN NUTTALL: I saw the match at our local pub in Sunnyvale, California, since it was televised live to subscribed business establishments in the US. Although the place was full, there weren't many Evertonians present. There were, however, quite a few Liverpool fans wishing us well – 'We'll miss the derby games if you go down' – but secretly hoping that Tranmere would replace us. Anyway, I went through the trauma like other Evertonians, not believing the state we had got ourselves into as a result of the two Wimbledon goals.

LOUISE WILLIAMS: We'd got to the pub early, anticipating a crowd. It was pretty full by kick-off, mostly with Everton fans on holiday in Cyprus. There was this bloke I remember particularly because he had a very large EFC tattoo on his arm. A load of 'mates' of his arrived to 'just stand here and watch you get relegated'. Even when things looked really bleak, this bloke was bravely retorting, 'Well, you'll be stood there a bloody long time.'

MIKE DUDLEY: I live on Long Island, New York, and I started listening to the BBC World Service. I was out in the backyard kicking a ball about with my son, who was almost four at the time. I couldn't believe it when we were one down immediately. When we went two down, I switched the radio off. I switched back on again just before half-time to learn of the penalty, but then had to take my son to his soccer match.

GUY JACKSON: On the day of the Wimbledon game I was in the darkroom as usual. I couldn't bear to listen to the game. At one point I went downstairs for a cup of tea. My friend's lodger was in the lounge in full Everton strip, listening to the radio. 'We're 2–0 down,' he said. He'd been crying. I did my usual thing of telling him not to worry, that we would score three before the end of the game and that he should go for a walk and forget about it. Secretly I was wondering how I would face him again after relegation.

LOUISE KELLY: We walked to the petrol station opposite the car park while Frenchie went off to buy a radio. While we waited, a Liverpool fan drove past laughing and took great delight in telling us we were two down. How could this be? A man and his son, aged about six, walked past. The son was in tears because they'd not got into the match. We told him the score, which only made matters worse.

Then there was hope. We heard a roar from Goodison and ambushed a guy in a car at the petrol station so we could listen to his radio. The four of us stood in silence. We had a penalty. Who was going to take it? 'Looks like Stuart.' There was silence, then there was a roof-lifting roar and four people were seen running madly around the garage forecourt.

MIKE BERSIKS: Then came Limpar's dive and the commentators started criticising the penalty award. This made me more livid but mostly filled me with a sense of extreme fear. Stuart scored it and I started smoking my friend's mum's Camels as my mood of extreme tension was lit by some small hope.

JOHN O BURNS: I'd reluctantly switched the radio back on and about 15 seconds later the crowd roared and my stomach seemed to rise into my rib cage. Commentator Alan Green said, 'Everton have a penalty, Limpar was fouled in the area.' I recall Bryan Hamilton and Alan Green saying that Limpar appeared to dive but may have been fouled anyway. Stuart ran up to take the penalty kick and the mighty roar from the speakers said the rest. 'Yeeeeessss!' I screamed. A draw was now possible. Luckily I have a high ceiling, or I might have punched holes in it.

MARK WILLIAMS: As we were walking up past Stanley Park we heard two roars. Some blokes came past in a taxi, shouting, '2–1, lads, 2–1!' From the double roar of the penalty award and its conversion, we assumed we'd got two in quick succession and were winning. We legged it back to the trees, where we ascertained that the score was indeed 2–1 – only no one pointed out to us until half-time that it was 2–1 to Wimbledon.

Dejected again, we decided to head back to Lancaster. I'll never forget that car journey for as long as I live. In the previous hour and a half I'd been through every emotion, from hope, to frustration, to despair, to hope, to ecstatic joy, then back to despair. The game sounded scrappy and the only utterances between us were 'we're going down, mate'.

LOL SCRAGG: Second half and we all felt a little more optimistic, but, as I remember, other results weren't going well for us.

Then it happened. I still can't believe that Bazza Horne scored a spectacular goal from what, 25 yards out. The guy can't *pass* the ball 25 yards, never mind shoot! When this rocket hit the net, I recall flying down about ten rows of the Glad seats in mid-air and getting used as a crash mat by anyone who'd followed me, but I didn't care!

GUY McEVOY: I remember thinking at half-time that none of these players seemed to care, that no one wanted to win. That no one on the field could be a true Evertonian, else they wouldn't be letting this happen. Then it all changed. One of those crazy moments that change your life. The ball found Horne 30 yards out, he controlled it on his thigh to take it past a man and then unexpectedly swung his boot at it. The ball curled into the top corner. Bedlam! Hope? Faith.

MIKE BERSIKS: The TV was replaying a missed Holdsworth header when suddenly it cut back to show a ball flash into the net off the upright. Barry Horne had scored and I let out a bellow which literally brought the police to the door! After my mate convinced the coppers that no one was being murdered, he came back to find me gibbering like a madman, praying in front of his TV for deliverance from the pit of relegation which had seemed a certainty mere minutes before.

OSMO TAPIO E RAIHALA: I remember being soaked in cold sweat, then suddenly, when the TV was showing a replay of a Wimbledon corner, Barry Horne gave us the lifeline. I remember him walking stony-faced and the other Everton players piling on him and trying to hug his head off. Christ, I loved the man like I'd never loved before!

MARK WILLIAMS: Just as I was coming to a roundabout at the end of the M58, a bolt from the blue. Out of absolutely nothing, Barry Horne fires a missile of a shot into the top corner and a red Cortina went careering across several lanes as I lost control of myself and very nearly the car. We went ballistic for a minute or so.

MIKE DUDLEY: I didn't get to switch the radio back on until my son's game was under way, which was maybe 20 minutes into the second half. There was no mention of the score for what seemed to be ages. Then the commentator let it slip that it was 2–2.

Next thing I know, the commentator says something about the roof being lifted off at Goodison. I was going bananas. All the parents standing around me were wondering why a grown man was standing listening to the radio with tears running down his face. I tried to explain to them when I had calmed down a bit, but I'm not sure they bought it.

JOHN O BURNS: I recall that Everton were somewhere near the penalty area. It then appeared that the speakers were popping as the crowd roared around my living-room. The commentator said something like 'the roof's blown off!' as apparently Stuart hit a weak shot that bobbled past Hans Segers. I stood up, both arms in the air, and screeched something. My stomach was in knots. I didn't know it, but tears were running down my cheeks. What was I doing here? I should be there! I should be with all of them! Internal emotional conflicts needed resolving, but not now. The match hadn't finished yet.

GUY McEVOY: The winner was as ridiculous as the equaliser was sublime. Stuart got a foot to it and Segers just seemed to lie down as it bobbled past. They all count. I remember that I didn't jump up and down. I just stood up straight with both arms in the air and let out the most enormous 'yes!' I've ever mustered. I must have been in that position for about 15 seconds. Even the girlfriend was jumping up and down, going mental. She was growing on me again . . .

OSMO TAPIO E RAIHALA: Diamond Stuart's half-tackle, half-shot totally baffles Segers and the ball is in the net. I started yelling, singing and shouting so madly that my neighbour came round and started thumping on my back door, asking, 'Did Everton score?' As I couldn't say anything understandable, he said, 'Wait, I'll get the champagne!'

MARK WILLIAMS: In the end, it didn't matter how the winner went in. All that mattered was that it did. What any non-footballing motorists must have made of the actions of two young men in a red Cortina on the M6 is something that I still wonder today. I'm sure that seeing a driver doing 80-odd in the fast lane whilst shaking both fists in the air and yelling his head off does not exactly inspire confidence.

RUTH GRIMLEY: My job at the radio station during the second half was to write up the headlines and keep the presenter informed of score changes. I had this computer screen and when goals went in anywhere in the country it would come up as a scoreflash. Every time one of these came up I just had to keep hoping that it was good news for us, yet carry on keeping up with the other matches. As you can imagine, I was in absolute agony until the second and third goals went in, when I could have kissed the computer screen.

LOUISE KELLY: Then the final whistle went. A guy fell out of a tree in front of me and when I turned round there were hundreds of people running out of the bushes. Most were crying, including us, and laughing and hugging everyone and everything in sight.

LOL SCRAGG: The scenes at the Street End will live with me forever. I don't think I've hugged so many men in my life!

GUY McEVOY: The final whistle triggered an orgy of hugging strangers all bonded by collective overwhelming relief. We were all aware that we had seen a true miracle. What had occurred would be written in history and one day we will bore our grandchildren with the tale of what we'd just witnessed. I didn't walk out of Goodison, I floated.

MIKE BERSIKS: I was in heaven. What a feeling of euphoria! I don't think I stopped trembling until 15 minutes after the game!

JOHN O BURNS: Relief instantly followed by concern. None of the key relegation-fighting teams were behind in their matches according to Teletext, and that's sometimes a few minutes behind the play. Everton can still go down if they all win. I simultaneously flicked the remote to change from Teletext to TV and the portable phone button to instantly call my mother.

The BBC had flashed over live to Goodison Park to witness the emotional crowd scenes as they all spilled on to the pitch with joy and relief. On the phone there was pandemonium, with all the children screaming and going wild. I remember my mum saying, 'Everton have won! They're all jumping up and down!'

But I knew that Everton were not yet safe. All the other teams could have scored goals in the last minutes. Were the celebrations at Goodison premature? The BBC flashed over to Stamford Bridge. The commentator was saying that Sheffield United were relegated. Total relief. The images were of the Sheffield United players trotting off the pitch, not appearing dejected. They learned of their fate in the dressing-room. Chelsea had scored in the dying minutes and sent Sheffield United into Division One.

OSMO TAPIO E RAIHALA: When the final whistle went and I saw the scenes of explosive celebration on the Goodison Park turf, the telephone started ringing and everybody wanted to call me and say how relieved they were. They were not only Everton supporters but other people who knew me and who knew how important this was to me.

ROY-KING MIAA: The final 15 minutes were pure, unadulterated torture. With my radio in pieces on the street below, no news could be gleaned from anywhere. Had we scraped the point? Had Ipswich lost at Blackburn? What about Chelsea and Sheffield United? Why do I do this to myself? I should be doing something less stressful like clog dancing in a snake pit.

Finally the results started coming through on Norwegian television. What did I see? Everton 3 Wimbledon 2! We had won, won, won! I roared with delight, jumped in the air and slammed my fist into the table as hard as I could. The table collapsed. My daughter, aged five, was sitting on the floor playing with her dolls and burst into tears.

I sang, I danced, I threw open the verandah door and roared out the news to all and sundry.

RUTH GRIMLEY: Instead of writing a headline to break Evertonian hearts, I had the pleasure of writing one about our great escape. With a couple of seconds to go, the Liverpool fan said that Wimbledon had equalised and it took me a couple of minutes to check that this was a heinous lie. When the final whistle went I had no one to celebrate with, but I still got a mention on air when the presenter made a comment about an Evertonian dancing with joy around the studio. I have never felt so happy in my life.

PHIL BOWKER: When I finally made it to the pub I remember pausing outside and thinking that I could just turn around and walk away. Nobody knows me, nobody is going to take the piss here. I can put off the agony of relegation until I get the Sunday papers in another 18 hours. I was sure we were going down. I took a deep breath and went in.

I didn't know how long I'd have to wait for a report to come on, I just knew I'd have to sit it out. I glanced up at the screen and there it was, in big white letters: Wimbledon 2. Relegation!

Why only the Dons' score registered when the Everton score was on the same screen I've no idea, but for a split second the nausea started to rise. Then I saw the 'Everton 3' bit and just couldn't believe it. I leapt into the air with a yelp and there followed a lot of beer buying and kissing of German strangers. And when a couple of guys at the bar told me that Everton had been two down, I didn't believe them. I was sure that we must have been coasting it at 3–0 up and let them back into it. Nobody comes back from 2–0 down to beat Wimbledon!

LOUISE KELLY: I had no voice for the rest of the weekend and went out and got absolutely blitzed. I had only been following Everton since 1989 and this had been one of the most exciting days in all that time. I don't want to go through it again, though. That was the only home game I missed during the entire season, and at first I was pissed off that all the armchair fans had come out of the woodwork and stopped me from getting in. But on the other hand it was great to see all the fans come out for the boys when they most needed it. I am sure that is what made the difference.

GUY McEVOY: The day took on an even weirder slant on the way home when my girlfriend did her best to ruin it all again by announcing that she was racked with guilt because she had two-timed me. Had she told me at any other time I would probably have been depressed for weeks, but I was too happy to care. When we got back I just told her to go away and let me party.

Ever since that game I've sat in the Top Balcony by choice. It now has spiritual significance for me. I've hardly missed a home game, fearful of what will happen if my faith ever strays again. I'll forever associate that day with a certain young lady and with the restoration of proper priorities in my life. I will forever be grateful for that Friday night row which was the catalyst for me going and having the chance to witness history. I will forever hope that I will never have to go through it again.

MIKE BERSIKS: One of the best, and worst, days of my entire life, and one which I don't want to see happen again as long as I live.

JOHN O BURNS: I don't know what I said to my mother but I told her I would speak to her later and put the phone down. Now I could relax and allow myself to stabilise and wonder why that situation was ever allowed to happen in the first place.

One week later I ended it with Ruth. She would occasionally do strange things like screech at me in pubs and in the street, which I thought was a bit off as I'd only ever been nice to her. She's now back in South Africa, which is the best place for her if you ask me. Three weeks after that awful day I met my present girlfriend Cheryl, from Zimbabwe. We went to the semi-final against Tottenham and the final against Manchester United together. She is an Evertonian. Since she came along, Everton have improved enormously. I can't help wondering if that free-fall to the brink of relegation was all Ruth's fault. It must have been Ruth's fault. Who else's could it be?

OSMO TAPIO E RAIHALA: It took a few months to fully understand what I (and all Evertonians) had gone through. The scenes from Goodison proved that nobody ever wanted us to be in the same situation ever again. The trauma was so deep and painful that it took the whole summer to recover.

I think that Everton FC has a responsibility to its supporters not to take us into situations like that of May '94. We promise our support in sunshine and storm and Everton will have to respond in the way we deserve. The Wimbledon match didn't change my life but it reminded me of how fragile an individual is when one clings to an institution like Everton.

ROY-KING MIAA: The phone was in use virtually non-stop for the next few hours. Either friends were ringing to congratulate me or I was ringing the news to anyone who would listen, including a few wrong numbers! I rang home to Liverpool and spoke to my brothers, two of whom had been at the match. They told me that at the final whistle, the tidal wave of emotion from the crowd was the most powerful thing they had ever experienced.

I sat down later and watched the *Sports Special* on Sky. What was Anders thinking of? The ball was on the way out of the danger area. Ablett's intentions were obviously light years ahead of his skills. Luckily the result went in our favour and the rest is history. I must admit that even today I get chills thinking about that game.

PHIL BOWKER: I'm not very good at taking the pressure of occasions like that. Someone mentioned that at 2–0 down they'd seen a 70-year-old bloke walking away in tears. If I'd been there I'd have been leaving with him! What a feeling, but never again!

LOUISE WILLIAMS: At the end, the guy with the Everton tattoo bought champagne for everyone and passed it around. Even mum got carried away and joined in the celebrations, although the effects of the sun may have played a part too. Anyway, a good time was had by all.

MIKE DUDLEY: As soon as I got home I was on the phone to my dad in England, a season-ticket holder in the Upper Bullens, who had just got home from the game. All I could get out of him was 'Fantastic! Fantastic!' It truly was.

GUY JACKSON: After a while I packed up in the darkroom and drove home, not even daring to listen to the radio. By the time I got there I was, if anything, less concerned with Everton's fate as with what I was going to say to my mate's lodger. I'd already prepared some sort of excuse when I went into my front room, took a deep breath and switched on the TV.

The irony of it all is that afterwards the lad thought I must have had some sort of ESP about the game, when in reality I'd been convinced we were for the drop.

MARK WILLIAMS: I went back to the girlfriend's to tell her that I was going out to drink champagne and she'd see me when *Match of the Day* was on. I ended up pissed but it didn't make me feel any better: nothing could have done. In a strange way it was just as good as the cup final. I think to appreciate glory, you've got to understand dejection. That's why Manchester United fans are so blasé about their success.

★ ★ ★ ★ ★

Southampton and Ipswich had both drawn, whilst a goal in injury time by Chelsea's Mark Stein had condemned Dave Bassett's Sheffield United to the First Division. Everton finished 17th, three places and two points above the relegation zone. Defeat at the hands of Wimbledon would have sent them down to the First Division for the first time since before rationing was abolished.

Sheffield United had been seconds away from safety. Mark Stein will never be able to show his face in the red half of Sheffield again. In the blue half, he'll never have to buy a drink again as long as he lives.

Howard Kendall has since returned to Goodison Park, the scene of his great triumphs of the mid-'80s, and departed again. He is now quite aggressively bald. You can't look at him without being intimidated by his baldness. Howard Kendall is probably the only person in the world who would actually look better with a Bobby Charlton scrape-over hairstyle.

Everton haven't won anything since that fateful day. At the end of the 1997–98 season they again avoided relegation on the last day of the season.

A Captain's Tale

HEREFORD UNITED 1996–97

On 21 May 1983, as Gordon Smith bore down on the Manchester United goal to inspire probably the second most famous piece of football commentary ever spoken, Brighton and Hove Albion were to come within a whisker of carrying off the FA Cup when the unfortunate Smith chose to pass rather than shoot beyond a poorly positioned Gary Bailey. The game finished 2–2 and the thousands of Albion fans who had travelled to Wembley from the south coast rose to acclaim their side's spirited performance. It was the culmination of a season that had seen the Goldstone Ground side relegated from the First Division but still reach the twin towers and give Manchester United the fright of their life. It was unquestionably the pinnacle of Brighton's long history.

Whilst Brighton celebrated an historic result earned in front of the entire nation, in the Welsh borders the players and officials of Hereford United were sweating on the outcome of their third application for re-election in the space of four seasons. The club had finished bottom of the Fourth Division on goal difference from Crewe Alexandra but still nine points short of safety, and although the re-election process was in general seen as a mere formality, an air of doom permeated the club. They could not really have complained had the League elected Maidstone United in their place.

However, Hereford survived the vote along with Crewe, Hartlepool and Blackpool; Maidstone's day would come years later with disastrous consequences. The foot of the Fourth Division and crowds that rarely rose above 2,000 were a million miles away from Jimmy Melia's white dancing pumps, helicopters to Wembley and inspiring wins over Manchester City, Sheffield Wednesday and, most notably, Liverpool at Anfield.

Yet these two clubs' paths were to cross in the most heart-rending way possible on 3 May 1997, when they met at Edgar Street in the first ever head-to-head battle for League survival. Brighton had tumbled from their 1983 heights to join Hereford at the bottom end of the Football League. On cup final days, pundits often comment that it's a shame there has to be a loser. But those losers live to fight again. The vanquished at Hereford that day stood to lose their most coveted possession: their Football League status.

It was a status that Brighton had enjoyed since 1920, Hereford for a mere 25 years. The Bulls' Football League place had been earned on the back of some epic FA Cup exploits, most famously on a crisp winter's afternoon in 1972 when the waif-like Dudley Tyler danced through the mud, Fred Potter saved everything that was thrown at him in the Hereford goal, and Ronnie Radford revealed his navel to the nation as he celebrated one of the most famous goals in FA Cup history. Malcolm MacDonald, his formidable sideburns and the rest of the Newcastle United side slunk home to Tyneside on the back of a 2–1 defeat inflicted by the part-timers from the Southern League.

Twenty-five years on, Hereford United entertained Brighton on the same energy-sapping pitch that had done for Newcastle United. Well, perhaps 'entertained' is too strong a word. No one in the 8,532 crowd or amongst the two teams could have called that game remotely entertaining. Too much was at stake. Everything was at stake. This was not just another game.

The media and most of the nation were behind Brighton. Their troubles had been widely documented, and the way their fans had united to rescue their club from its malevolent administration had been justly admired. They'd seemed dead and buried for most of the season, but a late surge on a wave of mass public support had resurrected their hopes of survival so that on that fateful final day of the season, Brighton, with a superior – or rather, less inferior – goal average than Hereford, needed a solitary point to survive. Hereford needed to win. Nothing else was good enough. Never, in the ten seasons since automatic promotion and relegation between the League and Conference had been introduced, had it gone down to the wire like this, the last two endangered clubs grappling with each other to determine who would cling on to their place in the Football League. Relegation between the divisions they could handle, but both sides peered nervously into the abyss of non-League football and, given their circumstances, possible extinction.

Brighton's troubles had begun back in 1993 when, around £3 million in debt, they were rescued by a package put together by a Lancashire businessman named Bill Archer. His controlling stake in the ailing club cost him just

£56.25, and the new administration immediately set about surreptitiously removing the clause in the club's constitution stating that no profit could be made by any individuals in the event of the sale of the Goldstone Ground. This was later reinstated only when the local press uncovered the move and published it to widespread horror on the south coast.

In July 1995 the Goldstone was sold to property developers, but, ominously, no alternative site had been found for the club who were then struggling in the Second Division. The fans began to voice their disquiet and were told, in a classic PR own goal that was to characterise the actions of the club throughout the entire affair, to 'stop whining' by the club's vilified chief executive David Bellotti.

As the club plummeted towards the Third Division, no news was forthcoming on where the club would contest the following season, when 90-odd years of history had gone under the tracks of the diggers at the Goldstone. Finally the club announced that they would be staying at the Goldstone for the 1996–97 season, finding nearly half a million pounds in rent to secure the lease from the new owners.

Brighton went into the season with the future of the club wholly uncertain. They had a suspended three-point penalty hanging over them following fans' protests after a game against York City the previous year, a doomed, crumbling, weed-infested stadium which had property developers outside revving their bulldozers and checking their watches all season, and were losing money hand over fist. And no one but the fans seemed in the slightest way inclined to do anything about it.

Hereford United were in slightly better nick, but only just. They still had a ground. Although deep in the financial mire themselves – they'd lost almost £1 million in three years – the 1995–96 season, Graham Turner's first in charge at Edgar Street, saw them reach the Third Division play-offs thanks to a tremendous late run which carried them into sixth place. Despite going out to Darlington 4–2 on aggregate in the semi-finals, there was an upbeat feel about the club in the immediate aftermath of the season. Two FA Cup ties against Tottenham had brought in much-needed revenue, and with things apparently buoyant on the field, relegation was the last thing on anyone's mind at Edgar Street as the new season approached.

The club's financial uncertainty was to take its toll, however. Ageing striker Steve White, whose goals had helped the club into the play-offs, departed for Cardiff when Hereford dragged their feet over his demand for a two-year contract. Tony James went to Plymouth and Richard Wilkins returned to Essex and his old club Colchester United. With a long-term injury to goalkeeper Chris MacKenzie, Hereford suddenly found themselves without the entire backbone of the side which had so convincingly reached the play-offs. It was then that Turner signed striker Adie Foster and his former protégé David Norton, who joined from Northampton Town.

David Norton has to be one of the unluckiest men in football. When you meet him, his genial nature belies the fact that his once-promising career was decimated by career-threatening long-term injuries, injuries that would have broken a less determined, less proud man. Whilst Brighton were on their way to the cup final and Hereford were rooted to the bottom of the Fourth Division, Norton was being plucked from schoolboy football in Wolverhampton to take up an apprenticeship at Aston Villa. He earned seven England youth caps on the way, breaking into the first team in 1984 under Graham Turner in a 3–0 win at Coventry City.

Injury was to dog his career from then on. 'I've had five operations on my left knee, two on my pelvis, a hernia op and four manipulative operations,' he says, 'and I've played for most of my career with a plate welded on to my pelvic bone. That's why I left Villa in the end, even though Graham Taylor had left a four-year contract on the table for me. I just thought it was time to move on. At big clubs like Villa, they don't wait for you if you get injured. They bring a youth kid in, or just go out and buy someone for 500 grand.'

After 50 games for Aston Villa, Norton left the club which had nurtured him and given him his First Division debut and moved on to Notts County. Once again injury was to blight his prospects.

'John Barnwell was the manager at County then. He'd managed Wolves when they won the League Cup in 1980, and I was always a big Wolves fan as a kid. But when I'd played about ten games, one of the operations I'd had on my pelvis whilst at Villa broke down and I was out for 16 months. With the ten months I'd missed at Villa through injury, that meant that I'd been out for over two years of the previous three.'

Norton doesn't elaborate on the extent of his injury, but going through some cuttings later I discovered that on more than one occasion the pain in his pelvis was so bad that he was physically sick, and his wife Tracey once fainted when she saw the agony her husband was suffering. Yet, despite being told to retire on three separate occasions, Norton displayed the resilience which was to prolong and characterise his time in the game and refused to give in. During his time in the treatment room, however, things were changing at Meadow Lane.

'Whilst I was out, the team started struggling and Neil Warnock was brought in as manager. He was a power player, he wanted players of a certain size, long balls, all that sort of thing. The footballers that John Barnwell had assembled were gradually weeded out and eventually I moved to Hull City on loan. They immediately made me captain and I joined them permanently the following season. That was probably my best time in football. Hull have a tremendous pitch and some great supporters who really took to me. I was enjoying my football, playing in different positions, both at right back and in midfield. I ended up playing over a hundred games for them.'

But the combination of financial insecurity and the constant travelling from his home on the outskirts of Nottingham to Humberside was eventually to take its toll.

'The distance to Hull was a problem, and then the financial situation at the club got worse and worse. They weren't sure if they could pay the players over the summer, so because of that I didn't want to move the family from Nottingham to Hull. City could have gone under at any time and I would have uprooted them for nothing. Often we'd be paid in cash on matchdays: whatever they took through the turnstiles they'd give to us. The supporters were literally paying the players' wages.

'When I was at Notts County I'd signed a two-year contract, got injured, recovered, signed a three-year contract and, on the basis of that, bought a house in Nottingham. Then, within a week of signing, with the ink barely dry on the contract, they said I could leave. My wife had given up her job in Birmingham, we were full of expectations, and before we knew it I was on my way again. So when I was at Hull, I couldn't risk going through that again. I was travelling up and down the motorway and it was taking it out of me, so eventually I decided to move on.'

After leaving Hull City, Norton hooked up once again with his boyhood idol, the man who had taken him to Notts County.

'John Barnwell was by then the manager at Northampton Town. I knew that they were struggling at the bottom of the league and I'd be dropping down a division, but I also knew that they were moving to a new stadium and the appeal of working with John Barnwell again made it attractive for me. I originally went on loan for a couple of months at the old ground, and eventually signed up full-time at the new Sixfields stadium.'

Ironically, the financial problems that Norton had experienced at Hull were to resurface at Sixfields as Northampton struggled to make ends meet at the new stadium.

'I didn't think it could be as bad as when I was at Hull, but it was,' he recalls. 'You always thought that Hull would pull it around because they're such a big outfit, and then you go to Northampton and the cheques were never on time and when you got them you had to pay them in straightaway in case they bounced. It was a terrible situation really.'

Once again Norton outlasted Barnwell's tenure, and once again he found himself unsuited to the new manager's style of play.

'When Ian Atkins arrived at Northampton, he soon made it quite clear that I wasn't going to be his type of player. Like Neil Warnock at County he was a power-play merchant – you know, long throws, set pieces, that type of thing – and it got to the stage where every time a number would go up for someone to come off, it was my number two. We had a few differences, but only on a professional level. When Northampton got to Wembley in the play-offs he phoned me up and invited me down to travel with the team, which was nice of him.

'But the only way I can play football is in the first team, and if you're not fancied you've got to move on, so in the summer of 1996 I spoke to Graham Turner at Hereford. After a long chat, I gave Graham my word that I'd sign for Hereford as soon as we could sort out the paperwork. It was then that Plymouth came in for me, offering as much money for a year as Hereford were offering for two years. But although I'd not actually signed anything, I'd given my word to Graham and that's how I came to be at Hereford. Graham had given me my debut in the First Division when I was at Villa, and that was the major factor that swung it for me. I also knew that Hereford had made the play-offs the year before, and I hoped to help build on that and help them win promotion.

'I was looking forward to the season, because I knew how Graham wanted to play. It was such a release from the long-ball power game at Northampton, being scrutinised for everything you did. Graham lets you get on with it, and allows you to flourish as a player, giving you complete trust in yourself to do what you want to do.'

Despite this optimism, early results went against Hereford. Following a 4–0 defeat at Swansea City, who had gone into the game on the back of six successive defeats, Graham Turner's side found themselves bottom of the table by mid-September.

'We went to Swansea following a couple of games where we'd lost by the odd goal but played really well. We arrived at the Vetch fairly confident of getting a result, but ended up with two players sent off and three goals down with half an hour gone. For the second goal, they had a guy called Torpey who buried a header in the top corner from an impossible angle, and for their third, our young centre-half Quentin Townsend had gone up for a cross with Torpey and for some reason just stuck his hand up and that was a penalty. I don't know what he was trying to do. So there we were, three down with two men off and half an hour gone.

'The boss said he'd seen it coming and had to do something about it. He brought in a new coach and from then on we went from a passing team able to play in a relaxed and confident manner to being totally demoralised. We went from a footballing side to one playing percentage football, getting long throw-ins from 30 or 40 yards, trying to get corners and goals from set pieces.

'The thing about the Swansea game was that three of the goals were down to individual mistakes rather than us playing badly, and I think that maybe it was a bit of a panic decision to bring the other guy in as coach. Hereford United were all about Graham Turner, and for a long period during that season he wasn't in full control of the coaching.'

A break in the league programme came when Hereford were drawn against the Premier League glamour side Middlesbrough. These were to be two of the three games that Norton missed all season, due to a freak injury.

'It was ridiculous really. On the Sunday night I'd been lying in bed with my legs together, and the position I was in caused a tiny ligament in my knee to inflame. I trained on the Monday, and it just got worse. Like a fool I tried to run it off, but soon it just went altogether, and I missed the Boro games.'

Hereford were thrilled at the prospect of playing at the Riverside Stadium, not least for the financial bonus it would give the struggling club.

'I can remember the lads warming up. I think they were out there at about half past six, they were that excited, and we weren't kicking off until a quarter to eight. Then the Middlesbrough players came out, with Ravanelli, Juninho and Emerson, and they all looked about ten foot tall – even Juninho, who's five foot nothing! They all looked so big, solid and well defined. You see them and you can't believe you're in the same vicinity, they are such megastars. I played at Villa with some of the players who won the League and European Cup and they were big stars then, but because of all the TV coverage on Sky and everything, the World Cup, the European Championships and the Italian coverage, these players today are just mega. And it's not just the fact that they are big stars, they're such amazing footballers as well. We got tanked 7–0, and I think Ravenelli could have had about 20 that night. On the one hand you're disappointed because they're scoring against you, but on the other you're admiring the ability and skill they've got.'

Back in the league, Hereford started to pick up points and soon lifted themselves away from the bottom of the table, whilst at Brighton events off the field were hotting up. A consortium led by Dick Knight was seeking to take over the club, but the existing administration were refusing to budge unless Knight and his associates could fulfil their conditions for the construction of a new ground, something they themselves had failed to do when selling off the Goldstone.

When Archer issued a press release on the day of Albion's home game with Lincoln City on 1 October stating that he had said no to the Knight consortium and that Brighton would share Fratton Park with rivals Portsmouth the following season, protests were guaranteed. When Lincoln scored, around a hundred fans ran on to the pitch and occupied the centre circle for a few minutes before returning to the terraces to the applause of the rest of the Albion fans. This was too much for the League, however, and Albion had two points deducted as punishment for the incident.

The following week Albion travelled to Wigan Athletic, a club situated close to Archer's home in Mellor, Lancashire. A group of around 200 fans travelled to Mellor and demonstrated peacefully outside his house. Albion lost the game 1–0 and went to the bottom of the league for the first time. Ten days later they entertained Hereford in the first instalment of the clubs' head-to-head encounter. The Albion fans were planning a mass walkout at a given signal in protest at Archer and Bellotti's refusal to accept Dick Knight's consortium, and with 70 minutes gone a single firework prompted a mass movement towards the exits.

'We knew what was going to happen,' says David Norton, 'but it didn't affect us in any way apart from scaring the shit out of us when the firework went off. As soon as the game was on, we forgot all about it.

'We knew it was an important game. We'd had a bad run and had to turn it around. Even though they were bottom there were people saying we wouldn't get a result, even one or two of our own supporters, and we went out there determined to do something. For most of the game it was perfect, with everyone doing their job, and we won 1–0. For me it was a case of going back to basics. Too many players had been playing as individuals rather than as team members. We had players who wanted to take three or four men on and have a shot or whatever, but when it broke down they were out of position. It looked good at the time but they didn't realise that once the move broke down we were all over the shop defensively, and that's why we lost so many games. But that day it went right and we got the result we wanted.'

The Brighton game saw Hereford start a three-match winning run, including an excellent 3–1 win over an impressive Chester City side at the Deva Stadium.

'Chester was probably our best performance of the season: we absolutely battered them. We played the long-ball game but we also played a bit of football,' recalls Norton. 'We knew we were too good to go down. We weren't thinking of relegation. We were actually thinking at this point, hang on, we could get in the play-offs here. At that stage we were within a couple of points of my old club Northampton. Naturally I wanted to be above them, so I was following their results and we were swapping positions with them. Of course they went up via the play-offs and we ended up getting relegated.'

That same day, the Brighton fans scored a notable victory when David Bellotti was forced to leave the ground early through the sheer weight of the protests against him. Hereford's next match brought their winning run to an end with a 1–0 defeat at Cambridge, a performance which, according to David Norton, was typical of Hereford's entire season.

'We'd already beaten Cambridge in the League Cup, and we ended up losing. Basically we were too undisciplined. That was what was so frustrating all season – we just kept giving so many bloody goals away through individual errors. You'd be in a game, everything's nice and tight, okay, you might not be a goal up or anything, but then somebody would run at our centre-half, he'd slip, they'd go round him and score. Or the ball would come across and someone would head it, and 99 times out of 100 in this league they go over the bar or into the keeper's hands, but against us they would fly into the top corner. When you're at the bottom, everything goes against you, every single error gets punished.'

The Cambridge game began a disastrous run of 15 games without a win for Hereford, a period that lasted a full three months. The squad was becoming more and more demoralised.

'It got to the stage where I didn't think we'd win another game all season. I'd never known anything like it. Training was awful. You'd never look forward to it; it was all long balls and corners. The philosophy was that if you got as many set pieces or corners as you could you'd score goals, but I think if you examined our ratio between goals and set pieces you'd find it was crap. The majority of the players were against it. If it wasn't for Dean Smith, who was the comic of the side, keeping us laughing, I think a lot of the players would have gone under during this period.

'It was getting to the stage where a lot of our mistakes were comical. I scored an own goal when we went down at home to Chester, whom we'd battered at their place. The ball had gone down the left-hand side and Gavin Myers was running on to it, tracking back. Nicky Law went to meet it and they banged into one another and fell over. The lad who Gavin was marking just ran on and crossed it, and I made a lunge for the ball. It was a great goal, left foot and everything, but in our own net. Even the gaffer was saying that he was sitting on the bench all the time just expecting something silly to happen. There were so many stupid incidents which for professional footballers were just unacceptable.'

The situation wasn't much better at Brighton. On the pitch the team were anchored to the foot of the Third Division and seemed certainties for the drop into the Conference. In November, the supporters staged a boycott of the home game against Mansfield which resulted in Brighton's lowest home gate since the war. A petition against Archer was delivered to the head office of his company, Focus DIY, whilst David Bellotti was having to be smuggled in and out of games to avoid the wrath of the Brighton supporters. It was curious as to why he kept turning up. Archer was rarely, if ever, seen in the vicinity of a Brighton game. Fortunately for him.

At the home game with Darlington on 3 December, Bellotti was chased out of the ground by angry fans on what many feel was the worst day of the season for the Albion. They lost 3–2 in a highly volatile atmosphere which left the club ten points adrift at the foot of the table and led to Jimmy Case being sacked as manager. The former Charlton player and manager Steve Gritt was appointed in his place, and the new boss was startled at the hostility he received from the fans who didn't trust anyone appointed by Bellotti and Archer. Results picked up, however, and Brighton entered the new year in a more optimistic mood.

Hereford were still trying to find that elusive victory to end their dreadful run, and when they lost 5–1 at Scunthorpe, David Norton was starting to despair.

'That was never a 5–1 game. Once again it was down to individual errors. All week the coach had been hammering into us to keep a clean sheet for the first 15 minutes. He reckoned if we could hold out for the opening period we could sneak a result. He kept going on and on about keeping a clean sheet for the first quarter of an hour. Anyway, I think the game was about a minute and a half old and they'd scored. You could see everyone on our side just cave in. I think we pulled it back, they went 2–1 up, we missed a great chance, then they went straight up the other end and scored. They came off saying that they didn't know how they'd beaten us 5–1. But once again it was down to individual errors.

'It's like when we got beaten 4–1 at Wigan in November. We'd played some of our best football of the season bar the away game at Chester. Andy De Bont, our keeper, had a goal kick on the left-hand side. I was on the right-back side and I'd been saying to him all the game, if I'm on give it to me, but the rules are, as every schoolboy knows, never pass across your own goal. I looked up all of a sudden and saw he'd tried to pass the ball to me. It went nowhere near me, their centre-forward read it, collected it and they scored to make it 2–0. In the second half they scored another two basically because we had to go up their end and try to save the game. Again we were thinking, how did we lose 4–1? It was kamikaze stuff.'

The following week, on 25 January, a change of tactics brought an end to Hereford's nightmare run of results.

'We won 1–0 at Cambridge. We changed the system from five at the back to 4-4-2 and turned in a great performance, really disciplined. We should have had two or three. Oh, it was like winning the FA Cup final, that one.'

A home win over Wigan followed, and a draw against Darlington and a 3–2 win at Barnet gave Hereford the feeling that the corner had been turned.

'The win at Barnet gave us ten points out of twelve. It was a good performance, and we thought that things would happen after that. There was even a sense that if we won four or five on the trot we'd be looking at the play-offs. Unfortunately, of course, it didn't happen.'

Although they still lay in 20th spot, the Hereford side never felt that they were in particular danger, especially when they came from behind to beat top-of-the-table Carlisle at Brunton Park in February.

'At home we'd gone 2–0 down to them but come back to 2–2. Warren Aspinall was in a one-on-one with Nicky Law, he slipped and Aspinall wrapped up the points for them in the last minute of the game. Up there we'd gone out thinking we could beat them, and before we knew it we were two down again, but we came back from it and the atmosphere on the coach back was the best it had been all season. Trevor Wood saved a penalty in the last couple of minutes and we defended really well, a brilliant result for us. It made that 15-game run worth it: one really good result making up for 15 bad ones. We knew that we could beat anyone on our day, and luckily Carlisle play a footballing game which suited us. We always played better against footballing sides.'

Meanwhile, the groundswell of support for Brighton was growing apace. On 8 February, whilst Hereford were winning at Barnet, a young Plymouth fan saw his idea for a Fans United day to show solidarity for the Brighton cause come to fruition. Eight and a half thousand fans showed up from clubs all over the country, with supporters even travelling from Holland and Germany to support the Albion. Roared on by their biggest crowd of the season, Brighton swept Hartlepool aside, winning 5–0. It was by far the Albion's biggest win of the season, and the five-goal haul took them ahead of Hereford in terms of goals scored. How much of a difference did Fans United make to the future of both clubs?

The Hartlepool game came as part of a sequence of five wins in eight games. Brighton were suddenly gaining on the rest of the division. They hit the headlines again thanks to a 4–4 draw with Leyton Orient at the Goldstone on 8 March, where Carl Griffiths's over-exuberant celebrations of the O's last-gasp equaliser led to two fans running on to the pitch to remonstrate with him and the referee. Hereford, meanwhile, were undoing all the good work from the Carlisle game with a 1–0 defeat at Doncaster Rovers.

'At Carlisle we'd taken maybe 60 to 100 fans and turned them over in a really good performance,' recalls Norton. 'We took a lot more supporters to Doncaster and they booed us off the pitch. What people have to remember, though, is that sometimes, like at Carlisle, things go well for you and sometimes things just don't happen. Doncaster was one of those games where we went there confident of getting a result. They were down at the bottom and it was a big game for both of us. People questioned our commitment for the game but I strongly disagree with that. It was a bottom-of-the-table clash and I think maybe Doncaster just wanted it a little bit more on the night.'

The defeat at Doncaster saw Hereford drop to 23rd place, with Brighton catching up fast. A draw with Fulham followed, with a trip to Hull City producing the same outcome. There were five games to go, and the last game of the season at home to Brighton was beginning to look more and more significant. A change in the backroom set-up at Hereford helped, however.

'From after the Doncaster game, Graham Turner took full control of the training again, and we only lost one of the last seven games,' says Norton. 'The atmosphere was better, and it showed in the results. The coach had been slating us, really having a go, saying that we were letting the gaffer down and had the wrong attitude and stuff, then he disappeared to Bahrain for a few weeks on a coaching assignment!

'We could have got something from the Fulham game. Then we played Hull City away and got another draw, but we'd had so many chances. The pitch up there is fantastic for playing football, and so many of our players were excellent on the day, we were certainly disappointed not to win. I remember the game particularly because I got such a fantastic reception from the Hull fans. I was almost crying. They were in turmoil at that point, with the chairman and manager under a lot of pressure, but their fans were fantastic to me.'

Three valuable points were picked up against Colchester, whilst Brighton lost at Scunthorpe.

'During the run-in it was always at the back of our minds that it would go to the last game, but we really thought we'd get out of it. In the Colchester game, they threw everything at us. It must have been a crap game to watch because we ended up just booting it as far as we could for the last ten minutes and got the result we wanted. We looked at the other results and thought, yeah, we're there.

'From there we went up to Scarborough, went one up, playing well, and then in the second half Gareth Williams, who's a mate of mine from Villa and Northampton, went up and put one in. I still say to him that he cost us our League status.'

Whilst Hereford were being held at Scarborough, a Craig Maskell goal was enough to give Brighton three valuable points at the Goldstone Ground. They were now just three points behind Hereford.

The Bulls' next task was to overcome Torquay at home, a tense encounter which saw the Gulls take the lead on the stroke of half-time, only for deadline-day signing Tony Agana to salvage a point for Hereford. It was a point for Torquay that ensured their survival. 'If we'd won that game then it would have eased the pressure a bit going into the games with Orient and Brighton,' says Norton.

Brighton picked up a point at Cambridge and on 26 April faced Doncaster in the last ever game at the Goldstone Ground. The Last Post was sounded, and the Brighton fans were encouraged by the presence of Dick Knight in the directors' box. Stuart Storer notched the only goal of the game, and the last at the famous old ground, to give the Albion a 1–0 victory.

On the same day, Hereford travelled to Leyton Orient, knowing that a win would keep them up.

'I think we took about 800 supporters to Orient and they made the noise of about 8,000. It was absolutely superb. We didn't really deserve to win the game and lost 2–1. Tony Agana came on and scored, and if he'd been on for a bit longer I think he might have got a result for us.

'At the end of the game I remember looking around the ground and looking at our fans and I thought for the first time, we could go out of the League here. It was a long walk back to the dressing-room. Before, when we'd lose a game, we'd think, well, we've got next week to turn it around, but the Orient game brought it home and I started to think we're in the shit here, we're really in it.

'I'd never thought we'd go down, even during that period where I didn't think we'd win another game. Teams who win leagues and promotions do it in the first half of the season because they pick up points, whereas the mentality of a lot of our players was that when you play a game early on in the season it doesn't matter, there's no real importance to it. It's only when you come into the last third of the season that all of a sudden every game is highlighted. At the start of the season, probably up until Christmas, a lot of players don't have promotion or relegation on their mind, because they're just thinking of the game the following week. The Orient game scared the hell out of me.'

And so the unthinkable was to happen after all. It was to be a 90-minute fight to the death at Edgar Street the following Saturday. The Orient defeat put Hereford into bottom place for the first time since September, as Brighton had somehow closed the gap and overhauled them. Both clubs were now on 46 points, but Brighton had scored three more goals. Hereford needed to win, Brighton just needed a draw.

'I'm sure that if Brighton had been playing at Gillingham at that point we'd have had nothing to worry about, but they had nearly 10,000 supporters at every home game in the final stage of the season. I mean, you've got to give them credit, they were absolutely marvellous at home, but I'm sure the support gave them the extra lift they needed in those final games at the Goldstone.'

It was to be an eventful week, and an extremely nervous one.

'All week, none of us slept. I don't think I slept a wink between the Brighton and Orient games.'

David's wife Tracey interjects, 'One night, David couldn't sleep. I think it was a couple of days before the game. He came downstairs at about four in the morning, put the telly on, and they were showing Brighton's goal against Doncaster. At four in the morning!'

Suddenly, Hereford found themselves in the media spotlight, and as club captain David Norton was in great demand.

'I think I did more interviews in that week than in my entire career! There was suddenly a lot of focus on us. For the first part of the week I was so nervous and edgy it was unreal, but then, from the Thursday onwards, all of a sudden I got this big-game buzz, and I couldn't wait for the match to come around.

'In the week leading up to the game you could see that the younger players were getting nervy and it was awful, just awful. There weren't many people in the country not aware of the situation. Even my daughter's school, where I've done some coaching, had organised a minibus, but I got them to cancel it in the end because there were rumours that the Brighton fans were going to cause trouble. If they were losing at a certain point, there were rumours that they'd try and get the match abandoned.

'Sky had wanted to show the game live, and it would have meant big money for both clubs, but Brighton said no. They were worried that if there was any trouble it would have been highlighted there and then. Then the League changed the referee and brought in one with more experience than the one they'd originally appointed.'

Finally the day of reckoning, 3 May 1997, dawned grey and overcast. Edgar Street was full to bursting as the teams ran out for what was unquestionably the most important match in both their histories. Graham Turner had made a surprise change in the line-up, dropping Trevor Wood in favour of Andy De Bont in goal.

'I thought it was a great decision. Trevor's confidence was shot and he was chipping away, making mistakes. He couldn't cope with the pressure, and he's an experienced keeper, a Northern Ireland international. The gaffer had said to me in the week that he was thinking of changing the keeper and asked me what I thought as captain. I said change him, Andy will be up for it.

'Blood vessels pumping, eyes focused, the crowd getting going, we were really ready for it. And the way we started the game, the pace of it, every player, even the substitutes, the manager, the coaches, the players not involved, everyone was so geared up for it. All of us were focused on one thing, and the energy there was incredible. We battered them in the first half, absolutely battered them.'

Hereford certainly had the better of the first half, but were restricted to one goal. Brighton's keeper Mark Ormerod tipped the ball over the bar from a header by Trevor Matthewson, and from the resulting corner Tony Agana's cross-shot was turned into the net by Brighton's teenage defender Kerry Mayo. The Hereford fans erupted: salvation was in sight. For Mayo, it was the most agonising moment of his short career.

'To go in just one goal up was disappointing, and then when the second half started we were still doing all right.'

Just after the hour, disaster struck.

'We had a goal kick. Andy scuffed it, I helped it on, it came back over our heads and our centre-half was running towards it. All he had to do was pass it, but instead he chested it down and tried to clear it. He scuffed it, and when the ball came across, the lad Maskell hit it against the post and Reinelt stuck in the rebound.'

Looking at a photograph of the goal, taken as Robbie Reinelt hit the shot that put Hereford out of the Football League, David Norton falls silent for the first time all afternoon. At the edge of the picture you can see his desperate lunge, some five feet behind Reinelt. In the background the Brighton fans are on their feet, many with their hands on their heads in reaction to Maskell's shot hitting the post. Reinelt is a good two feet off the ground, caught at the precise moment of striking the ball. The long silence in David Norton's living-room makes the picture seem even more poignant. The silence becomes deafening.

'That's me there, with the skipper's band on,' he says, eventually, pointing at his prone figure, small pieces of mud frozen in mid-air dislodged by his hopeless tackle. 'I must have dived in from about ten feet away, that's how desperate it was. Awful.'

He falls silent for a few seconds. Ten months later, in the peace and quiet of his Nottinghamshire home, the noise and pressure of that fateful day, and that fateful moment in particular came flooding back.

'Awful,' he says again. 'Seeing that brings it all back . . . when they signed him, I knew he'd be a good player for them. Incredible.

'Looking at the TV coverage, I think we had a good case for offside. When I'd helped the goal kick on and the ball came back there was a lad offside, and when our centre-half tried to clear it and scuffed it there was a man offside, and I'm sure the lad stuck the ball in from an offside position. But you only see this when you watch it afterwards on the video. I think Maskell was offside when he hit the first shot.

'After they got the goal we had two good opportunities. Adie Foster had a great chance at the death. Any other time and he'd have buried it, the most important goal he'd ever score, and he hit it straight into the keeper's arms.'

That late miss was to cost Hereford the game. The television coverage showed Graham Turner, apoplectic on the touchline. 'Come on,' he's shouting, 'plenty of time, there's plenty of time!' Just as he says it, the referee blows the final whistle. In a rare sensitive piece of television coverage, the picture turns black and white and goes into slow motion. The sound of the crowd fades into silence, and all you can hear is the sound of a human heartbeat. Turner's expression turns slowly from panic and desperation to sheer unadulterated despair.

Brighton's Steve Gritt, by contrast, screamed with delight and hurtled on to the pitch to embrace his players in turn. Hereford's players slumped to the ground.

'I can't describe the feeling, you just go numb,' says Norton, visibly moved even ten months after the event. 'In the past I've heard people saying that they feel like they've had their insides ripped out and I've thought, yeah, right, but there's no other way to describe it. You just go completely numb. It's the worst feeling in the world.

'At the end of the game I was on my knees just staring at the pitch. One of their players, Dave Martin, whom I knew from Northampton, lifted me off the ground and put his arms round me. I was just totally limp. Before I knew it I was on everyone's shoulders – the fans had picked me up. I was just trying to cover my face. That was on the telly and everything.

'We got back to the dressing-room, and it was just horrible. There were 12 to 15 blokes bawling their eyes out. I'd never known anything like it. I was in the shower room just screaming my head off. There were experienced lads in there just numb; they couldn't believe what had happened. Words can't describe the feeling and the atmosphere in that dressing-room.

'Eventually I dragged myself out to the gaffer's office, and he was just sitting there. "Norts," he said, "I'm going to have to resign." He just looked devastated. You could still hear the Brighton fans singing outside. Eventually a few of the other lads drifted into the office and we managed to talk him out of jacking it in. We all felt empty, but there was a feeling that we wanted to put everything right.

'From there we went to the players' lounge and then I went to the Sportsman's Club, where the supporters were, because I wanted to show my face. There was this one supporter there who said to me, "I can't believe you players. We're all out there upset and crying and everything, and you didn't come out and do a lap of honour or anything."

'I said, "Hold on a minute, mate, you've got 15 grown men crying their eyes out in there. They think it's the end of the world. Do you think we really want to go out there and do a lap of honour? We're all totally devastated." I was just so angry, and then he started slagging off one or two of the players, saying they didn't want it and weren't bothered and all this, and I just didn't need it. Then the club chaplain came up to me and just gave me a massive hug, and Tracey turned up and just held me. They used that on the telly as well, but you're not really aware of it at the time.

'Andy De Bont was absolutely crushed. He'd blamed himself for scuffing that goal kick, yet he'd had an exceptional game. The goal kick was his only bad kick of the game. We dropped him home, Tracey and I, and he just cried non-stop in the car for a whole hour.

'At the end of it, it wasn't down to Andy's clearance or Adie's miss at the death, it was down to all the mistakes we'd made all season. We all have to take responsibility for Hereford going down. The gaffer's taken his share, I've taken mine as captain. I think in any other season, with 47 points we wouldn't have gone down. If you look at our points total, with 47 points you don't expect to go out of the League. You wouldn't even expect to get relegated, with three going down. But we all knew the system before the start of the season and we'd finished bottom of the pile.

'It's been a disastrous time, but you make your decisions and you have to believe in them. I believed I was going to Hereford to win promotion. To be relegated out of the Football League was the worst thing in the world. It'll always be with me. I think that with any team going out of the League, if you speak to the players involved they will be hurting, and you don't think you'll ever get rid of the feeling.

'I was at Aston Villa when they were relegated from the old First Division. I missed the run-in through injury, but I remember we went down when we either drew or lost against Sheffield Wednesday. There was a numbness, but you knew that Villa were a big club and had a very good chance of coming back. But nothing in football is worse than going down out of the Football League. I've been told to retire three times and had twelve operations, the lowest points of my life, but they don't come near being relegated with Hereford.

'And it doesn't just affect me, it's everybody. Tracey, the players – the only good thing is that you're all in it together. We went for a drink and a meal afterwards, about five players, the wives and girlfriends and a couple of parents. We had to share it even though we didn't want to be there.'

'We decided we didn't want to be on our own,' says Tracey, 'and it was just awful. Chris Hargreaves was just devastated. We'd been away since the Friday, and of course when we got back all the neighbours came out, but we were just trying to get into the house without anyone seeing us. We got in and played the answering machine, and because we'd been away since the Friday there were all these messages saying don't worry, you'll win, you'll be all right. Then after the game there were all these messages of condolence. It was just terrible. When I went back to work on the Tuesday, I think it was a bank holiday weekend, the people I work with just said, oh well, never mind. They couldn't appreciate what we were going through.'

It took a few days' reflection for David Norton to fully understand the enormity of the events on the pitch at Edgar Street that day.

'Relegation's a subject that hits every footballer and football fan,' he says. 'But once it happened to us, we felt as though we'd just been forgotten. We never really got too much of a mention until the final week, and then once we'd gone, there was no support. Brighton had supportive coverage all the way through, and would have had this year as well if they'd gone down instead of us, but we've been totally forgotten.

'You see our supporters at places like Carlisle, and now at grounds in the Conference, and their commitment is just unbelievable. And their feelings, they've got it with them all the time and they're just craving some success. It's a way of life. It's a way of life for a footballer as well, but on the other side of the fence we've got supporters who live and die for Hereford United. It's the same all over the country: all their attention is on football from Saturday to Saturday. If we win, the fans have a great working week; if we lose, they're really brassed off.

'It's the same for the staff as well. At a small club like Hereford everyone's got the same feelings, from the secretary to Colin who does the pitch. Even the girl who does the teas and coffees for the players, she feels it as well. The wives and girlfriends, they felt that last week with us; every single thing we went through as players, they went through as well.'

Rather than brood upon what might have been, Norton immediately set about preparing to take Hereford back up the following season, hoping that the rest of the squad would be with him.

'We had a get-together. We still had a bit of money left in the players' pool, so I wrote to everybody. I was worried everyone would go their separate ways, and thought if we all got together we could talk things through. I organised a bit of a buffet and the gaffer asked if he could come along as well. This gave him the chance to speak to one or two of the players. The message I wanted to get across was that we'd got ourselves into this, and it was our responsibility to get us out of it again. I asked them where they thought they'd go anyway – not to a good football club paying good wages, that's for sure.'

David Norton cuts a stark contrast to the footballing mercenaries of the Premier League. The supermen he'd seen at Middlesbrough seemed a million miles away here at the bottom end of the football ladder. David Norton is a player who once had the world at his feet: a first-team place at Aston Villa, England youth caps, a future England manager offering him a long-term contract. Injury and circumstances had left him struggling to hold together a squad that had just been relegated from the Football League. The irony isn't lost on him.

'Top to bottom in ten years, basically, isn't it? From playing for Villa at Anfield, drawing 3–3 after leading three times, to the game against Brighton, captaining the Hereford side that was relegated out of the League.

'I'll admit that at one stage I thought, my God, I can't play in the Conference, but the thought of going down, the faces of those Hereford supporters, weighed up against the opportunity for personal gain, there was just no question that I'd leave. Your own personal pride should tell you that you've got to do your best. I was captain when we went down, and my pride told me that I had to captain Hereford back up again. Too many people go down and immediately want to move on somewhere else. I think you've got to have a bit more responsibility and see it through.

'I took a wage drop to come to Hereford. I changed our mortgage to a fixed-rate mortgage to help pay my way purely because I wanted two years of enjoyable football.'

After all his battles against injury, David Norton at least deserved that. But even that was to be denied him.

'I knew Graham Turner, I knew one or two of the players and I thought Hereford United was a club with the potential to win promotion to the Second Division. Unfortunately it all went the wrong way.

'The first week after we went down was a nightmare, but after that, once I'd got the meeting together with the lads, I was just so up for it. I wanted to get back training straightaway – right back in the middle of May, this was. I didn't think there could be any more motivation to get back up than what happened at the end of that season.'

The opportunity for David Norton to take Hereford United back into the Football League was cruelly snatched away barely half a dozen games into the new season, when his injury-blighted career was finally ended on the training ground. All the years of struggle, the constant pain and battles for fitness that he had endured, it all came to an anti-climactic end on a windswept training ground in October 1997.

'We were training the day before a game against Stevenage Borough. We were doing a few one-on-ones, which is funny, because you don't normally do those the day before a game. I was tracking Brian McGorry and he was turning me inside out. I was staying with him, but just at the death he got half a yard on me and I lunged at him full stretch. My knee hit the ground before it should have done and it pulled the tendon away from the bone. I didn't allow it to heal properly. I played a game against Colchester in the FA Cup and just felt a bit tired, but then trained for two or three days when I should have rested it. That was it, the end of my career. Originally the club were going to pay for an operation, but then when the gaffer looked into the financial situation he was told the club just couldn't afford it. Even though I'd only missed three games, over my two-year contract my ratio of games played wouldn't be enough with a long-term knock. That was what made my mind up, really, and I announced my retirement not long afterwards. Everything that's happened to me in the last two years you wouldn't expect to happen in an entire career.

'It's been the same for Hereford as a club this season. We've had Tony Agana out, Ian Foster's been out for four months, I've been out and had to retire, Trevor Matthewson was out for twelve weeks, Brian McGorry, our engine room in the midfield, he got some mystery virus and you couldn't get any energy out of him. The financial side of the club is all over the place and we've gone five or six weeks with no wages. It just seems like everything's another brick in a wall put up against the gaffer and Hereford. But the gaffer just goes from strength to strength, and wants to play a big part in rebuilding the club. The supporters are very passionate, they want to win the Conference so badly, and I think the club's got a chance next year.'

But for all his desire to oversee Hereford's return to the League, David Norton is reduced to watching from the sidelines. The Brighton game was to be his last in the Football League. Unlike many players, however, he refuses to be downhearted, despite the fact that the tremendous potential he had as a youngster has not been fulfilled. He now has ambitions both inside and outside the game.

'I'd love a crack at management,' he says. 'I believe I've got a lot of ability, but I haven't fulfilled the potential that I had, and maybe it's got to come out a different way. It might be coaching, it might be something else, but I believe in myself, the ability I have, and you've got to go on to the next thing.'

'David's very well thought of,' says Tracey. 'Every club he's been at he's been well thought of, not just as a good player but as a good professional. The manager said the other week at a supporters' forum that David is the best pro he's ever met.'

Despite the catalogue of injuries and disappointments that marred what could have been a successful career, David Norton's friendly, laid-back manner disguises a grim determination to succeed, to make up for the opportunities that have passed him by through no fault of his own. He loves the game, loves football being played the way it should be played, and takes great pride in his work. His enthusiasm for the game is unabated.

'You've got to be honest with yourself and put everything you've got into it. I had injuries that should have finished me years ago, but I found ways around them. I was doing yoga more or less every day for five years. That was the only way I could carry on playing. There's no way you can kid yourself. You have to prepare yourself. If you prepare yourself thoroughly you'll get somewhere.'

His ill luck didn't end with his playing career, however. Shortly after sustaining the injury that finally ended his playing days, Norton's father died. Then, a couple of months later, the small sports equipment printing company he had started, Montana Designs, lost everything in a burglary.

'We'd got it together at a friend's property at the back of his house, everything got going nicely and then we were burgled. They took the lot. But we got it going again and now I've moved it into the house.'

I search his expression for some sign of strain, exasperation or even defeat, but the sparkle is still there. He even chuckles as he recalls the burglary. David Norton refuses to be beaten, on or off the pitch. In his life as well as his career, he continues to battle against the unfair doses of adversity that seem to come his way.

'Everything had to be put on hold. Then with my dad dying, my injury as well, trying to train but falling short all the time, it was awful. But I've got my family, I've got my daughter and that's the most important thing. At the end of it football is just a game, but that game is so important to so many people. My only regret is not being able to take Hereford United back up.'

It's evident that the most frustrating thing for Norton is that this final injury, one unconnected with the pelvic trouble that had dogged his career, deprived him of the opportunity to put right what happened to Hereford United. It's a burden that is obvious, even behind his outwardly jovial nature. The steely determination which fuelled his battles with injury will stand him in good stead for the future. That very morning he'd been for an interview with a company hoping to set up a chain of football schools of excellence, and his old club Notts County have been in touch about the possibility of coaching youngsters at Meadow Lane. So despite the setbacks and bad luck, the future looks bright for David Norton. 'When I'm a top manager, make sure you come back and interview me,' he calls after me as I leave.

Hereford United will probably return to the Football League. David Norton won't, at least not as a footballer. That incredible occasion at Edgar Street was to be the last time he stepped on to a football pitch as a Football League player. Leafing through his scrapbook, looking beyond the dodgy '80s hairstyles, Norton's memories are mainly of injuries, struggle and pain. The majority of the cuttings are tributes to his courage and determination; one even shows him receiving an engraved goblet in recognition of his bravery in fighting the career-threatening injury he sustained at Notts County. Injury cheated David Norton out of a successful football career, but you won't find a trace of bitterness.

In the Norton living-room the only reference to his long career is a small framed photograph, not the centre-piece of the room but hanging modestly next to the kitchen door. Taken during his time at Northampton, the picture shows him with the ball at his feet, striding determinedly forward, gazing upfield, looking for an opening, searching for the next opportunity.

David Norton isn't finished yet, not by a long way.

Armani Jackets and Scruffy Jeans

MIDDLESBROUGH'S MISSING POINTS

'It seems every club has its price, but what a price! Fancy a club like Middlesbrough paying as much as that for a single player,' said the newspapers.

'A truly sensational transaction,' said the FA chief.

Juninho? Emerson? Ravanelli? Gazza? You're about 90 years out. The newspaper was the *Athletic News* of 20 February 1905, and the FA chief was W.C. Pickford, all three-piece suit, watch chain and bristling moustache. The transaction that caused so much furore was not the import of another overseas star at an inflated price, but the signing of the genial Wearsider Alf Common from Sunderland, just around the corner, to become the first ever £1,000 footballer.

Boro, second from bottom of the First Division and without an away win for two years, were trying to buy their way out of trouble and did so in the most spectacular fashion, smashing the transfer-fee record for a player who had cost Sunderland a third of the price when they had signed a homesick Common from Sheffield United a few months earlier.

Unlike Boro's superstars of the 1990s, however, Common managed to keep Boro in the top flight: on his debut at his old club Sheffield United, the portly striker scored the only goal of the game. At the end of the season Middlesbrough stayed up by two points. And they'd turned up to all their matches that year, so were able to keep all their points.

Eighty-one years later, on the opening day of the 1986–87 season, Middlesbrough were lining up for a home game with Port Vale in the Third Division at the Victoria Ground, Hartlepool. The Official Receiver had padlocked the gates at Ayresome Park as a financially crippled club awaited a new consortium to bail them out of the mire, and the trip along the coast was necessary for Middlesbrough to fulfil their fixtures and avoid expulsion from the League. Expensive signings were out of the question. The main pre-occupation for the 3,500 fans present that day, the lowest crowd in Boro's history, was the question of whether they would still have a club to support the following week. New all-seater stadia, world-class players and season-ticket sell-outs within a decade were not even pipe dreams; groundsharing with a club traditionally so far below Boro that they couldn't be considered rivals, in the lower reaches of the Third Division, in front of a cynical hard-core of under 4,000 was the grim reality. The phrase 'Cellnet Riverside' was more likely to concern the hawking of the club's goalnets around the shipyards to raise a few quid than anything else.

Exactly ten years later, with doom long ago averted, Middlesbrough were lining up against Liverpool as members of the cash cow that is the FA Premier League at their swanky new stadium with a team packed with Brazilian and Italian internationals. The noughts on their bank statements were in black, not red. It was a long way from Hartlepool.

Boro won successive promotions in 1986–87 and 1987–88 and arrived in the First Division a little too quickly. Down they went. Three seasons followed in the new First Division, until promotion was won again under Lennie Lawrence. Once again Middlesbrough lasted only one season in the top flight, and in 1994 they appointed Bryan Robson as manager. Robson took Boro back into the Premier League at his first attempt.

On 3 November 1995, Robson pulled off an amazing coup when he signed the Brazilian Footballer of the Year Oswaldo Giroldo Junior, or Juninho as he was to become immortalised on the back of thousands of replica shirts and in tattoos in the ensuing 18 months. The national press immediately reached for their dictionary of clichés and came up with numerous ill-informed com-parisons between the supposed cultures of Brazil and Teesside. Needless to say, the words 'samba' and 'beach' were bandied about with all the restraint of Ainsley Harriott plugging his latest cookery show, whilst words like 'poverty' and 'national debt' were strangely missing. Middlesbrough, mean-while, from the cosy offices of London, was a wasteland; mutants prowled the smog-bound streets in arctic temperatures, the products of overexposure to the chemical pollution from the region's numerous noxious fume-emitting chemical plants. Juninho was swapping a life of non-stop sun-drenched partying with a little football thrown in for what Michael Herd of that well-known Teesside journal the *London Evening Standard* described as 'one of the most ravaged industrial landscapes on earth'. Michael Herd has probably never been further north than Highbury. The attitude of the London-based media was understandably to engender feelings of deep paranoia at Middlesbrough, feelings which were to work against them in the coming months.

Juninho, five foot five in his stockinged feet, became an instant hit on Teesside. Signed by Robson, who is much admired in Brazil, from São Paulo for £4,500,000 (or 4,500 Alf Commons), Juninho grinned, charmed and played his way into the hearts of the traditionally cynical Middlesbrough fans. Rarely has there been such unadulterated adulation for a single player.

Hopes were high at the Riverside following the 1995–96 Premiership season, especially when Robson announced the signing of another Brazilian, Emerson, from Porto for £4 million. This was immediately followed in July by the capture of Italian international Fabrizio Ravanelli from Juventus for another club record fee of £7 million. Middlesbrough were spending wildly: there were rumours of an £11 million bid for Fiorentina's Argentinian international Gabriel Batistuta, and Ravanelli's weekly wage alone was rumoured to be somewhere between £26,000 and £42,000, depending upon which newspaper you read. Could they buy their way to success?

The club had in ten years gone from an affectionately regarded sleeping giant, playing to meagre crowds in a vast, echoing stadium, to a behemoth of wealth and glamour, with fans talking in hushed whispers of a place in Europe. Boro were a big club not because of their record on the field, but because they have a big, loyal support. The trophy cabinet had always been bare – Tommy Docherty's Molineux Japanese prisoner of war was rumoured to have taken up residence – with only a couple of Second Division championships and two Amateur Cup wins in the nineteenth century troubling the local engravers. Oh, and the Anglo-Scottish Cup in 1976, of course.

Middlesbrough seemed to have existed perpetually in the shadow of their more illustrious neighbours Sunderland and near-neighbours Newcastle United. Now, they had suddenly become a force in the Premiership, on paper at least, backed by high finance and with a spanking new ground to boot. Boro fans' traditional air of resigned self-deprecation was replaced with a new vigour, a feeling that, after a hundred years of teasing, Middlesbrough Football Club was at last going to provide them with something to celebrate.

On the opening day of the season, a sun-drenched capacity crowd at the Riverside Stadium watched their Italian international striker bang in a hat-trick in a thrilling 3–3 draw with highly fancied Liverpool. A week later Juninho bagged his first of the season in a 1–1 draw with Nottingham Forest. West Ham were thrashed 4–1 and Coventry 4–0 in the space of seven days at the Riverside, and in mid-September, following a 2–1 win at Everton where Boro came from behind to steal the points, Middlesbrough sat handily placed in sixth position. Ravanelli was averaging a goal a game, Juninho one every other game, and Boro fans were dreaming of a place in Europe the following season.

Geoff Vickers, a lifelong Boro fan now resident in St Albans, Hertfordshire, runs Middlesbrough Supporters South, an organisation for Boro fans exiled in the south of England. MSS travel to every Boro game, home and away, through travel arranged by Vickers.

'Yes, a European place was on our minds at that point,' he says. 'The pre-season signings of Emerson and Ravanelli had sparked off a massive feeling of anticipation which was fuelled by the first game of the season, the 3–3 draw with Liverpool. The Ravanelli hat-trick, the shirt over the head thing, that got everybody up. In September we brushed aside West Ham and Coventry and were definitely playing with the assurance of a top-six side.'

Robert Nichols, editor of the Middlesbrough fanzine *Fly Me to the Moon*, the first fanzine to reach 200 issues, was similarly optimistic. 'For the first time since the days of Jack Charlton in the '70s, we thought we had a team of contenders. We'd unearthed an absolute gem in Emerson and thought he would be the top midfielder in the Premiership, we had the European Cup winner Ravanelli scoring regularly, and Juninho was really starting to shine.

'We were full of hope, and then came that week in early September when we played West Ham and Coventry off the park. We were playing scintillating football and actually converting it into victories. We went away to form team Everton and Robson was quoted as saying this was the real test. We came back from 1–0 down to win 2–1, including a Nicky Barmby lob. We didn't win another game for months!

'I have to say that in early September we thought we could be outsiders for the title, things were beginning to look that good. As for the cups, well no one in Middlesbrough talked about cups. We had too many bad memories.'

The Everton win was followed by a 7–0 pillage of Hereford United in the Coca-Cola Cup, making a total of fifteen goals in three games for Boro. But then things started to go wrong. A 2–0 reverse at home to Arsenal was followed by a 4–0 stuffing at Southampton. The Saints hadn't won a game all season and had picked up just two points, but a brace from Matthew le Tissier helped to bring Boro's flyaway start to a juddering halt.

Geoff Vickers recalls the game. 'Actually, we had a lot of the play at the Dell but missed a penalty, and at the end Barmby hit the underside of the crossbar. The defence, however, was particularly weak, and we missed skipper

Nigel Pearson. We were cruelly exposed, and the defence that day contained two players who were never to play for us again: Phil Whelan and the ridiculous Branco.'

The first cracks in Boro's season were beginning to appear. Whilst they were magnificent in attack, the defence looked flimsy, particularly when the opposition ran at them. 'We tried a few changes at the Dell,' recalls Robert Nichols. 'Phil Whelan played; he'd been red-carded there the season before and he really felt the pressure of the weight of history. Also it was patently obvious to everyone except the management that he was nowhere near good enough. Branco started at left back having starred in the two Coca-Cola Cup games with Hereford, but at Southampton he looked painfully slow.

'We weren't too downhearted, because everyone felt it was just one of those days. Just one of those games where nothing goes your way. In hindsight, however, there was already a lot wrong in the camp. Middles-brough flew off to the Far East on a tour, and you have to question doing that mid-season. By the end of the tour, Branco had gone, John Hendrie had gone and Barmby was on his way. Clearly something had gone off out there. There must have been arguments.'

Barmby joined Everton for £5.75 million, with Robson claiming he was 'too similar to Juninho', whilst Ravanelli was publicly linking himself with any club that happened to be doing well at the time. Predictably, results didn't improve. Boro threw away the lead twice at Sunderland and crashed 3–0 at home to Spurs. A 0–0 draw with Wimbledon at the Riverside saw skipper Nigel Pearson pick up an injury that would keep him on the sidelines for most of the season. The antithesis of Boro's glamour boys, the former Shrewsbury Town and Sheffield Wednesday defender was a rock at the back. Robert Nichols describes him as 'the backbone of the side. He is like the manager on the pitch: he leads, he talks and he commands respect from his team-mates. The defence was often all at sea without him and the team would often fragment into a group of individuals. Nigel's presence throughout the season would have prevented Ravanelli from bleating about the defence (would you dare criticise Nigel Pearson? A formidable bloke indeed) and Nigel would have demanded 100 per cent attitude on the park. As fans we were disheartened by the players' attitude at the end of games; with Nigel around he would always insist that they come over and applaud our supporters. Without him they'd just troop off.'

Vickers agrees. 'This was the time when I called us the "split" team. We were a bit like a guy wearing an Armani jacket and a pair of torn, scruffy jeans. We had a quality team going forward, but without Pearson our defence was just not good enough for this level. Players like Chris Morris, Neil Cox, Phil Whelan and Derek Whyte had been found wanting too often, and Steve Vickers lost a lot of confidence without Nigel alongside him.'

'Almost as importantly,' continues Nichols, 'Middlesbrough became sidetracked with the fruitless pursuit of Barcelona's Nadal to replace Nigel. We knew an ordinary centre-half was not good enough: we needed a captain. But Barcelona led us on and then right up the garden path; the chase didn't go cold until several months later. People were so certain he'd join that Ladbrokes had him down in their odds! Meanwhile, we kept shipping goals and shedding points.'

In the first week of November, Middlesbrough were convincingly beaten at St James' Park, a result which pushed Newcastle to the top of the league but left their near-neighbours floundering in 15th place.

Three days later, Emerson went back to Brazil to visit a sick aunt. Whilst there he announced that his wife couldn't settle in England and that he had played his last game for Middlesbrough. 'If they insist I return I will simply refuse to play,' said the midfielder. Five days later, Juninho told the Italian press, 'If any offers were to come in from Italy, I would want to discuss them. The real problem with English football is its structure. Even the tiniest club in Italy is better organised than over here.' Meanwhile, Liverpool were apparently that week's destination for Ravanelli. Boro's dream team looked to be falling apart by the day.

Nichols recalls, 'We woke up to headlines screaming things like "Emo says I quit". We were then dragged through the dirt nationally and internationally. We were bemused, sickened and extremely downhearted. This man was an absolute star; we felt the world would cave in if he left.'

'There were all sorts of stories circulating in the press, who were stoking up the "Boro fall to pieces" headlines,' says Vickers. 'Agents were constantly lurking and the club had to issue frequent denials of the latest rumours. Ravanelli was opening his mouth over in Italy, where he was on international duty, and criticising the training facilities. He'd established himself as a bit of a rent-a-quote by now, and so we didn't really take much notice of the stuff he was coming out with.'

Robert Nichols was less charitable. 'The whole thing appeared to be coming apart at the seams,' he says. 'The dream was fast turning into a nightmare and in the meantime the team was losing game after game.

'The media outbursts seemed to be developing into a pattern. Every time Robson or club officials were away there would be reports in the press, so they couldn't immediately refute them; Ravanelli and Juninho would later deny them; Ravanelli's were always taken from interviews he gave whilst away on international duty. Now we didn't know who to trust. Everyone was constantly on the defensive. Team spirit must have been in tatters. They needed big Nigel in the dressing-room.'

At Christmas, Middlesbrough hadn't won a game in the Premiership since the victory at Goodison way back in September, a run of 12 games without a win which yielded just four points. On 14 December Boro were hammered 5–1 at Anfield and slipped to 16th place. Ravanelli announced that Middlesbrough were unable to avoid the drop.

A week later Middlesbrough were due to visit Ewood Park to face Blackburn Rovers. Boro, however, were decimated with injuries and a flu bug, a situation that put no fewer than 23 players out of contention, as if the club wasn't demoralised enough. Robson announced that he didn't have enough players fit to put a team out, and sought to postpone the game. A call to the Premier League two days before the match was due to take place drew a noncommital response, with the League's Rick Parry apparently pretending to be out, so Boro felt justified in not turning up at Blackburn.

Robert Nichols was relieved to hear that the game was off. 'We'd just been slaughtered 5–1 at Anfield and the team looked in total disarray. Robbo looked visibly tired and had just been publicly humiliated by being thrown out of a wine bar in Stockport on a bouncer's back, a wine bar that he'd just opened. Everyone was under real pressure, and the fans felt it too. With the Blackburn game off we could relax for the weekend and not have to worry about taking on fast-reviving Blackburn away. I didn't think a great deal of it at first because teams are often said to be on the verge of calling off games because of flu. Wasn't this just the same?'

Geoff Vickers felt the same way. 'Remember we were coming off the back of a 5–1 hammering at Anfield. I think the club thought we stood no chance of beating another struggling team like Blackburn. Games had been called off due to illness before, we had given 36 hours notice, but the communication channels between club and League appeared to be problematic, to say the least. I remember first hearing from a colleague at a work Christmas party that the game was off and I immediately thought, "We can't do that; what's going on?" A feeling that later turned out to be well-founded.'

Middlesbrough were vilified in the press, receiving scant sympathy from a media who seemed determined to knock them down at every turn for having the temerity to challenge the established order. 'We were being attacked from all quarters and defended the decision,' says Vickers.

Boro's paranoia was exacerbated by their indignation. The club felt victimised and persecuted. In hindsight, Robert Nichols concedes that the club could have handled the situation better than they did. 'Obviously you can't deny it was a massive mistake, as was the way we prepared for the hearing and the subsequent appeal. We shouldn't have stormed off on a wave of publicity to George Carman, we should have tried to quietly broker a deal. I still feel terribly let down by the Premier League, though. I don't understand why they sought to punish us. We have alleged time and time again that the club had sought advice but were misdirected on the day. The Premier League has never had to explain its actions: why did Rick Parry and his assistant pretend to be out of the building when the club called Premier League headquarters? We were apparently told we could go ahead and call the game off. If you read Boro chairman Steve Gibson's letter to the Premier League, to which, incidentally, he never received a reply, you'll realise that the Premier League's own guiding body did nothing to help us and were extremely heavy-handed over the whole situation.'

Both Vickers and Nichols agree, however, that the game shouldn't have been called off. 'God knows why we didn't play the game,' says Nichols. 'We did have 15 players, we could have put out a side. We should have waited until the day of the game when the flu epidemic would have reduced the squad further; what could the Premier League have done then?' It was a situation that was to have grave repercussions come May.

The rest seemed initially to have done Middlesbrough good: on Boxing Day two goals from Juninho, returning from a month's lay-off with injury, steered the team to their first win since September, completing the double over Everton with a 4–2 victory. The next three games were lost, however, and left Middlesbrough bottom of the table for the first time. Then, on 14 January, the Premier League announced that Middlesbrough's punishment for failing to fulfil their fixture at Blackburn Rovers would be a deduction of three valuable points. Ravanelli, helpfully, ran straight to the newspapers. 'Middlesbrough are going down,' he said. 'It saddens me to say it, but the situation is truly tragic.' He stopped just short of asking them to print his agent's telephone number.

Bottom of the league and with three points fewer than they'd thought they had, it was a double blow which could have finished Boro's season there and then. 'We thought we were completely doomed,' says Robert Nichols. 'We were stranded way below the pack. But what it did was produce an astonishing fightback. We were shocked, completely dumbfounded, at the time of the hearing. We'd expected a fine, yes, but a three-point deduction? No way. The whole town was numb and then very, very angry. We fought back as the situation galvanised us into action. Already paranoid that the world had it in for us, we protested and all pulled together, on and off the pitch. Chairman Steve Gibson talked to the squad and management and we roared back against Sheffield Wednesday 4–2.'

Geoff Vickers picks up the story. 'It was a siege mentality that led Steve Gibson to call a crisis meeting which included the club management, the staff and the players on Friday 18 January. The next day we took Sheffield Wednesday apart 4–2. Juninho sparkled and the crowd showed its undying support. The chant "stand up if you love Boro" started at this game and became a recurring theme ['even in the directors' box,' interjects Nichols], and I had tears welling in my eyes when the whole ground stood up in unison. Steve Gibson was standing too: his rallying call had worked, and the morale of the club was boosted a great deal.'

'We would show the bastards,' asserts Nichols, 'and survive in spite of them. We also thought we could get the ruling overturned. We knew the world of football seemed to be against us, but felt the sentence to be a draconian, knee-jerk reaction. Surely they had to reconsider? It was unjust and excessive.

'The media gloating made us very insular and deeply paranoid, but it pulled us together as a community. It was as if we were taking on the world. In a negative way we began to feel increasingly cursed. Referees were against us too, and I'm sure that this paranoia clouded the club's vision in its strategy to win back the points.'

The club was confident that on appeal the three points would be restored. Geoff Vickers organised the Middlesbrough Supporters South Christmas party, held in London in February to coincide with an away match at Wimbledon. 'That night Keith Lamb, the club's chief executive, assured us that the three points would be restored. We all believed him because the penalty was very harsh. We remembered the 12 points that Spurs had had deducted a few seasons earlier, which were eventually returned in exchange for a heavier fine. We thought that maybe now the Premier League had been seen to flex their muscles they'd give us the points back and double or triple the fine.'

The Boro fans certainly did their bit, mobilising themselves into a campaign that saw 18,000 protest cards being filled out and delivered to the headquarters of the Football Association in London. Geoff Vickers was one of the supporters who took the sackloads of cards to Lancaster Gate in early February.

'I was quoted at the time as saying that the motto on the FA flag was "Fair

Play", and that that was the treatment we wanted. On the very same day Shrewsbury Town were given permission to call off an Auto Windscreens Shield match due to illness and injury. There was never any doubt at the time that we'd get the three points back.'

If Boro were struggling in the league, however, by February they were flourishing in the cups. In the Coca-Cola Cup they'd seen off Hereford United (10–0 on aggregate), Huddersfield Town and Newcastle United, and would also account for Liverpool and Stockport County before losing in the final to Leicester City after a replay, and they'd overcome Chester City and Hednesford Town in the FA Cup. Wembley beckoned again when Boro went on to defeat Derby County and then Chesterfield in two classic games in the semi-finals. The cup runs were to prove a welcome distraction from the tribulations of the Premier League, but were to take their toll in terms of the huge number of games to be played as the season wore on.

'We didn't feel that the cups were having a detrimental effect on the league until after the Coca-Cola Cup final,' says Vickers. 'The 1–1 draw with Leicester meant that after a gruelling extra half-hour we faced another fixture. Tiredness did creep into the league performances and certainly accounted for key defeats at Sheffield Wednesday, home to Sunderland and at Spurs.'

'At first the cup games really helped,' continues Nichols. 'It took our minds off the dogfight and helped boost confidence and morale amongst the players and supporters. We'd never previously reached a Wembley final and never got past the quarter-finals of the FA Cup. When we achieved these goals it was historic and a tangible achievement for the club. Things were only positive. On the other hand, there is no doubt that we lost game after game following cup wins. We'd hammer Chester 6–0 and then lose at home to bottom club Southampton. It happened time after time.

'At the time I thought the positive aspects exceeded the negative, but, looking at the record books, we lost about five league games after cup wins. So in hindsight it's obvious that it was tearing the heart out of our survival cause.'

March proved to be a good month on the pitch for Middlesbrough. Early in the month Ravanelli's second hat-trick of the season contributed to the 6–1 stuffing of Derby County at the Riverside, Leicester were then beaten at Filbert Street, and Blackburn and Chelsea left Teesside pointless. These four league wins on the trot were interspersed with the FA Cup quarter-final win, again over Derby. 'We'd reached our first ever semi-final, and we didn't lose another league game until 19 April,' enthuses Vickers.

'We were on a roll,' continues Nichols. 'Robson got the Manager of the

Month award and Juninho was playing like a world-beater. He was taking teams apart on his own: his performances at Leicester and in the home game with Chelsea must be amongst the most complete ever seen in the Premiership. We had pulled together both on and off the pitch and now we were showing everyone what we were capable of in the league and in the Coca-Cola Cup. We felt sure that this spirit would carry us through and at this stage we were confident that we would finish comfortably above the drop zone.'

On 26 March, however, Middlesbrough's season was dented yet again. Steve Gibson and Bryan Robson arrived at the appeal hearing to be told that the three-point deduction they'd been so confident of retrieving would remain in place. The appeal had failed. As he left the hearing, a stony-faced Robson was given, with crass bad timing, the Manager of the Month award. He didn't smile for the cameras.

Geoff Vickers thinks Boro were made scapegoats. 'I think the FA had made their minds up to make an example of Middlesbrough. The press were very much anti-Boro. We'd hired top lawyer George Carman QC and they hated us for it. Mind you, he was the most expensive flop ever.'

'It was a terrible blow,' laments Nichols. 'A real shock. Even the football pundits had seemed confident that a compromise would be reached. Despite the blow, we still thought we could stay up. We were playing so well, and with the players we had we knew that we were better than the teams around us. It would have been nice to relax with the Coca-Cola Cup final.'

A week later came the draining game with Leicester City at Wembley. Apparently on the way to a famous victory, Boro conceded a late equaliser to take the game to extra time and eventually a replay at Hillsborough. Seven days later, Second Division Chesterfield secured a semi-final replay with Boro, when Jamie Hewitt's goal in injury time of extra time made the final score 3–3, and three days later Boro endured another strength-sapping period of extra time in the Coca-Cola Cup final replay, going down to a Steve Claridge goal. Three high-profile, hard-fought games in ten days had gone to extra time. The Boro players were shattered.

'The fans were left absolutely drained, so God knows what it did to the players,' says Nichols. 'There was just one devastating disappointment after another, and I'm sure it got to us mentally as well as physically. We lost a crucial home game with Sunderland after the Coca-Cola defeat: we were totally drained and unfocused. There is no question that the extra times were instrumental in this defeat. The Sunderland result was important and I thought we were down.'

'Without doubt,' agrees Vickers. 'The Leicester and Chesterfield equalisers were crushing blows, for they meant more games that we didn't need. The defeat at home to Sunderland was the real downer: I thought that was that.'

Robert Nichols asserts that the Coca-Cola final was a crucial moment: 'We were leading with two minutes left and Coventry were a goal down in the league to Liverpool. Victory for us and defeat for Coventry would have ensured our survival, of that I am completely convinced, but a last-minute goal by Dion Dublin gave them a vital win.'

By the end of April Middlesbrough were in deep trouble at the foot of the Premiership, but had finally overcome Chesterfield to reach their first ever FA Cup final, their second Wembley appearance of the season. However, two days later, Boro met Spurs at White Hart Lane.

Playing so soon after the semi-final was seen as another example of football's grudge against Middlesbrough.

'Being forced to play Tottenham on the Thursday two days after the replay was cruel and wrong. The game should have been delayed at least 24 hours, but Alan Sugar insisted that it went ahead. We were tired, but still should have won. That defeat extinguished our hopes.'

Geoff Vickers left White Hart Lane a dejected man. 'When we lost 1–0 at Tottenham we traipsed out of the ground convinced that we were relegated. We faced four matches in eight days and needed a minimum of nine points from a home game with Aston Villa and away games at Manchester United, Blackburn Rovers and Leeds United. We were exhausted after three games in seven days: a Tees-Wear derby, an FA Cup semi-final and a vital match at Spurs.'

With four games left, Boro were in desperate trouble at the foot of the table, and hadn't scored in their previous three matches. Aston Villa were the visitors for Middlesbrough's last home game of the season, when Boro clinched the points with a last-minute penalty to make the score 3–2.

'It was our last shot and once again we decided to really go for it. We used the cup experiences to make the Riverside a cauldron of noise and give the players a lift, and there were flags, scarves and banners everywhere,' recalls Nichols. 'We ripped into them and went 2–0 up, then they came back to 2–2 and we were awarded a last-ditch penalty. Half the crowd couldn't watch.'

Geoff Vickers wasn't one of them. 'It's funny, really, I usually get very tense at matches and under normal circumstances wouldn't have dared look at Ravanelli's last-minute penalty. In the end I thought I've gone through so much this season anyway, and watched fairly calmly. If he'd missed, we were down.'

That left Boro with three away games at Manchester United, Blackburn

Rovers and Leeds United. All daunting prospects for a team fighting for its life.

'The foreign players said goodbye to the Riverside with a lap of honour, which was a bit ominous,' recalls Nichols. 'Few people thought we'd get anything at Old Trafford, and three away games in a week was surely beyond our flagging squad. Yet the thing about that season was that with every match our hopes would lift again, at times almost from the grave.'

Remarkably, Middlesbrough went 3–1 up at Old Trafford within the first 40 minutes as Juninho, Emerson and Craig Hignett each found the target. Roy Keane made it 3–2 before half-time, and Ole Gunnar Solskjaer rescued a point for the champions midway through the second half. 'United could have clinched the title if they'd won that day,' recalls Geoff Vickers. 'In the end we were happy with a draw even though we had been 3–1 up and playing well.'

Robert Nichols agrees that this was a point gained by Boro rather than two lost. 'To draw at Old Trafford has to be seen as a point gained, but we could have won the game. As it was we gave ourselves renewed hope, but at the enormous cost of losing Ravanelli with a hamstring injury.'

Having come away from Manchester United with a valuable point, Boro's next opponents were Blackburn Rovers. They travelled to Ewood Park for the rearranged match from December when Boro were consuming Lemsip by the bucketload and cancelling their transport to Lancashire to stay in the warm. Five places above Boro, Rovers went into the game having chalked up just one win in their previous seven matches. For a team with a less hectic schedule, this match could have been easy pickings, but exhausted Boro couldn't break down Rovers' defence. Late in the game, referee Paul Durkin fanned the flames of the conspiracy theorists by waving away claims for a penalty when Juninho was felled in the area under a clumsy challenge by Colin Hendry.

'It was a definite penalty,' remembers Geoff Vickers. 'Paul Durkin had denied us clear penalties earlier in the season at Derby County. It was just the latest in a long line of events that seemed to conspire against us.'

Robert Nichols recalls, 'We were all so wound up for this one it was unreal. If we had attacked them they would have cracked, and we were absolutely incensed by the refereeing. It was a penalty, and we'd have stayed up if we'd put it away. Bloody Blackburn! The Boro fans had desperately wanted to win this one because of the three points and the unsavoury comments made by Tony Parkes about the postponement. But on the day, we never really went for it.'

Which left Boro with one game to play, at Elland Road. With Forest already down, four teams were in danger of filling the two remaining relegation places. Coventry City seemed to be the favourites for the drop; on the Saturday morning they occupied 21st position with 38 points, the same as Middlesbrough but with an inferior goal difference. The Sky Blues travelled to White Hart Lane. Two points ahead of both Coventry and Boro in 19th place were Sunderland, who faced a tricky encounter with Wimbledon at Selhurst Park. Southampton, on 41 points, travelled to Aston Villa. Even a win might not have been enough for Middlesbrough, whilst a draw or a defeat would send them down whatever the results of the other games.

'Going into the Leeds game we thought that we could do it,' says Nichols. 'All we had to do was win: someone else is bound to slip up. Sunderland will probably fail, we thought, they'll not beat Wimbledon, and Coventry are down anyway. Leeds were crap: they couldn't score. They'd only scored seven since January. A win at Ewood Park would have meant we'd only have needed a point out of this game.' Geoff Vickers had also analysed the table. 'Sunderland had to win and we didn't think they were capable. Coventry needed both of us not to win.'

At half-time, Leeds and Middlesbrough were locked at 0–0, as were Wimbledon and Sunderland, whilst Southampton were losing to a Richard Dryden own goal at Villa Park. Coventry, thanks to goals from Dion Dublin and Paul Williams, were winning 2–1 at Spurs. If things remained that way, Boro and Sunderland were down.

With 13 minutes left, the unthinkable happened and Leeds scored. Within two minutes, Juninho had equalised. Boro still kept up their hopes. The most traumatic season in their history was going right down to the wire. At Selhurst Park, Jason Euell put Wimbledon ahead against Sunderland with five minutes to go. Coventry were clinging grimly on to their lead. Southampton were still losing, but with Boro drawing and Sunderland losing, they looked safe.

The final whistle sounded across the nation and brought Boro's season to a tragic close. The players collapsed to the turf: Middlesbrough were out of the Premiership. Juninho, who'd given so much all season, sat head down and motionless, completely drained as the rigours of the season finally caught up with him. Tears rolled down his cheeks and on to the Elland Road pitch. 'It was one of the saddest moments I've experienced watching football,' says Vickers. 'In the end, we'd played badly, Juninho apart.'

Robert Nichols was numb. 'The dream had cracked and everything had been destroyed. The final indignity was watching the players board the coach to streams of abuse from Leeds fans who'd stayed behind just to mock them. We had gone out to entertain all season, been thoroughly lambasted by the media and football fans everywhere, and a negative team like Leeds, who'd contributed nothing to the season, had ended up sending us down. Is there no justice?

'We were empty and broken-hearted. Juninho and Ravanelli would go. So would Emerson (good riddance). The wheels had come off the club, and nobody cared about the cup final the following week.'

'We knew that relegation would mean losing Juninho, our hero,' says Vickers. 'The game just epitomised our season: Juninho as a one-man cavalry charge. Players like Beck, Freestone and Stamp just weren't on the same planet as him.

'Nobody was looking forward to the cup final. We were down, yet facing a match that everyone had dreamed of for all the years I've supported the Boro. It was a strange, horrible feeling.'

Robert Nichols tried to salvage something from the gloom. 'I spoke to Eric Paylor, a reporter on the local *Evening Gazette*, and tried to start a rallying cry for the FA Cup. Look, I said, let's at least win the FA Cup and retrieve something from the season where we had created this great team of entertainers.'

Alas, there was to be no silverware at the Riverside that season. Roberto Di Matteo waltzed through the Boro team and buried the ball in the back of the net before a Middlesbrough player had touched it. The deflation in the side was tangible. The heads dropped instantly: Middlesbrough had nothing left to give.

'There was no way we were going to win the FA Cup,' says Vickers. 'There were stories of unrest in the camp, players fighting on the team coach, that sort of thing, and the supporters just weren't up for it. The "three points" chants at the start of the game were the highlight but our excitement lasted precisely 42 seconds.'

The recriminations over the three points continued long after the season had finished, with Steve Gibson threatening legal action for their return. Whilst this may have caused a few hearts to leap into mouths in the city of Coventry, where the supporters emerged from their latest survival hangovers, there was never really any question that Boro would get the points back.

But surely the three-point fiasco just disguised the fact that Middlesbrough just weren't good enough, that they had proved to the football world that you couldn't just buy your way to success? That a team has to be built, and that you can't put a bunch of highly paid strangers in the same colour shirts and expect them to go straight out and win things?

'The three points was a mask that hid our shortcomings,' agrees Nichols. 'For all the money spent and the quality of players in our squad, we should have been pressing for a European place, and our cup success demonstrated what might have been. There is no doubt that we should have been contenders, three points or no three points, and serious questions needed directing at all levels at the club. Once again, we had failed to preserve top-flight status, and were relegated from the top division for the third time in a decade. And it really hurt.'

Geoff Vickers echoes these reservations about the side. 'I can't forget the pathetic form we had shown early in the season. Nobody can deny that the defence wasn't strengthened quickly enough – Festa didn't arrive until January – but our form in the second-half of the season was that of a solid, mid-table outfit.

'But at the end of the season, we shouldn't have gone down. Over the 38 games we'd earned enough points on the field to stay up. As a team we were better than Forest, Coventry and Sunderland, and on our day we were classier than half the sides in the Premiership.'

Nichols agrees. 'We didn't deserve to go down because of the injustice of the three points and because of what we'd achieved in a football sense. But we did deserve it on every other level. We had been absolute garbage for weeks in the soft centre of the season and took too long to turn it around. As Craig Hignett said, the league table doesn't lie. But with the three points issue, perhaps it does.'

At the end of the season, it was expected that Boro's three big overseas stars would leave the club. Juninho was a talisman to the Boro fans: the diminutive Brazilian had shown not just his phenomenal ability, but a passion for playing the game and for playing for Middlesbrough. Even since his departure for Atletico Madrid, he is still eulogised at the Riverside, with commemorative books and videos devoted to him still doing a brisk trade at the Boro shops. Not bad for someone who played a little over 50 matches for the club.

Ravanelli and Emerson, however, did not receive the same level of worship. Ravanelli had whined his way through the season, thumbing through the *Rothmans Yearbook* to see which club he would decide were interested in him next, and, although he came up with the goals, he scuppered Boro's cup final by declaring himself fit after his hamstring injury when he patently wasn't. The shop window of a Wembley final was too important for him to miss, but the move backfired when he limped off early in the game.

Emerson's majestic performances in the early part of the season earned him many admirers, but after his unlicensed sabbatical to Brazil he was not the same player. In the run-in in particular, he strolled around the middle of the park, spraying misplaced passes all over the place and showing not the slightest inclination to break sweat. Boro fans were not happy, and for once the Teesside supporters and the press were united in opinion. These players were happy to bank more money in a week than most of the supporters would see in a year, but were disinclined to actually earn it. Things had come a long way since the days of Alf Common, who would train in the mornings and spend the rest of his day wrestling and shadow boxing to keep himself in shape.

'Ravanelli should never have played in the cup final,' says Vickers. 'He wasn't fit and showed himself to be self-centred with no commitment to the team. Emerson's announcement after the final that he was staying shocked us all.'

'There was real animosity towards Emo and Rav,' continues Nichols. 'These world-class players should not have dragged the team down, they should have been an inspiration. They hadn't put the effort in when it mattered and you don't pay out millions for that. You only have to look at the outstanding contribution made by Juninho to see how much the other two let us down.

'But we were prepared to forgive. We're quite forgiving people, us Boro fans. Emerson had been playing on an injury and Rav had at least scored a good few goals. We wanted to believe!'

Surprisingly, Ravanelli and Emerson were still at Boro when the new season began in the Nationwide League. Whereas Liverpool had been welcomed a year before, Charlton Athletic were the first visitors to the Riverside this time. The Addicks led for much of the game, but Ravanelli scored what was to be his last Boro goal to give the Teessiders a winning start. Emerson eventually departed for Tenerife, and Ravanelli joined Marseille.

It had been a long and traumatic season for Middlesbrough. Whilst they felt genuinely hard done by, the actions and reactions of the club had won them few friends. No football fan likes anything more than seeing one of the rich clubs come spectacularly unstuck. Boro fans would have been in the same position themselves not so long ago. The glee that accompanied the failings of Newcastle United and Blackburn Rovers in recent years was now focused on Middlesbrough as they stamped their feet, spat out their dummy and had tantrum after tantrum. Steve Gibson, in an interview with *Fly Me to the Moon*, was later to rue, 'Many of the statements put out weren't really considered, and PR is now something we're looking at.'

Having never reached Wembley before in their long history, Boro did it twice in the same season, but on neither occasion emerged victorious. Nichols

191

regrets, 'The FA Cup would have been the cause of great celebration. It would have been the first silverware in our history, and to be able to buy scarves and shirts with "Middlesbrough FA Cup Winners 1997" on them would have been an enormous lift for everyone in the area. Playing in Europe for the first time would have been exciting and we would have had far more to look forward to than the pit of doom which opened beneath us at the end of the 1996–97 season.'

At the time of writing, Boro are poised for a swift return to the Premiership; by the time you read this they'll probably be there. They will no doubt have learned a great deal from their 1996–97 experiences, and the long-suffering Boro fans will have realised that building your hopes up too high will only give them a longer way to come crashing down. Even when you sign Paul Gascoigne.

Middlesbrough supporters are used to having their hopes dashed, but the 1996–97 season was the ultimate tease. Not only did the season crash around their ears, but their new status as one of the game's fat cats left their supporters incredulous at the amount of scorn and vitriol poured upon them from all quarters of the football world.

It's tough at the top, as Middlesbrough will no doubt discover again and again.

Are You Watching, Macclesfield?

MANCHESTER CITY HIT ROCK BOTTOM

As football surfs towards the millennium on a wave of popularity and prosperity, with grounds full to bursting and everyone piling on to the bandwagon, it is perhaps surprising to hear that one lifelong fan is turning his back on the club he has followed since the age of nine. A club which has seen its share of triumph and more than its share of disaster and humiliation. A club that has watched its neighbour and fiercest rival become an unimpeachable fortress of success and wealth. A club of proud tradition, a club long regarded as one of the giants of the game. A club at the lowest point of its long history. Huw Evans won't be going to see Manchester City again until they are worthy of his support.

'I no longer have a football team,' says Evans, a 32-year-old civil servant from the Middleton area of Manchester. 'I really mean that. I said it right after the Stoke match. I can't go and see them now, there's just too much gone on. I'm not going to see City again until they are back in the Premier League because they don't deserve it. They won't deserve my support until they're back in the Premier League. They've had too much money off me, too much time and support, all that kind of thing. Obviously you can't change your team, you just can't do that, but I think you could stop supporting them.'

Raised on the exciting City side of the mid-'70s, Evans has experienced the ups and downs of a lifetime's support of Manchester City, a blind devotion exercised long before it was fashionable to be a football obsessive. Devotion is a characteristic trait of Manchester City supporters, whose unfailing attendance kept City's gates around the 30,000 mark even as they were relegated to the Second Division for the first time in their history, and it is a trait that Evans feels has to change if City are to make any progress at all.

'I remember when I was really young, about ten I think, and there was about 40,000 at the match, which in those days wasn't a sell-out. I was in the Kippax with about 25,000 others and I remember this bloke – he was probably about 25, although he seemed much older to me then – saying to me, "We didn't let them down, did we? Look at the Main Stand." It was half full or something, but on the Kippax we hadn't let them down. It's that mentality that's got to change.

'I've heard people saying that the only reason the gates stay so high is that it's the one thing that United can't have a go at us about. I don't believe that. I think people honestly feel that if they don't turn up they're somehow letting the club down. But when clubs like Celtic and Newcastle became too complacent and then saw their gates drop to ten or twelve thousand, they suddenly realised, hang on, we've really got to do something about this.'

When a Manchester City supporter advocates sacrificing the one thing that their Manchester rivals cannot lampoon them for, something is obviously seriously amiss. Manchester City's recent history is one of boardroom strife, a revolving door to the manager's office and a series of mishaps that, with hindsight, made the club's relegation to the Second Division at the end of the 1997–98 season all but inevitable.

The series of events that led to City's demise can be traced back to the late '70s. The unassuming and affable Tony Book, a former Manchester City player still involved with the club and a great favourite with the fans, was replaced in 1979 by the flamboyant figure of Malcolm Allison. Allison had been part of the championship-winning set-up of the late '60s as assistant to Joe Mercer, and in the eyes of City chairman Peter Swales, obsessed with asserting City's dominance over their rivals at Old Trafford, he was the man to establish Manchester City as the biggest, most successful club in the land.

Unfortunately, as Swales would later admit, Allison was lost without the influence of Mercer. He dabbled unsuccessfully in the transfer market, signing Steve MacKenzie from Crystal Palace for a quarter of a million pounds before the teenager had even made his full debut for the Eagles and Michael Robinson from Preston North End for £750,000. After a long chase, Allison secured the services of Steve Daley from Wolverhampton Wanderers for nearly £1.5 million, then a record for a transfer fee between two British clubs. In March 1980 Swales stumped up a staggering £1.25 million for Kevin Reeves from Norwich City. Results didn't match City's vast investment, however, and before long Allison was on his way out of Maine Road. Swales's dream of overhauling Manchester United had claimed another casualty, and he honed his expertise in filling out P45 forms.

The legacy of Allison's spending, sanctioned by Swales, was to dog City for years to come, and, despite an appearance in the 1981 FA Cup final where they were undone by possibly the most famous cup final goal ever, it was to be City's last real crack at the big time. The signing of Trevor Francis for over £1 million in 1981 under John Bond, possibly only completed because Swales found out that Manchester United had tabled an offer that the player would find difficult to refuse, and extensive ground development plans stretched City's resources further still. Injury was to restrict Francis's appearances in a City shirt, and despite the odd inspirational performance his time at Maine Road did not justify the fee. Francis was on a massive wage, an annual six-figure sum that City couldn't hope to meet, and during 1982 the club's precarious financial position began to make itself plain. With Francis soon departing, City's crowds dropped to around 28,000, and with the transfer market now commanding ridiculously inflated sums, mainly thanks to their own profligate spending, the Blues found it difficult to compete. The resignation of John Bond following a 4–0 defeat at Brighton and Hove Albion triggered an alarming drop down the table. Bond's assistant John Benson took over, but he was never going to be more than a temporary measure.

City went into the last game of the 1982–83 season on the back of nine defeats in thirteen games. At home to Luton Town, they needed just one point to ensure their survival and condemn their opponents to the Second Division. Huw Evans remembers the occasion well.

'It had been one of those seasons, but nobody seriously thought we were going to go down. There was no way we were going to go down. We'd last been relegated in the early '60s, so most of us had never known anything but the First Division.

'Maine Road was packed. I remember getting the bus down from Middleton, and normally there'd only be about ten or fifteen of us on it, but that day it was full.'

Luton went at City right from the start, whilst City seemed content to sit back and play for a draw. City's fans became restless. 'It was a bit of a laugh to start with, but as the game went on and Luton kept on at us, the ground started to go quiet,' remembers Evans.

Then, with five minutes remaining, Luton manager David Pleat brought on Yugoslav international Raddy Antic. Antic had been on the field for less than a minute when Brian Stein sent in a hopeful cross. City goalkeeper Alex Williams came for it but could only palm the ball to the edge of the penalty area, where Antic sent in a shot that flew into the bottom corner via a deflection. There were 86 minutes on the clock, and Maine Road was stunned into silence. You could hear the shouts of the Luton players.

'It was such a shit goal,' says Evans. 'It seemed to go in off about eight people in slow motion. Oh, it was a nightmare. We were in the Platt Lane that day, and although I don't remember much about the match, I remember the goal. It kicked off at the end, with really terrible fighting on the pitch. I remember Brian Stein fighting with a City fan. I kind of knew this lad, and he and Brian Stein were just punching seven bells out of each other on the pitch.'

Luton's David Pleat skipped on to the pitch, a curious half-run, half-jig as he rushed to congratulate his captain Brian Horton, a future City manager, an enduring image which has been a godsend for comedy football video compilers ever since.

'I didn't see Pleat but I remember all the Luton players just legging it off the pitch. A mate of mine was crying his eyes out, we couldn't believe it. We were only about 16 or 17 and we'd never known anything like it. Bloody Luton. And now we're playing them in the Second Division.'

To compound City's misery, within a fortnight Ron Atkinson's United had carried off the FA Cup. The gulf between the two Manchester giants was widening, much to Swales's horror.

'We'd really got ourselves relegated in about 1979,' recalls Evans 'when Swales sacked Tony Book and Malcolm Allison came back and spent all that money on Daley and Reeves and so on, players who just weren't up to it. After that things went rapidly downhill, although we actually had quite a good team when we went down: Tommy Hutchison, Tommy Caton. It was a good team but, typical City, one that was badly managed.

'The crowd are crap, too. They don't help. The atmosphere at Maine Road can be terrible because we get on the team's back if we're not three up inside ten minutes. Because of that Swales would sack a manager as soon as the crowd got a bit restless and appoint a succession of weak managers. Yes, 1979 was when it started going wrong, and that's why we went down in 1983.'

Predictably, the Luton game spelt the end of John Benson's time as manager. In order to maintain his desire for a higher media profile than United, Swales sought to bring in a well-known manager, a strong character who would lead City back into the top flight and launch a concerted challenge for major honours. City, though, were in dire financial straits, a situation not aided by relegation to the Second Division. After Swales's philanthropic tolerance of Allison and Bond's transfer activities, the club were believed to be losing over £1,000 per day in interest alone.

Into this monetary mire waded Billy McNeill, Celtic's European Cup-winning captain who had gone on to become a successful manager at Celtic Park. McNeill packed the side with Scots, and although City's first campaign in the Second Division saw them finish ten points behind promoted Newcastle in fourth place, the feeling was that City would go up the following season.

'When it became clear that Chelsea, Sheffield Wednesday and Newcastle were going up, we knew that it would be us the following year. I remember the last home game of the season, Cambridge United I think it was, and we knew that next year we were going up. Even with players like Derek Parlane and Jim Tolmie in the side.'

The 1984–85 season was a successful campaign for City, culminating in promotion after the last game of the season thanks to a 5–1 hammering of Charlton at Maine Road in front of a full house. City's celebrations were muted somewhat, however, as news filtered through of the terrible disaster at Bradford.

Manchester City's first campaign back in the top flight was memorable only for a dramatic appearance in the Full Members Cup final the day after achieving a 2–2 draw in the Manchester derby. City went down to Chelsea in a 5–4 thriller. The following season, however, saw the seeds of disaster sown early in the campaign. Just seven games into the season, at the end of his tether with certain factions in the City boardroom, Billy McNeill departed for Aston Villa. Freddie Pye had been appointed director in charge of team affairs, but he and the manager clashed constantly, and when Pye got together with close friend Ken Bates to bring Gordon Davies to Maine Road without consulting McNeill, it was the last straw. Doug Ellis waved his chequebook and the Scot was away.

Huw Evans recalls the mood amongst the fans at the time. 'It was a bit of a killer. I think he made a bit of a mistake there, McNeill. I remember at the time City considered themselves to be a much bigger club than Aston Villa, so in our eyes he really had no right to go there. I was 20 at the time, and at that age, as a City fan in particular, you think your club is the biggest in the world. I still do, in very odd moments these days. But when that sort of thing happens, when McNeill went to Villa, you start to realise that whatever your history, your club's not the force it once was.

'When I grew up in the '70s, there was only really Liverpool who seemed to be a lot better than us as a team and bigger than us as a club, but by the mid-'80s even Chelsea had a better team than City — and you know you're in trouble when even Chelsea are better than you . . .'

Once again, Swales's stopgap came from inside the club, as Jimmy Frizzell took over. City soon went bottom as the season lurched towards its inevitable conclusion. With no money available and unrest off the field, City were relegated after a 2–0 defeat at West Ham United, having won just eight games all season. Jimmy Frizzell was pushed upstairs to the post of general manager, making way for former Norwich City coach Mel Machin to become the latest incumbent of the manager's position and keep the man who engraves the brass plates for the Maine Road office doors in employment. A stabilising first season, in City terms at least, saw the club finish in ninth position, the campaign including a 10–1 hammering of Huddersfield Town. The fans, Huw Evans included, began to feel slightly more optimistic.

'Yeah, that season was the start of a revival at City, really. There were a few young players coming through like Andy Hinchcliffe and Andy May from the youth team. At that time City were so skint that they started playing their youth-team players. Even though we didn't go up that year we knew we had the makings of a good team. We should have won that league the year after.'

City made a poor start to the 1988–89 campaign, failing to register a win until a 2–1 victory over Brighton and Hove Albion in late September. However, a sudden improvement in results saw City surge up to fifth place in the table at Christmas. In a sign that the mood amongst football fans in general was changing for the better after the dark days of hooliganism, City took 12,000 fans to Stoke City on Boxing Day, most of whom were accompanied by large inflatable bananas. City fans were one of the instigators of the inflatable craze that swept the terraces during the late '80s, and its pinnacle came at the Victoria Ground that day. Even the City players took to the field with inflatable bananas under their arms.

'I don't really remember how it started,' says Evans. 'Everybody says to me it was for Imre Varadi, because people had started calling him Imre Banana.'

Each club seemed to have its own inflatable: later that season television cameras at Plough Lane captured the scenes in the away end at the Wimbledon v. Grimsby Town FA Cup tie, which seemed to be almost entirely populated by a shoal of inflatable haddock.

The wave of optimism buoyed the City team to such an extent that they went into the penultimate game of the season knowing that a win over AFC Bournemouth would take them back into the top flight. A 3–0 half-time lead for the home side sent City fans into rapture, only for the visitors to claw the game back to 3–3 and send City into their final game still needing a draw to be certain of going up. A late Trevor Morley equaliser gave the Blues the point they needed against Bradford, and City were back in the First Division.

Despite Machin strengthening the side during the summer of 1989, the Maine Road club found the going difficult in the top flight, and City went into their meeting with Manchester United in mid-September in bottom position. Somehow, City rattled in five goals against their fiercest rivals, a game that will live long in the memory of everyone from the blue side of Manchester.

'That game was the best ever,' says Evans. 'We eventually finished 17th, I think, but that result sparked us off and led to us pulling away and out of trouble. Paul Lake was just outstanding that day. I've still got the radio commentary on tape, and every two minutes it's "Lake beats so-and-so, Lake threads the ball through" – he was just everywhere. Clive Tyldesley's the commentator and it's well known that he's no lover of United, so it makes for great listening. Seems a long time ago now, though.'

However, despite a win in their next match, City's results soon nosedived once again and, following a 1–1 draw at Selhurst Park with Charlton Athletic, Machin was shown the door by Swales, who bemoaned the fact that the departing boss had never established a rapport with the Maine Road faithful. Huw Evans sees the sacking as typical of the late City chairman.

'It was classic Swales, wasn't it? Machin wasn't that bad a manager, and he refused to pander to the fans, which is fair enough. But it was typical of Swales's weakness: a bit of abuse and the manager goes. Every time. You'd shout for Swales's head, and the manager would go. That's where City fans are bad, I think. We know we've got a bit of power at the club. City know we could all turn around tomorrow and say that's it, we're not coming any more – which I wish we'd do, really. Celtic and Everton did it, went down to bad gates and then came back. But the number of sackings that Swales instigated – and there were certainly quite a few – was definitely influenced by the opinions of the fans at Maine Road.'

Despite unsuccessful approaches to former City striker Joe Royle, then overseeing Oldham Athletic's brief sojourn in the top flight, Swales announced that City's new manager would be Howard Kendall. Kendall, who had managed Everton to their successes of the mid-'80s, came back to English football following a spell in Spain at Athletic Bilbao.

Soon after his arrival, it seemed that Kendall was trying to reassemble his old Everton squad at Maine Road. Peter Reid and Alan Harper arrived from Queen's Park Rangers and Sheffield Wednesday respectively in time for Kendall's first game in charge, ironically at Everton, with City still bottom of the First Division. The match finished 0–0, a decent result, but Kendall soon incurred the wrath of the City fans by bringing in Mark Ward, another former Everton player, from West Ham United in exchange for Ian Bishop and Trevor Morley. 'We were incensed,' says Evans. 'Ward never wanted to play for City, we all knew that. Every City fan knew that all the time he was there, and it was no surprise that he went as soon as Kendall did. Morley and Bishop were dead popular; Bishop in particular had gelled well with the lads who'd come through from the youth side like Paul Lake, Ian Brightwell and David White. And Kendall seemed to have something against Clive Allen: he was in the reserves all the time, banging in three or four goals every game, giving 110 per cent, and Kendall wouldn't give him a game, the man who only about three or four years earlier had scored 47 goals for Tottenham. It was just inexplicable.'

Despite these unpopular moves, Kendall did succeed in hauling City out of trouble. The signing of Niall Quinn from Arsenal for £800,000 completed the team Kendall assembled to preserve City's top-flight status. The football hadn't been pretty, but City were at least safe from relegation.

During the close season Kendall strengthened the side further, bringing in goalkeeper Tony Coton and, controversially, Neil Pointon from Everton in exchange for Andy Hinchcliffe. 'That's probably when we started selling good players in earnest and replacing them with bad ones,' asserts Evans. 'I mean, look at Hinchcliffe: he's been in the England squad, almost made the World Cup, and he's obviously highly thought of. But Neil Pointon? Soon after we went down I counted 15 former City players plying their trade in the Premiership. We had a full first-team squad of ex-Blues in the top flight, and we were in Division One. From around this time, everyone we sold we replaced with somebody much worse.'

Early results were mixed, but a 3–3 draw at Maine Road in the Manchester derby did not endear Kendall to the City faithful. With the Blues 3–1 up with just a few minutes remaining, the manager pulled off Peter Reid and threw on Ian Brightwell. In the remaining minutes United scord twice to earn a point. Later that week, City bowed out of the League Cup at Arsenal, whilst Everton were losing to Sheffield United. The outcome of the Goodison side's defeat was the sacking of manager Colin Harvey. It was a dismissal that was to have immediate repercussions for City, as shortly afterwards Kendall walked out of Maine Road and returned to Everton.

Huw Evans's opinion of Kendall has not mellowed with the passing years. 'I'm not sorry for what's happened to him since. I've got absolutely no time for him. When he walked out on City, there was pure, intense hatred of the man, which was given full vent when he first came back to Maine Road with Everton. All through the game the City fans were chanting "Fuck off,

Kendall", and a mate of mine who watched it on Granada said that was all you could hear all the way through the match. He'd stitched us up, basically, and all that talk of City being a "love affair", I mean, what a load of bullshit.'

Buried within the City fans' disgust with Kendall's departure was the frustration that under his tutelage the team had actually started to show signs of progress. Once again the hopes of the fans had been left in tatters. Kendall had substantially revamped the playing side at Maine Road, bringing in his own players and changing to a less flamboyant style than City fans had been used to, but one which produced results. Before he left, City fans were finally beginning to believe that they had a manager capable of taking the club back to the heights to which they had been accustomed many years before. The fact that yet another manager would now have to come in and commence a rebuilding of the squad was too hard for them to swallow, and to them Kendall was nothing but a traitor, a Judas.

Keen to see the progress instigated by Kendall continue, the fans called for the promotion of Peter Reid to the hot seat. Swales concurred. 'If it was going to be anybody, we wanted Reid. We couldn't face the start of another rebuilding process. Presumably Joe Royle was linked with the job – he usually was – but at least Reid gave us a sense of continuity and stability.'

Despite the managerial upheavals, City managed to finish the 1990–91 season in fifth position. 'Higher than United,' as Evans is quick to point out. 'We finished fifth two years running, but football was actually pretty terrible then, wasn't it? These were the Graham Taylor years, people like Carlton Palmer were internationals, and City were good enough to finish fifth in what was a mediocre First Division. Even so, it was the highest we'd finished since 1978, and we thought we were back where we wanted to be. At last the club seemed to be well managed.'

Memories of City's transfer-market disasters were revived when Reid smashed the club's record fee, laying out £2.5 million for Keith Curle, Wimbledon's lanky defender. Despite an encouraging start to the 1991–92 campaign which saw City top the table in the early weeks, the new year saw their form nosedive amid rumours that all was not well off the field. Peter Reid had brought in Sam Ellis as his assistant and there were stories that the new man was not popular amongst the players.

'Yeah, there were lots of rumours,' says Evans, 'stuff like Tony Coton injuring his wrist punching Ellis in training, and Niall Quinn was meant to have had his nose broken by Michel Vonk. I think Ellis was a bit of a hard case, and some of the players didn't take to him too well which led to a few problems in the dressing-room.'

201

Despite the rumours, fifth place was achieved again, with City fans taking some comfort from the fact that their rivals across the city were pipped to the title by Leeds United, whom City had thumped 4–0 as recently as April.

Just prior to the start of the 1992–93 season, Reid matched the record fee he'd created the year before, shelling out another £2.5 million for Wimbledon full-back Terry Phelan, whilst Rick Holden arrived from Oldham in exchange for Neil Pointon and Steve Redmond. The fans found it odd that Reid chose to bolster the defence when it was in midfield that City were lacking depth.

'We were doing what Liverpool were doing a couple of years back with John Barnes: everything was going through Peter Reid in midfield so the rest of the team had to play to his pace, and the guy was 36 years old. And who do we sign? Not a midfielder, but another defender!'

Despite these misgivings, City's top-five finishes in the two preceding seasons left Evans optimistic about his club's chances for the forthcoming campaign. 'This is how bad it is being a City fan, right? I'd looked at our first six fixtures for the 1992–93 season and thought, hey, we can get 18 points here. We'd all turned up for the first game against QPR, and it was Sky's first live Monday night match. In fact it was the first season of the Premier League. There were fireworks and dancing girls, and then the Red Devils parachuted on to the pitch! Everyone was just chucking things at them, it was hilarious. The Red Devils at Manchester City. I don't know who'd done that particular bit of market research, but they couldn't have done any worse than that if they'd tried.'

The game finished 1–1, beginning a season of mixed results. A few victories were ground out, but City fans were growing restless with the physical nature of the Reid/Ellis school of football. 'They were basically just chucking it up to Quinn, and I think Paul Stewart was there then as well,' remembers Evans. A good run in the FA Cup was terminated by Tottenham Hotspur in a quarter-final played at Maine Road which was more memorable for crowd disturbances than the game itself. Evans cites that game as typical of the situation at City at the time. 'That game showed how poor we actually were,' he says. 'Whenever we played a decent side, they'd show up our weaknesses, and we got beaten 4–2. We were never really in that game at all.'

The crowd disturbances were an expression of the years of disappointments and false dawns that City fans had been forced to endure. The game saw the opening of the new Umbro Stand at the Platt Lane end and was meant to be the latest instalment in City's march to Wembley and the FA Cup. The whole occasion was an unmitigated disaster. The crowd trouble put them on to the back pages for the wrong reasons, and Swales's dream of emulating the

Blues' rivals were shattered as United continued their march towards the Premiership title. Until now Swales had always been buoyed by the fact that although City had won nothing for many years, they had still won the title more recently than United. Alex Ferguson had come within a whisker of losing his job after the 5–1 gubbing at the hands of City, but the Old Trafford club persevered with Ferguson's methods, in direct contrast to Swales's hire-and-fire style, and the Red Devils went on to dominate the English game for the ensuing seasons.

'Every year, one more thing that we had to hold on to over United goes away,' says Evans. 'It used to be winning the championship more recently, but that went. The 5–1 was wiped out when they turned us over 5–0. Every year it just becomes worse and worse. Even that thing about City having more fans in Manchester than United, I don't think even that's true any more. There are definitely more United shirts parading around Manchester than City shirts.'

The fact that Swales's constant promises of City's domination of their rivals were looking less likely meant that the pressure on Reid and Ellis to deliver was greater than ever before. United had won the title; they were the best team in the country. City fans, fed up with constantly being asked to be patient, were growing more and more unhappy with Swales and he knew it. In his 20 years at the club, City had achieved virtually nothing. The constant turnover of managers was making the club a laughing stock, and was shown up as folly by the achievements of Alex Ferguson, who had overcome early problems to establish himself as one of the greatest club managers in football history. The pressure upon Swales to resign was increasing with each passing game.

'Just before the 1993–94 season, City appointed John Maddock as general manager. He was a journalist and was paid about 60 grand basically to take the flak from Peter Swales. It didn't work,' remembers Evans. Maddock soon made himself immensely unpopular as he apparently deliberately tried to undermine Reid's authority. He insisted to the press that he was in charge and had the power to hire and fire. In his desperation to appear as more than a mouthpiece for Swales, he became widely regarded as an arrogant megalomaniac. Even the players expressed their displeasure with the way he was handling the affairs of the club. Eventually Reid sought a clear-the-air meeting with Maddock and Swales. When the meeting closed, Reid left the room without a job. Two weeks into the season, City were managerless once more.

Huw Evans was flabbergasted. 'Two weeks into the season and you sack the manager. I mean, what is going on? It's just constant panic stations at City all the time; it has been for years now. We're a 24-hours-a-day crisis club. There's never a period where you can say, okay, let's just level off here and take stock for a while. That never happens, because as soon as results go the wrong way the fans are shouting for the manager's head.'

The usual suspects were bandied about as possible replacements: Royle, Steve Coppell, Dave Bassett and even Terry Venables were all linked with the post. Maddock's comments that City were about to appoint a top-flight manager with a proven track record caused excitement amongst City fans who had been desperate for such a boss since the days of Mercer and Allison.

At the televised game against Coventry City on 27 August the media speculated upon who Reid's successor might be. The list of top-flight managers who had never managed City was growing ever shorter, but there was one face in the crowd that night whom no one had linked with the job. Jaws dropped in the control room as the cameras picked out Oxford United's Brian Horton in one of the Umbro Stand executive boxes. Whilst the fans spent most of the game calling for Swales's head, the media sought to confirm whether Horton, a member of the victorious Luton Town side at Maine Road in 1983, would be the new boss. The end of the game saw the announcement that Brian Horton was indeed to be the latest occupant of the manager's chair at Manchester City. The fans, expecting a Venables or a Bassett, were incredulous. In their view, Brian Horton was not fit to manage their club.

'We didn't know who he was, basically,' recalls Evans. 'At least before we'd always had managers with a reasonable reputation, but nobody knew who Brian Horton was. His first game was Swindon away, I think, and everyone was just taking the piss. But I suppose he was all we could afford at the time.'

That match at Swindon brought a welcome 3–1 victory, although the beleaguered Swales was nowhere to be seen. Just five days later, however, it was announced that former hero Francis Lee was launching a takeover bid for the Maine Road club. Lee was a veteran of over 300 games in a City shirt and a member of the great side of the late '60s and early '70s. He was perhaps best known for his prowess from the penalty spot, which earned him the nickname of 'Lee One Pen'. An England international, he left City after a disagreement with Swales over the methods of manger Ron Saunders in 1974 to join Derby County. Lee retired from the game in 1976 to pursue business interests in paper manufacture and as a racehorse owner. In an article in the *Daily Mirror*, he now announced his ambitions to put Manchester City back on the map, promising big money and that he would run the club 'from top to bottom like a winning team'.

The supporters were delighted. 'It all happened quite quickly,' says Huw

Evans of the news. 'When Reid went there was a solid body of opinion for Swales to go. Reid's dismissal was the final straw. So when Lee threw his name into the ring the fans were obviously delighted. A great ex-player with the reputation of being a shrewd businessman, seemingly with plenty of cash. Most of all he was a part of the best team City has ever had. Obviously you're going to shout for him.

'I think there's a feeling amongst football fans that chairmen don't know anything about football. Here was a chance to have a chairman who knew about football and who knew about Manchester City. But footballers are famous for being footballers, not good chairmen. I think it was just seen as an opportunity to get rid of Swales, which everybody wanted.

'We'd heard loads of rumours over the years, Saudi takeovers and so on. At one stage there was talk of Philips, who were our sponsors at the time, taking us over and turning us into the British equivalent of PSV Eindhoven, but nothing ever came of it. So when Lee came along it finally looked as though there was a viable option, and he became the first credible contender to oust Swales.'

Given the choice between Peter Swales, a member of the increasingly unfashionable old school of football chairmen who had presided over a pretty miserable 20 years at Maine Road and given City the reputation of a club which appointed and sacked managers on a whim, and Francis Lee, a hugely popular ex-player, relatively young, with the football knowledge and capital to take the club into the next millennium, it wasn't difficult to see why Lee was so popular amongst the fans. He represented the light at the end of a long, dark tunnel, the chance of a fresh start, the opportunity to put the nightmare of the Swales years behind the club. 'Lee was promising people like Mike Summerbee and Colin Bell; the boys were going to be back together again like in the good old days. That was the feeling,' says Evans.

Horton's first home game in charge was against Queen's Park Rangers, and when Lee arrived he was swamped by a tide of adulation from the City fans. Swales, in contrast, fielded a barrage of abuse surrounded by police in the directors' box. City swept to a 3–0 victory.

It soon became clear that Swales would obstruct Lee's attempts to take over the club. Many saw this as characteristic stubbornness, but, with the benefit of hindsight, Huw Evans detects a certain perceptiveness in the actions of the beleaguered chairman.

'The City fans never twigged this at the time, but Lee appeared to be stalling. He didn't try and buy 51 per cent of the shares; instead he tried to broker a deal with Stephen Boler, who'd been one of Swales's cronies, so that he controlled rather than owned 51 per cent. We should have thought, hang on, he's not paying that much for the club, about £3 million or so, and if he's going to be such a big investor in City, why can't he buy 51 per cent of the shares outright?'

Swales intimated that there was another interested party, which muddied the waters further, but details never emerged and Swales carried the identity of this mysterious figure to his grave.

At the club's Annual General Meeting in October 1993, Swales made it plain that he was not prepared to listen to any more offers from Lee. Huw Evans is of the opinion that these were the last, desperate measures of a desperate man determined to cling on to power at all costs, a power that was all he had left in his life.

'I don't think Swales was a particularly successful businessman, so he'd made most of his money from Manchester City. Through this he became involved with the FA. It's notable that he died shortly after he left the game. City were his life. Once he left the club he didn't really have anything left, so in a way I can understand why he wanted to cling on and keep Lee out. He was putting stories about that Lee's supporters had abused his mother whilst she was in a hospital bed, and that he'd had bricks through his windows, all that kind of thing. If any of that was true then it probably made him realise just how hated he actually was, so eventually he went.

'Jack Walker had come into the game by then. He'd pumped a load of money into Blackburn Rovers, signed a top manager and signed top-class players, and it didn't look like happening at City as long as Swales was in charge. You looked at Blackburn and you looked at City and you thought, well, Lee's the only option really if we're going to emulate a club like Blackburn Rovers. I do think in hindsight that we weren't actually as optimistic about Lee as was portrayed at the time. We were just hoping for a miracle, and Lee was the only one around – but he had to be better than Swales.'

To compound the misery of the City fans after the AGM, the Blues threw away a 2–0 lead over Manchester United at Maine Road to go down 3–2. That game cost Huw Evans £150. 'We'd been 2–0 up at half-time and I was with two Reds. I gave them odds of 10–1 at half time: one had a fiver, the other a tenner, so I ended up 150 quid down.'

Results were going against City when on 29 November Swales stepped down as chairman of the club, announcing that he would remain on the board to co-ordinate a new regime that would not include Lee. However, as the negotiations continued into 1994, it became inevitable that Francis Lee's consortium would assume control of the troubled club. It took until early

February for Lee and his associates, former City player Colin Barlow and John Dunkerley, to take up positions on the board. Lee pledged to sort out the club's finances and keep them in the Premiership. Although he promised that no players would be sold, he didn't intimate that money would be made available to strengthen the squad.

The first game under the new regime saw Maine Road engulfed with blue and white balloons, with Lee saluting the fans from the directors' box. A 2–1 victory followed, but the euphoria off the field could not disguise the shortcomings on it. Few expected Horton to survive long under the Lee regime, and results were certainly doing nothing to give him any kind of job satisfaction. Despite the signings of Uwe Rosler from Nurnberg and Paul Walsh from Portsmouth, City's Premiership status was by no means assured. A 2–1 victory over Newcastle sparked a late-season rally, and City finished the season in 16th place.

The 1994–95 season proved to be no better: despite a good start, City found themselves struggling. A particular low point was a 5–0 hiding at Manchester United which wiped out the memories of 1989 for the United fans. Going into Easter, City were once again peering nervously over their shoulders. Whilst a 2–1 win over Liverpool and a 3–2 victory at Blackburn Rovers helped to ensure survival, another season of struggle had not endeared Horton to the City faithful. A spineless 3–2 defeat to lowly Queen's Park Rangers on the final day of the season ensured that Horton would be the latest manager to leave Maine Road.

'Lee was always going to get rid of Horton,' recalls Evans, 'He was always going to sack him. It was a bit of a relief, to be honest: we felt that, finally, something good, something positive, was going to happen. When Lee came in it was like when a new manager arrives. You think, okay, we'll give it till the end of the season, then we'll see what the new boss is going to do. That summer of 1995, everyone was hoping to see better things.'

The media paraded their usual shortlist of candidates, a list which included Bobby Robson and George Graham. Once again, sources at the club promised a big name. Colin Barlow hinted that a European place was City's short-term target, and that the new manager would have to have the experience to achieve that goal. City's fans waited with baited breath to find out who the new messiah would be. They were disappointed to find out that it would be Alan Ball. Ball's record as a manager is less than impressive, featuring a number of relegations, and he had no managerial experience of European competition either.

'Alan Ball was the first time the alarm bells rang amongst City fans,' recalls

Evans. 'He had no pedigree as a manager and you started to think, is this the best we can do? It probably was at the time, though, because no one wanted the job. It was then that Francis Lee having all his mates around him at the club started to seem like a bad idea. Instead of recreating past glories, it was just a load of yes men. Also, there was always a strong feeling that Lee had a lot more say in the selection of the team than he perhaps should have done.'

One move by Lee that would pay off for the fans was the signing of the Georgian international Georgiou Kinkladze for £2 million.

'I remember there was so much press about him, that this was the greatest player Manchester City had ever signed, and I was thinking, oh yeah, here we go, it's Steve Daley all over again. I really thought he'd only be there about six months and then we'd flog him on to Bolton or someone. Or Oldham, who were like a City B team. But as it turned out he was amazing. I mean, what a player. He did all the right things press-wise as well – you know, always phoning his mum and stuff – when he actually seemed to spend most of his time writing off Ferraris.'

Ball also brought in Kit Symons from his old club Portsmouth and the German international goalkeeper Eike Immel from VfB Stuttgart. Evans was wary of City's imports.

'Immel wasn't bad; I mean, he was certainly good enough for us, but we'd signed more than one player who was supposed to have a good international pedigree and then couldn't kick a ball straight. Michel Frontzeck was just one in a catalogue of bad signings. He was one of the worst City have ever made. The weird thing is that the fans know immediately that these players are no good, but it seems to take managers a year or so to notice. Frontzeck was certainly one of those.

'But Ball was actually assembling a half-decent side. Lomas was still there, Garry Flitcroft, players who have since gone on to better things, so God knows how we got relegated that year. Well, apart from Alan Ball being involved, that is.'

City's opening spell of the 1995–96 season was a disaster. A 1–1 draw with Tottenham on the opening day was followed by eight consecutive defeats which left the club anchored to the foot of the Premiership table. City faced Liverpool in league and League Cup games within three days of each other, which ended 4–0 and 6–0 to Liverpool respectively. After the latter game, Ball scored a spectacular PR own goal by stating how much he had enjoyed the Liverpool performance. A mini-revival in November saw Ball receive the Manager of the Month award, but after Christmas City were soon back in trouble. The FA Cup provided welcome respite and City progressed to the fifth round, where they faced Manchester United at Old Trafford.

After half an hour, United fans were reeling at the rare spectacle of Peter Schmeichel being comprehensively lobbed by Uwe Rosler. However, soon afterwards United won a corner and, as the cross came over, referee Alan Wilkie blew his whistle. The ever shy and retiring Roy Keane immediately went berserk, believing he had been penalised. When he saw the referee pointing to the spot, his arms, previously raised in protest, suddenly waggled with delight. No one could understand why Wilkie had awarded the penalty, including Huw Evans.

'It was the day they opened the new stand and we were in there with a load of screaming Reds. They got a penalty and to this day nobody's ever known why it was awarded. There was a huge brawl: Curle and Cole were fighting, Quinn was trying to leather Keane – and they were in the same Irish team! Quinn really hated him, you could tell by the way he went straight for him.'

United went on to win the game 2–1, but City bounced back in the league with an inspiring 3–3 draw with high-flying Newcastle United, a game which saw Kinkladze at his brilliant best. Huw Evans recalls that City were then lumbered with 'big-club syndrome'.

'Everyone was trying to compare us with Everton after their escape two years before, saying that we'd pull through. There's always this feeling that when it comes to the end of the season and there's, say, five clubs in danger, the three smallest ones will end up being relegated regardless of their positions at the time. I think that season we had the usual suspects like Southampton and Coventry City, and even Wimbledon were in trouble at one point. But everyone was saying we'd be all right, and we were too good to go down.'

Going into the last game of the season, at home to Liverpool, City occupied the third relegation spot with 37 points. Southampton and Coventry City had the same total but superior goal differences. Southampton were at home to Wimbledon, Coventry were at home to Leeds. All City had to do was gain a better result than either one of them.

Before the game, a minute's silence was observed for Peter Swales who had died that week of a heart attack at the age of 62. Although a figure of hate throughout much of his reign, no one could deny that Swales was City through and through. The club was his life. His ambition was to be better than Manchester United, and it was this obsession which led him to fire a series of managers and land City in the predicament in which they found themselves at the time of his death. He was a chairman from the old school, a throwback to the old days of local businessmen running the club for spiritual rather than financial gain. He had become an anachronism by the time he was ousted by Lee, a sad figure clinging on to power because it was all he had left to live for.

Huw Evans recalls Swales's final pronouncement with a wry chuckle. 'You know what Swales said before he died? He said, "The last thing I want is for City to go down." If you look at it another way, that was in fact the last thing he got. It's true, that; it was in the *Manchester Evening News*.'

Unfortunately for City, Liverpool took an early lead when Steve Lomas turned a McManaman shot into his own net. Liverpool were performing notably below their best, and rumours abounded that they were keen to see the Blues survive. They appeared to show little interest in taking the game by the scruff of the neck and capitalising on their early lead. Eventually Ian Rush made it 2–0, but City fans remained confident that their side could overhaul the deficit against such lacklustre opponents. With 20 minutes remaining, Kinkladze went down under a heavy challenge in the area and Rosler smashed home the penalty. Eight minutes later, Kit Symons equalised with a header. City were back in the hunt.

'It was two each and Liverpool were going to let us win,' recalls Evans. 'Lomas put through his own goal, then Rush scored a ridiculous second, but we fought back to 2–2. Then the word got around that that was good enough.'

Tragically for City, the rumour that Coventry were losing turned out to be unfounded. However, the word didn't filter through to the City bench, where Ball was instructing his players to play keep-ball to see out the remaining minutes. Lomas was shielding the ball near the corner flag when Quinn, who had been substituted, discovered that Coventry were in fact drawing and that City needed a win to stay up. He hared along the touchline, screaming at his team-mates, but to no avail. City couldn't find a winner and were relegated.

Huw Evans was there. 'Everyone always says "typical City", but that really was typical City. We could have won that game easily; there was nothing in it for Liverpool. They had the cup final coming up and so no one was going to dive in and risk getting injured. As for the Coventry score, I guess that 36,000 people just got it wrong. You hear players saying all the time "My maths isn't that good", but surely it couldn't have been that bad? With all the time they spend in the bookies, you'd think their maths would be pretty good!'

The City players were grief-stricken, none more so than Niall Quinn. The Irish international apologised to City fans that evening on *Match of the Day*, showing rare humility for an international footballer. Quinn's attitude is not forgotten in Manchester.

ARE YOU WATCHING, MACCLESFIELD?

'Everyone at City has still got so much time for Niall Quinn,' says Evans. 'I remember once United were playing in Europe, Barcelona I think it was, and they interviewed Niall Quinn on *Grandstand*. They asked him if he was going to wish United well in their European game and he said, "Look, I'm a Manchester City player, of course I'm not going to wish them well." I thought fair enough for that because most players would have said, yeah, I hope they do well, to keep promoting that myth that everyone hopes United do well in Europe because it's good for the game.'

The City fans were understandably far from satisfied, particularly when players of the calibre of Walsh, Phelan, Flitcroft and Coton left the club. The only signing was Gerry Creaney, much to the incredulity of the City fans.

'Why sign Gerry Creaney?' asks Evans. 'If you want a big donkey up front you just play Niall Quinn, don't you? We weren't a terrible team that season. When we went down we had the basis of a very good side, one that should have stayed up. But again the fans have got to take some of the blame. The crowd at Maine Road are just terrible. If you go away with City it's just a bit of a laugh, a few songs, cheer if we score, but at home the fans are on the players' backs straight away and it's got to affect them. You turn up out of loyalty, but the trouble is you turn up, see a poor team playing poor football and you get frustrated.'

Before long, Quinn and Curle joined the exodus.

'Curle was bad at City. Just as Whiteside, Robson and the others were supposed to be big drinkers at United, and that was partly why that period was never successful for them, well, Curle was apparently always out on the town. I knew a lad who signed for City a few years ago, a forward who came from Shrewsbury during Horton's time. He said he arrived in Manchester at this glamour club and he was just out on the piss every night with Keith Curle. I mean, that's no way to play football, is it? I was glad when Curle went, I'd had enough of him by then, but Flitcroft, he was our best player.'

Once again, City's finances came under heavy scrutiny. It became clear that players were being allowed to leave in order that the wage bill be trimmed. This was met with disdain by City fans.

'If you own a business that's been as unsuccessful as City over the past few years, you wouldn't expect to be making any money out of it, not straight away. But Francis Lee was making money and the people he was employing were making money out of Manchester City, and I just think that's totally wrong. Football chairmen are supposed to lose money if their team's that bad, then cream it off when things go well. That's how it's supposed to work. But

Lee wouldn't spend money to get us out of trouble, he just wanted to cut the wage bill by selling our best players and bringing in rubbish.

'City have developed this classic routine. They sign a couple of players cheap and then go on about how much potential they've got and how much they're going to be worth in a few years' time. I remember we signed one lad who was apparently going to be the first £10 million footballer, and I can't even think of his name now. I think he came from Exeter or somewhere. It's a way of fooling the fans that you're buying someone with tremendous potential, that this is the way to buy footballers. They buy rubbish, tell you they're going to be great footballers and then sell all the best players to get the wages down. And it works.'

City's 1996–97 season was to be cataclysmic from start to finish, although any suggestion that City were to finish in the bottom half of the table would have been greeted with widespread mirth at Maine Road before the campaign kicked off. Huw Evans was one of thousands of City fans confident that the worst times were behind the club.

'When we went down I thought we'd romp that division. It was at the time when people were really starting to say in earnest that there was this huge gulf developing between the Premiership and the Football League. We went down having drawn a game with Liverpool that we could so easily have won and having beaten Villa away, which is always a difficult game to win. And we were thinking, well, we've got bloody Ipswich in the first game, we'll hammer them. We'll hammer everyone. But it became apparent quite early on that that wasn't going to happen.'

City's opening match saw them scramble a 1–0 win over the Suffolk side, but this was followed by a single-goal defeat at eventual champions Bolton Wanderers, a result that flattered City. A 2–1 defeat at Stoke City followed, with both sets of fans uniting in their chants against manager Ball.

Within days Ball had resigned. Once again, City had lost their manager in the opening weeks of the season. Asa Hartford took over in a caretaker capacity, but after a run of three defeats in four games City faced a trip to Third Division Lincoln City in the League Cup. City were outplayed and outclassed by the Imps and despite taking a first-minute lead went down 4–1. A club with Premiership aspirations had been comprehensively shafted by a bunch of Third Division also-rans. The Imps' manager John Beck showed canny foresight when he commented afterwards, 'Manchester City need guts and determination to get out of this crisis. They may have to go down to the Second Division to sort themselves out.' His Lincoln side also won the return leg at Maine Road, this time by a single goal to nil.

Soon afterwards, Francis Lee thought he had found his man when Dave Bassett accepted the job of manager at City. Having shaken hands on the deal and announced it to the press, Bassett went home, slept on the decision, then informed Lee that he had changed his mind.

'He's a pretty shrewd guy, Dave Bassett,' says Evans, 'and I think he'd had a peek at the books, asked what could be done over the next year or so and realised that he was on a loser from the start. It was the same with George Graham, who was also linked with the job. I think they asked what the potential was, found out that there wasn't any and thought, well, sod that, then.'

Amid speculation that City would never find a new manager, in October the former Crystal Palace manager Steve Coppell accepted the job. His first six games saw City achieve some inconsistent results: two wins, a draw and three defeats. Suddenly, unexpectedly, Coppell announced that he was leaving Maine Road for medical reasons, as the stress of management was proving too much. This didn't stop him from returning to Crystal Palace and guiding them back into the Premiership.

'That was always a bit suspect, but what can you say?' asks Evans. 'Once again the phrase "typical City" springs to mind. He seemed a reasonably intelligent bloke, Coppell, and we thought perhaps he could handle Francis Lee, because there was all this talk of Lee interfering with team affairs, but he obviously couldn't.

'This really was a period when City were a bit of a joke. I think we got so many managers that year because a new manager always wins his first game, and that was what kept us up! But Coppell was a big name, and no one really cared that he'd been a Red. He'd done well at Palace, taken them to the cup final and what have you, and then he recovered sufficiently to take them back into the Premier League that season.'

Coppell's assistant Phil Neal was put in temporary charge during a period which saw City descend to 21st place in the First Division, their lowest ever position. A 2–0 reverse at Barnsley in December spelled the end of Neal's tenure, when the dour figure of Frank Clark arrived at Maine Road. At last City looked to have got their man. They had, after all, tried everyone else.

'I thought that appointing Clark was going to be a great move. I remember reading Ian Ross or David Lacey in the papers at the time saying that by a ridiculous twist of fate City had ended up with a good manager. I agreed. Through some bizarre events that season, we'd actually appointed a good manager with a decent track record, somebody who'd needed a club and who would surely do well for us.'

Clark certainly seemed to bring out something in the City players and results took a significant turn for the better. There were even hushed whispers that City could make the play-offs, whispers which reached Huw Evans.

'We did start playing well for a while, and even though we never quite pulled away from the bottom half of the table, we really pulled up. I remember thinking that the First Division is a tough division and that the teams that go up usually lose 12 or 13 games a season, so I thought that if we strung a few results together we could still finish in the play-offs. We finished 14th in the end.

'I would say that 1996–97 was the worst season in our history, worse even than the following season when we went down to the Second, because that was when we finally got rid of all our decent players, apart from Kinkladze. I think the relegation season that followed was a product of the season before. We should have gone down then; we were certainly poor enough to go down.'

The arrival of Clark had lifted the spirits of the long-suffering City faithful. At last they had a manager they felt was worthy of the club, and he'd instilled a sense of self-belief in the motley crew that made up the playing staff. Not surprisingly, the hopes of the City fans were high as the 1997–98 season dawned. Huw Evans was one of those looking forward to the new campaign.

'I think that every football fan is optimistic at the beginning of a season. Come August you always think that it's going to be your year one way or another. We still had Kinkladze and Rosler and we were thinking, apart from Middlesbrough and Nottingham Forest, who were the good teams? We started off dodgy but beat Swindon 6–0 in September, and they were second in the table at the time. We followed that with a 3–1 win at the City Ground and we thought, well, we've had a bad start but we can obviously beat these teams and do well. And that was when people started saying that Clark had run out of ideas, that he'd just lost it. But I think the fans just got on his back too much in the end and he thought, sod it, I'll easily get a job elsewhere.'

A disillusioned Clark was eventually fired to make way for former striker Joe Royle, the man who had been linked with the City job every time it had become vacant over the previous ten years. Which was quite a few times. Clark left with a parting warning to Royle.

'It will take a very long time to sort things out at that club,' he said. 'I made a start and, given time, I would have done it. But the results in the interim had to be better than I was getting. It's a rat-infested place. The whole situation is summed up by the fact that the chairman could not say with any kind of confidence that he could keep secret for 12 hours the fact that he was sacking a manager and bringing in a new one.'

The first chants of 'Lee out', unthinkable a few months before, were heard at Maine Road. David Makin, a major shareholder at the club, announced on a radio phone-in that he would lead a campaign to force Lee out. The beleaguered former player, piqued that the same people who had welcomed his arrival four years earlier had turned on him so vociferously, eventually gave way in March to David Bernstein, the head of the French Connection clothing empire.

Royle's first task as manager was to announce that the mercurial Kinkladze would be sacrificed in order to avoid relegation, although this was a prospect already being contemplated by the City faithful. Royle had a quintessentially English attitude to the inspirational midfielder. 'People have clung on to him because he does things that mere mortals can only dream about,' he said. 'What he seldom does are the things that ordinary players do. He seldom tracks back, tackles, gets back in the shape of things or trains hard. Some people say that the problems have arisen because Gio doesn't get the support he needs from the team, others say it is because the team hasn't had the support from him.'

Whatever the excuses, Huw Evans and the City fans were beginning to think the unthinkable. That Manchester City could be relegated to English football's third division.

'By Christmas you knew. I'd never really thought that we'd go down. Well, you just don't think like that, but the results were so bad. People just kept phoning me up saying that City were going down. There's that whole thing about humbling the bigger clubs, the ones who still have pretensions of being a major force and all that. Even my girlfriend's dad – he's a Cambridge City fan, you know, they pull in 250 people every week – even he was ringing me up on a Saturday evening and saying, eh, your boys are going down – and his lot were struggling at the foot of the Dr Martens League!

'If anything, the Birmingham match in December was the turning point. That was when we realised that our luck had run out. We went 1–0 up in the 88th minute and lost 2–1 in the 97th. I think you know your name's not on the cup that season when that happens. I suppose, looking back on it, we were always going to go down. That's what City do – they go down.

'I didn't even get any enjoyment out of United being knocked out of Europe and losing the title. It was that serious. I really didn't give a toss, when normally I'd be supporting their opposition. Before, it just meant so much. I've even got a Fenerbahce shirt in my cupboard, and I was down the

Topkapi Kebab House the night they drew 3–3 with Galatasaray. This year even that didn't matter. The one thing that does annoy me, though, is that if you go to the pubs in Manchester, the City and United fans hate each other as you'd expect; we are still their biggest rivals. But the United fans who live in London, or Outer Mongolia or wherever, for them Liverpool are their biggest rivals. It does get on my nerves a bit, that, the feeling that City aren't United's rivals. They still are in Manchester, and that's where it counts.'

On 25 April City faced Queen's Park Rangers at Maine Road, knowing that defeat would send them down to the Second Division for the first time in their history. Royle recalled Kinkladze, who had started just two games under the new manager and who hadn't played for six weeks. It could have been his last hurrah in a City shirt, as he was destined for Ajax at the end of the season.

Within a minute of the kick-off, Kinkladze drilled a 30-yard free-kick into the bottom corner of the net. Just six minutes later, keeper Martyn Margetson handled a back pass and former City striker Mike Sheron hammered the ball into the net for the equaliser from the resultant free-kick. On 22 minutes Jamie Pollock headed a cross past Margetson for a farcical own goal. City hit the bar twice in the space of three minutes before Lee Bradbury scored from close range to make the score 2–2. A point wasn't really enough and City knew it. They went into their last game at Stoke City knowing that even a win wouldn't be enough if Portsmouth, managed by Alan Ball, and Port Vale both won. Stoke themselves were in with a shout of staying up – well, actually more of a whisper than a shout.

David Bernstein, the new City chairman, had announced that City would be finding their own training facility instead of continuing to play on the council-owned site they currently occupy, former idol Joe Royle was in charge, and Lee and Swales were fading memories. However, City still had 90 minutes of the season left to ensure that they stayed in the First Division. 'If we go down, the problems will take on even more proportions because then the players I had in mind to bring in next season might not fancy the Second Division,' Royle told the press. 'The purse strings would be tightened because the crowds would be less, so you end up chasing your tail again. We have got to hope for a phoenix-from-the-ashes job.'

The match at the Britannia Stadium was a sell-out, the first at Stoke's new stadium. There was a series of scuffles in the stands around kick-off but the two sets of fans eventually settled to watch their teams' destinies played out before them. City took a first-half lead through Shaun Goater, but by the time Paul Dickov made it 2–0 early in the second half it had become apparent that Alan Ball's Portsmouth and Port Vale were both securing comfortable away victories and that both City and Stoke would be relegated. The final result, ironically one of City's best of the season, a 5–2 win, was purely academic. 'Are you watching, Macclesfield?' sang the City fans. The game ended in an atmosphere of utter dejection as the players went through the motions for the final time that season. Huw Evans watched the game on television.

'I still thought before the game that if we won we'd be all right. We played some lovely football that day – okay, we played some lucky football as well – but fairly early on it was obvious that we weren't going to stay up even if we'd won the game. I knew Ball would just go mental if we stayed up and Pompey went down. I've never hated a man as much as I hated Alan Parry that day – apart from Howard Kendall, obviously. But he was saying, 'All the financial directors of the Second Division clubs will be rubbing their hands with glee,' and I was thinking, fuck off!

'So next year we're playing Macclesfield. I don't want to talk about that, it's just too much. Macclesfield is a big City area. Stockport, Macclesfield, everywhere on the south side of Manchester is a huge City area, so all the locals who aren't City are going to love it. It'll be like the '50s again, all those Lancashire derbies: Preston, Blackpool, Bolton. All the players will be wearing baggy shorts and smoking Woodbines.

'Seriously, though, if you look at our results, we had some thumping wins and some really stupid defeats. We'd get to about sixth or seventh from bottom and you'd think, right, two more wins and we'll pull away enough to look back with a bit of breathing space, but we'd always get up to a certain point and then come down again. We couldn't string results together at all. When you're at the bottom and you're losing, it doesn't matter so much because the teams around you aren't winning either. But teams do get away and the number of clubs in trouble gets smaller and smaller as the season draws to a close. Huddersfield pulled away, Tranmere pulled away and in the end it was down to us, Reading, Port Vale, Stoke and Portsmouth.'

The future for Manchester City is uncertain, but surely they won't stay long in the Second Division. Huw Evans is quite sure of what City need to do.

'I don't think they're that good, to be honest,' he admits. 'Royle's talking about cutting the playing staff, but every manager says that when he comes in. Mind you, he did make the point that there were 50 players on the books when he arrived, and I suppose, if you think about it, when you've had six managers in a couple of years and each of them has made three or four signings, you end up with all these players who don't know what they're doing there.

'I think that if they do that, and get rid of the old boys' network at the club, then they've got a chance of getting it back together. I don't want to hear about takeovers, you know, Rick Wakeman, Oasis, the Sheikh of wherever. I think they should get management consultants in to sort out the mess, go around the whole club staff and ask people what they're actually doing for Manchester City. I hate management consultants, but I reckon if they looked at the staff at City they could weed out so much dead wood. I bet City have got more staff on their books than United have. They need to pull that club apart and put it back together again, and if people don't like it then that's tough.'

He suggests more drastic improvements. 'The whole club has got to change, even the ground. We've got to move – the ground's a shambles. We've got four stands and none of them match. We've got the massive one on the Kippax, and this horrible one on the Platt Lane which holds about 50 people. Then we've got the old main stand with the Aero roof. I remember when we bought that roof, it cost a million quid or something, and everyone was asking what was wrong with the old one, especially us on the Kippax who had to stand and look at it every week. Then we've got the North Stand, which was the height of fashion in 1974, but now it just looks like something that was the height of fashion in 1974. It's a terrible ground now, a right mish-mash. It's not a patch on Bolton or Derby, the new grounds that are springing up after the Taylor Report. City have got no hope of emulating that as long as they're at Maine Road.'

But until such improvements are implemented, until City have got themselves back in some sort of order, Huw Evans doesn't want to know.

'I'll tell you what sickened me most after that Stoke game. It was hearing the City fans singing "We'll support you evermore" and cheering the players who'd let City down so badly that season. I looked at the players coming off the pitch at the end and I thought, you lot are on about five grand a week, and we're cheering you after you've done this to us. And there were so many City fans there applauding them, and I was thinking, you're stupid, you're all fucking stupid.'

It was then that Huw Evans decided that enough was enough. Manchester City didn't deserve his support as long as the players weren't fit to wear the shirt. Amidst all the hype about football supporters' blind devotion to their clubs, the idea that if you don't wear your club's shirt day in, day out you're not a real fan, and the belief that you have to blindly cheer on your team through defeat after pathetic defeat to prove that you are a true supporter, the case of Huw Evans shows that this image so beloved of the media is garbage.

Here is a true Manchester City fan, someone who has stood on the terraces and sat in the seats at Maine Road through good times and bad, seen his club become a national laughing stock and decided that enough is enough. That is true support. Huw Evans loves Manchester City with a passion made evident through the anger and frustration that ploughs through his affable exterior. No doubt he will one day return to Maine Road. But until Manchester City get their act together, they may lose many more Huw Evanses. Surely they can't afford to do that?

Even though the game is more popular than it has ever been, when it starts losing fans like Huw Evans alarm bells should be ringing. Unless Manchester City pull their finger out, until they dismantle the club and rebuild, they cannot rely on the thousands turning out every week. Complacency is a dangerous thing. If the clubs continue to believe the hype that people will be queuing around the block come hell or high water, they will be brought back to earth when football's not trendy any more.

You can only push people so far. Huw Evans, one of Manchester City's most devoted fans, is fed up with being patient, fed up with excuses and fed up with seeing his club reduced to a laughing stock.

Losing the Huw Evanses of this world is a bad sign for the game. Is the bubble about to burst?

Epilogue

FOR WHOM THE BELLE VUE TOLLS

It is the day of Doncaster Rovers' last match in the Football League. After a four-hour drive from south London, I have produced my tenner at the turnstile only to discover that they've made the game all-ticket. All manner of pleading comes to naught, and although I've travelled hundreds of miles to get within 20 yards of the pitch, I'm not going to see the game. I'm not the only one. Although the ground has a capacity of around 5,000, barely 3,500 people are inside, swollen deceptively by the presence of many Colchester fans, who still have an outside chance of going straight up.

A policeman sent me to the club office to plead for admission, saying that the club had insisted on the all-ticket restriction. As I joined the ticketless souls outside the ticket office, we were told by a harassed-looking woman that there were no tickets available as the club had been forbidden by the police to sell tickets on the day of the match. Eh? I asked if the game was actually sold out, or whether they just weren't prepared to let people in who hadn't bought tickets in advance (despite the fact that the all-ticket restriction hadn't been publicised outside Doncaster). The woman in the ticket office didn't know. We weren't going to get in. Two middle-aged men held their heads in their hands. They'd been to every other Football League ground in the country, and just needed Belle Vue to complete the set. They weren't going to get in either. Why the game was all-ticket was a mystery. But the bigger picture was far more important than me not being able to get in.

The plight of Doncaster Rovers has not received the attention it should have. It appears that Brighton and Hove Albion have the monopoly on the 'small club's fans battle against malicious ownership' stories in the national press, but the way in which Doncaster Rovers have been allowed to deteriorate to the extent that they were relegation certainties at the start of the season deserves wider recognition. The half-hearted protests on that last day were the desperate actions of broken fans. A mock funeral procession arrived at the ground, complete with undertaker. Once the procession arrived in the forecourt of Belle Vue, however, there were just a few chants and clenched fists from the people at the front for the benefit of the photographers, whilst the rest of the procession melted away in search of programmes and their places on the terraces.

On one side of the forecourt a gaggle of sorry-looking elderly people waving placards were being berated by a Doncaster fan. It turned out that the pensioners with the placards represented the local Conservative Party and had been sent to Belle Vue in order to drum up support for the forthcoming local elections. A Rovers fan was verbally belabouring one of the huddle about the brow. 'Where've you been till now?' he asked with a pained expression. 'It's no good coming to the funeral, you should have tried to stop the funeral happening in the first place!' The old boy who'd borne the brunt of the tirade looked bewildered. Having anticipated a quiet afternoon's leafletting and waggling his placard at fans arriving for the game, he eventually spluttered, 'But . . . we didn't know about it.'

And therein lay the protestors' biggest problem. Brighton had been a novelty; they had satisfied the media's coverage of life in the lower divisions for the foreseeable future. Their inventive protests and fallen-giant status gave them an angle, but in the southern-dominated media, who really cared whether Doncaster Rovers survived or not? Their dreadful results merited the odd chuckle on Radio Five's *Sports Report*, but outside Doncaster the fans' protests fell on deaf ears.

Doncaster Rovers have never really set the game alight. Their list of honours features three Third Division (North) championships around the time of the Second World War and a couple of Fourth Division titles in the '60s. Brighton, of course, had their First Division days and an FA Cup final appearance relatively fresh in the memory. But Doncaster Rovers, ensconced at their crumbling Belle Vue ground, had never captured the imagination of the footballing public.

Rovers' last season as a Football League club – let's face it, they are pretty unlikely to return – was a statistical treasure trove: the club used 45 different players, won just four games all season, were relegated by 15 clear points, conceded 113 goals and scored 30. They didn't win a match until December, when just 864 people saw Rovers beat Chester 2–1. Their leading goalscorer

Prince Moncrieffe rattled in eight goals. Yes, worth a chuckle at the end of *Sports Report*, but not much else.

The reasons for Rovers' demise are rooted in the actions of Ken Richardson. Describing himself as the club's 'benefactor' rather than chairman, Richardson has avoided formal links with the Doncaster Rovers company, save for being a shareholder. He is currently awaiting trial for conspiracy to cause arson after two people were caught clumsily trying to burn down the stand at Belle Vue one night in June 1995. The hapless duo immediately fingered the Doncaster 'benefactor'. It was not Richardson's first brush with the law: in 1984 he received a suspended prison sentence and fines totalling £45,000 for conspiracy to defraud following a horse race at York in 1984. A horse purporting to be Flockton Grey romped home by 20 lengths at 10–1 – only it turned out that the horse was actually a ringer called Good Hand with which Richardson was involved. Richardson had also owned and closed the Northern League team Bridlington Town, which triggered an FA investigation.

Although Richardson denies direct involvement in Rovers, the three directors of the club are his daughter, his niece and an old friend. The general manager of the club, Mark Weaver, a man possibly more unpopular with Rovers' fans than Richardson, if that's possible, is also a friend of Richardson.

Belle Vue is rather inaccurately named. With its weed-strewn terraces and decrepit grandstand, the only thing the sad old ground has going for it is its location. Situated opposite Doncaster racecourse, Belle Vue used to stand alone surrounded by waste ground. However, in the last few years a cinema, a leisure complex and an Asda superstore have sprung up around the ground, increasing the value of the land on which Belle Vue stands by a considerable amount. A couple of years ago an advertisement appeared in the *Daily Telegraph* offering the ground for sale. Given that the ground is owned by Doncaster Council, it was a baffling move by the club's administration, but one that maybe betrayed the reason for their involvement.

On the field, Weaver has been picking the team, whilst Richardson was credited with keeping the club up in 1996–97 in spite of the efforts of player-boss Kerry Dixon. Dixon had replaced Sammy Chung as manager at the start of the season, with Chung arriving at the ground for Rovers' first game only to be told that he wasn't the manager any more. The squad has been run down, players have been released, and by the end of the season the players were only required to report to the club on matchdays as the coaching staff had all been laid off. One of Weaver's neighbours played in goal for one game. So many players were used by Rovers in 1997–98 that only nine made appearance totals that reached double figures.

Thus Rovers went into that last game a broken team and a broken club. Colchester fans, rather out of place in the depressing surroundings with their blue and white wigs and balloons, looked sheepish as they trooped off their coaches and into the ground. Of course, Doncaster lost. Colchester missed out on automatic promotion. The whole day was an anti-climax from start to finish.

In a move that showed characteristic petulance by whoever it was that made the game all-ticket, the gates weren't opened until the final whistle had gone. Entering the ground at last, having spent most of the afternoon in a local pub or kicking pebbles around the Belle Vue forecourt, I saw a small knot of supporters gathered in front of the stand to chant at the empty directors' box. 'He burnt our stand, he's hated by the fans,' they chanted. 'We want Richardson out.' There were defiant chants of 'Rovers' and 'Yorkshire' before the players trooped into the stand to be greeted like heroes. Throwing their shirts to the fans, the players looked shattered. Although relegation had been confirmed mathematically three weeks earlier, they still looked devastated and humiliated. Whoever it was that cajoled them back out to applaud the supporters, it was a noble gesture. The fans appreciated that it wasn't the players' fault that the club faced a tumble through the Conference into the lower reaches of non-League football. As the team trooped dejectedly back to the dressing-room, the fans stayed in front of the stand for a while longer before finally dispersing with a collective shrug.

Much has been made of supporters' fights to save their clubs: Brighton and Hove Albion, Charlton Athletic, AFC Bournemouth and others. The Doncaster fans looked broken. The media has all but ignored them.

Whilst the rich clubs get richer, smaller clubs are being run into the ground. The relegation of Doncaster Rovers could spell the end of the club. Okay, they've never won the FA Cup, they've never won the League. They have won the Yorkshire Electricity Cup, but somehow that doesn't really count. However, Doncaster Rovers means the world to its fans. It's the fans who built the club, the fans who sustained it. What right does anyone have to take the club away from them? If Doncaster Rovers disappears, it will be a black day for football.

Relegation can seem like the end of the world. It isn't. Nothing like it. At least most relegated clubs will start the following season, albeit in reduced circumstances. For Donny fans, relegation from the Football League is just the natural conclusion to a series of events designed to drive their club into the ground. In the face of the possible death of Doncaster Rovers, they are finding it hard to keep believing.